Faces of Grief

Stories of Surviving Sorrow and Finding Hope

Sherry L. Hoppe, Ed.D.

PINEROSE PRESS

Chattanooga, Tennessee

Faces of Grief
Stories of Surviving Sorrow and Finding Hope
by Sherry L. Hoppe

Pine Rose Press, L.L.C.
8909 Rostis Lane
Chattanooga, Tennessee 37421

http://www.pinerosepress.com

ISBN: 10:0-9849135-6-4

Cover design by Kacie Yates.
Cover photograph © Sherry L. Hoppe, 2011

Printed in the United States of America.

Dedicated to the Memory of

Hannah Bruning
Anne Campbell
Cleo Dalrymple
Dennis Durrance
Tiny and Vivian Durrance
Jason Fowler
Kelly Gibson
Paul Goldberg
Sharon Gilley Grant
Wayne Groce
Bob Hoppe
Anna Stone Hill
Kermit and Helen Howard
Mike Johnson
Daniel Johnson
David Kennedy
Tira Chapree Nation
Chester Oliver
Grover Phillips
Jimmy Phillips
Floyd Phillips
Johnny Ransom
Debby Levan Ransom
E.J. (Butch) Stone III
E. J. Stone Jr.
Anna Watson
Doris Watson
Garland Watson
Charlie Wright
Jonathan Wyatt
Missy Yates

ACKNOWLEDGMENTS

As I interviewed people for this book and then tried to do justice to their stories, I was both saddened by tragic losses and uplifted by the strength and faith of those who have found a way to go on with their lives despite deep anguish. For their willingness to share how they survived their journey through grief, I am deeply indebted to:

Nita and Walter Bruning
Gordon Campbell
Flavia Fleming
Diane and Gary Fowler
Debbie Gates
Hazel Gibson
Darlene Glenn
Joy Goldberg
Judy Hubbard
Linda Johnson
Marsha and Curtis Johnson
Connie Kennedy
Pam Lane
Muffin Liskovec

Wanda Martin
Marcia Nation
Aileen Oliver
Melissa Pierce
Alisa Poorbaugh
Jerry Ransom
Suzanne Rushworth
Bo Watson
Shelby Watson
Carla White
Kay Wilson
Vicki Wyatt
Sylvia Yates

Special thanks to Mildred Gilley, Jayne Groce, and Don Yates for allowing stories of their loved ones to be included.

Table of Contents

SECTION ONE

FACES OF GRIEF

SECTION TWO

STORIES OF SURVIVING LOSS AND FINDING HOPE

Nothing is past; nothing is lost
One brief moment and all will be as it was before
How we shall laugh at the trouble of parting when
we meet again.

Henry Scott Holland, English, 1847-1918
Canon of St. Paul's Cathedral, London

INTRODUCTION

If it were not for hopes, the heart would break.
Thomas Fuller, English churchman, historian, 1608-1661

Death — a simple five-letter word, one short syllable — but the upheaval in its wake echoes like an earthquake, massive and devastating, shaking our soul in a way no other emotion can emulate. At its deepest, grief is wordless. We try "empty," "lost," "heartbroken," and countless other formations of letters, but none seem adequate for the anguish threatening to drown us in a sea of sorrow. It is at such times, as Helen Hayes wrote, "We turn to poets, philosophers, and playwrights to articulate what most of us can only *feel* in joy and sorrow. They illuminate the thoughts for which we only grope; they give us the strength and balm we cannot find in ourselves." Knowing this, whenever Hayes felt her courage wavering, she rushed to renowned writers because they gave her the "wisdom of acceptance, the will and resilience to push on."

Faces of Grief follows the path Hayes trod, seeking thoughts from great writers for the journey through grief, for moments we feel numb, immobilized, and alone in our sorrow. At other times, when anger erupts, coming from our soul in a screech like a cry bellowing from the bowels of the earth, we use our own words — expressing anger at the heavens that our loved one was taken, anger at the departed for leaving us alone; anger at ourselves for not making the best of the time we had together. When our rage subsides, when we are ready to deal with the range of emotions ricocheting around us, we may find insight and understanding from the words of well-known writers.

Those on the other end of the spectrum — the small number of individuals who feel relief at a loved one's death — may also need help. Perhaps the deceased suffered through a terminal illness, and death was a longed-for release. Or maybe the person just made our own lives hell on earth. Some also face the guilt of being comforted — perhaps even thankful — the person is no longer present. Even with liberation from an unbearable situation, the passage through grief must be traveled — a way must be found to deal with the absence of the person now gone forever from this earth.

Whatever the situation, the faces of grief are as inimitable as the person who died. The visages take many different shapes — child, teenager, young adult, middle-aged, elderly; parent, offspring, sibling, spouse, grandparent, friend. On grief's countenance, features are formed by the circumstances of death — whether from natural causes, suicide, accident, addiction, violence; sudden or anticipated. A promising life stolen by pills; a freak accident in a neighbor's yard; a young soldier blown apart by a roadside bomb; a beautiful college student ravaged by leukemia; a child struck by a drunk driver; a wife felled by a heart attack; a brother whose kidneys failed; children burned to death. These are the images of death, mirrored in our faces of grief. Each face has a story, and each story has a message for someone in need of help while walking through the shadows of sorrow.

This book presents not only the wisdom of well-known writers but also shares the perspectives of more than twenty individuals who, having experienced devastation in the valley of death, have begun their climb back to the mountaintop. Ordinary people who have found strength to go on with their lives, though the fabric of their existence may forever be woven with poignant threads of grief and sorrow. These courageous stories are testimonies of hope — hope that even though we will never get *over* our sorrow, we can get *through* it.

From whence does hope spring? How do we cling to it in the midst of the greatest loss of our lives?

Hope can come from within or from people we know. It can come from books we read or sights we see. It can come from fervent faith, even when death's dark winds buffet our beliefs. As George Iles said, "Hope is faith holding out its hand in the dark." With one exception, all of the people interviewed for this book found solace — some sooner than others — in the hope they will someday be reunited with their loved one.

Life's lessons about dealing with grief, about searching for hope when we feel hopeless, surround us daily — in the splendor of nature, in the inspirational lives of friends and strangers, in religious books, in the words of poets, philosophers, and playwrights, and in the depth of our souls. The goal of this book is to open the doors to some of those places for you, guiding and sustaining you through the depths of your grief to the other side. As Henry Scott Holland, Canon of St. Paul's Cathedral in London, wrote, our loved one is waiting for us, "for an interval, somewhere very near, just around the corner. All is well."

SECTION ONE

FACES OF GRIEF

Author's Note:
When an individual's name is followed by the + symbol, a personal story can be found in Section Two. *Stories are arranged by type of loss in alphabetical order by first name.*

Chapter 1

GRIEF TRANSFORMS US

...You know nothing about Hope...whom fools have called deceitful, as if it were Hope that carried the cup of disappointment, whereas it is her deadly enemy, Certainty, whom she only escapes by transformation.

George Eliot, English author, 1819-1880

Like George Eliot herself, these words require pondering. We desperately want the certainty of death to be transformed by hope—hope that we can survive our loss because we hold a greater hope: Someday, in another dimension, we will be reunited with our loved one. Getting to that conclusion, believing it and accepting it, being transformed by it, does not always come easily.

One moment our loved one is alive, and then, in an instant, in our presence or absence, the last breath is drawn; the body is stilled, never to move again, never to smile or laugh with us, never to comfort or support us, never to hold our hand or sit next to us, never to surprise or dismay us. In an instant, our lives forever altered. All we have left is a shadowy silhouette that once was full-bodied, a short scene from the life we shared.

I remember after my husband died I frantically tried to remember his face. I would stare at his picture, then close my eyes and will myself to see him. But only the sky blue of his sometimes steely and sometimes playful eyes appeared; the image of his face stubbornly refused to come forth. Alarmed, I tried to picture him sitting in his leather chair beside me, but all I saw was vacant space. No matter how hard I tried, I couldn't envision him unless I was staring at his picture. It was so disconcerting I put his photographs everywhere so I could catch sight of him wherever I turned. My ability to see without a physical image had been transformed by my grief, so I created shrines to keep the face I loved tangible and near.

Similarly, Gordon+ tries to evoke an image of his wife, but all that comes forth is a fuzzy picture. To actually see Anne, he must have a concrete photograph. He looked at her every day for more than two decades, and then the next day after she was gone, he couldn't see her clearly in his mind. Perplexing. And it hurts.

Grief alters us in myriad ways — how we view the one who is gone, how we see ourselves, how we look at life, and how we relate to others.

A mother loses her only child and is suddenly no longer a mother — no child to hug, no bruised knee to kiss, no tiny body to help dress for a party.

An accident snatches a teenager, and we question whether fate or God stole him away. We wonder why our child was chosen and not another. The word "mother" or "father" never sounds the same again, even if we have other children.

A child's father dies in front of him, felled by a heart attack, and he doesn't understand why other kids still have their dads. His future ravaged, he faces life with a new family — strangers who want to take the place of his father — *and* his mother who had died from cancer five years previously. How much should one child have to bear, the little boy's cries wordlessly shout.

A sister watches her brother die slowly of kidney disease, and she laments his loss, knowing she will never be a "sister" again — at least on planet earth. The once sapphire-blue sky they shared over the ocean now black and turbulent.

Those left behind view life through darkened lens, the coming years bitterly transmuted. We see how much revolved around our lost loved one — the center of our world. Suddenly, the earth spins crazily on its axis, a gaping hole throwing it out of balance. Thunder from a threatening sky no longer sounds strong and forceful, its voice now muffled with melancholy.

Robert Crais, in his novel *L.A. Requiem*, penned these words: "Suddenly the way you see everything is different, as if the world has changed color, hiding things that were there before and revealing things you otherwise would not have seen." After death invades our lives, we think differently, we see differently, and we act differently. The whiteness — what was pure and good and wholesome — is now black, bottomless, and bewildering. The transformation hits like an eclipse, swiftly and totally, before the moon moves away from the sun, exposing the blinding light of reality — our loved one has departed this life never to return. The speed of this shift in the way we see life is shattering.

Maxine and Lloyd Yates had five children, all healthy, full of life, and treasured beyond measure. After a drunk driver swerved and struck 11-year-old Missy at their mailbox, Maxine could not speak, too shocked, too shaken to face the awful reality. She wanted to reverse the earth's spin and turn time back to the point when Missy started her fatal walk to the mailbox so she could hold her back. She wanted to retreat into herself, hide from the bitter emptiness she felt. But she had to go on, to look after her family; even so, the vacant place in Maxine's heart was so huge the other children could never totally fill it. It remained a sacred place, never to be invaded or forgotten — just a place she visited in the quiet of the evening as she looked out from her back porch over the rolling farmland.

Though she went through the daily routines of caring for her large family, Maxine never got over Missy's death. She was transformed; forever watchful over her remaining children; forever wary something might happen to another of her brood. To see her, she appeared happy tending the others in her clan, but inside a looming dark hole in her soul held a steady, if unseen, vigil.

≈

In another part of Georgia, many years later, another couple faced a series of dramatic challenges with their handsome, charming young son. Their trial began when, at the age of 15, Jason was diagnosed with aplastic anemia. Over the next few years, Diane and Gary+ felt helpless as their vigorous, vibrant child slowly lost his vitality — and his independence. Then, an answer to prayer — a bone marrow transplant offered new life, but it was just a reprieve before the worst storm of their lives struck with deadlier force than the others they had met head-on and survived. This tropical-strength storm's aftermath left their lives forever changed—a beloved voice never to be heard again. The silence of the absence was palatable.

As I listened to Jason's parents tell his story, I recalled the correspondent in Stephen Crane's short story, *The Open Boat*. A fictionalized version of a real-life experience in 1897, Crane tells of being capsized at sea, left with three other sailors in a small open boat that wasn't much larger than a bathtub to fight waves "most wrongfully and barbarously abrupt and tall." Like I perceived Jason did, these men, after tossing in the furious sea for days, felt the tempting hand of safe harbor more than once, only to be thrown back into "a squall, marked by dingy clouds, and clouds brick-red, like smoke from a burning building...."

Once when a lighthouse appeared and then vanished on the horizon, the correspondent cried out: "If I am going to be drowned—if I am going to be drowned—if I am going to be drowned, why, in the name of the seven mad gods who rule the sea, was I allowed to come this far and contemplate sand and trees? Was I brought here merely to have my nose dragged away as I was about to nibble the sacred cheese of life?"

And so Jason and his family must have felt after tasting the goodness of life once again after his successful transplant before "tall black waves swept forward in a most sinister silence, save for an occasional subdued growl of a crest."

In Crane's story, a man came running and bounding into the water as the ocean spit the correspondent from the grip of the undertow into knee-deep water. Giving the weak man "a strong pull, and a long drag, and a bully heave at [his] hand," the savior pulled the correspondent to shore.

The undertow of graph versus host disease sucked Jason under in the waves of this life, but he never lost sight of the lighthouse signaling the way home. Waiting there, to pull him safely to shore, was Jason's Savior.

~

Maxine and Lloyd lost their precious daughter in an instant as she went to get the afternoon mail; Diane and Gary lost their beloved son after an extended battle they never anticipated fighting. Both families faced fissures that could never be filled.

But parents' love for their children never dies—it just waits in anticipation of life together in a different realm. The final transformation has now come for Maxine and Lloyd, who have been reunited with Missy. Diane and Gary know they will someday have a joyous reunion with Jason. They are in no hurry—they have two other children and three grandchildren to watch over and love. But when the time comes, they will rejoice as they see Jason running to greet them with an excited smile and an exuberant hug.

Whether our bereavement is for a child or a parent, a sibling, a spouse, or other loved one, that same hope exists for all of us. The love we once shared remains alive within us until we, like the one who left this earth before us, find ourselves transformed once again—this time to love at a higher level than we have ever known.

Hermann Hesse wrote, "The call of death is a call of love." He believes if we answer that call in the affirmative, death can be sweet. Then and only then can we accept death as one of the great eternal forms of life and transformation.

Chapter 2

I MISS YOU SO MUCH

And can it be that in a world so full and busy, the loss of one weak creature makes a void in any heart, so wide and deep that nothing but the width and depth of eternity can fill it up!
Charles Dickens, English novelist, 1812-1870

Our world is populated with numerous friends and family members, but the one we lost leaves such a void we often cannot fully embrace the ones who are still with us. As much as we love them and they love us, they are not an adequate substitute. Everywhere we go, every sight we see, every word we hear, is shaded by absence.

The sights of ordinary and special times...mothers shopping with their children, couples holding hands under a restaurant table, fathers watching their sons play ball, families celebrating holidays...are sights and times ripped out of our lives.

These denied experiences shape our days and sting sharply in our soul. Like Bengali poet Rabindranath Tagore wrote, "In our desperate hope we go and search for her in all the corners of our house. We find her not." This desperate hope: we see a child at a distance and think it is our own; we see a crowd on television and search feverishly for the face of the parent we loved; we hear the phone ring, and we think our son is calling; we see an empty chair at the table, and the vacant place speaks silently of the one who was.

We are alone in a way we have never been alone before.

As Mark Twain declared, "The mind has a dumb sense of vast loss — that is all." Our willpower is not sufficient to shut down our thinking — what we have lost consumes and colors every thought. We miss seeing our loved one's face. We miss hearing his voice calling our name, feeling her touch on our arm to get our attention, seeing his eyes stretch wide in wild excitement.

Josephine Humphreys, an American novelist, describes it as being "catapulted" into a whole new existence. "The sky was different. A ham sandwich was different." Important or mundane, every sight we see and every object we touch no longer seems the same.

Suddenly, we must learn to do things our loved one always did for us. Linda+, just months after her husband's sudden death, had to open up their swimming pool alone—a task she and Mike had always shared. She had to make financial decisions, go to church by herself, take her car to be serviced. The list of new experiences, new responsibilities, is endless. Sonja O'Sullivan, the Irish champion runner, has her own list, saying those left behind have to "learn how to open bottles, move the furniture, open stuck windows, go home alone, investigate the noise in the night, eat alone, be sick alone, sleep alone…sing alone." Little things we took for granted; big things we never thought about having to do ourselves. The one we had counted on to be there for us has left us to fend for ourselves.

When a parent dies, even adult children sometimes still feel the urge to call for advice or solace long after the casket is closed and covered with clumps of clay. We lose a sibling, and we mourn he will never play with our children. Our teenager dies, and our heart wrenches with the realization she will never bear us grandchildren. Absences strike every chord of the future, sounding dissonance where once was harmony.

English author Daphne Du Maurier wrote: "The evenings were the hardest to bear. The ritual of the hot drink, the lumps of sugar for the two dogs, the saying of prayers—his boyhood habit carried on throughout our married life—the good night kiss. I continued the ritual, because this too lessened pain, and was, in its very poignancy, a consolation."

Many spouses miss such evening rituals more than anything else. Both Linda and Shelby+ recall with affection and sorrow about sharing their day's events with their husbands. "Catch up" time that seemed so casual and unplanned now leaves a huge hole at the end of their day. Spouses often find the absence of companionship—at night or any other time—the most difficult part of living alone. Gordon+ misses lying in bed with his wife, doing crazy things like trying to remember all of the songs in *Mary Poppins* and then singing them. It was just one of the fun pastimes he and Anne enjoyed together. Parents also miss the friendship and camaraderie of their child. Hazel+ treasured the times her son Kelly would stop by her house, sitting at the kitchen table, just filling her in on what he had been doing. She misses going places with him—hopping on his plane to head to a concert or just going to a local fair or other event. Now she sits alone, watching the sidewalk he used to tread to her door, staring at the place where he always sat in her living room. Such recollections cause us to wonder how we can bear to go on living. Even bright sunlit days have overcast skies. Restlessly, we trudge the drab days, longing for the face we adored, the companionship we cherished, the activities we shared.

Alone.

The missing makes us miserable; but, if we can but pause to shift from the darkness in our soul to the beauty in the life we shared, the missing may become mellower.

~

I speak from experience.

During an interview for a book on my husband's life and historic trial, A Matter of Conscience: Redemption of a Hometown Hero, Bobby Hoppe, I was asked what I missed most about my husband.

My answer was simple: Everything.

But then I went on to enumerate everything I missed about Bob:

I miss his beautiful blue eyes.

I miss his charming and sometimes devilish smile.

I miss sitting beside him in our library reading, Bob with a marker and pen in hand, highlighting and underlining parts he wanted to remember, stopping to share a profound passage with me.

I miss sitting with him on our patio at sunset, recounting our day's events, with a chilled glass of Reisling.

I miss traveling with him, exploring foreign lands and discovering new vistas in our own country.

I miss his teasing.

I Miss You So Much

I miss the way he liked to surprise me with unexpected gifts.

I miss his holding me in bed at night as I fell asleep. And, I miss how he willingly warmed my cold feet, even if he did gasp when I put them on his legs on a chilly winter night.

I miss the rituals we shared, funny ones and poignant ones. We loved to ride the rails, and it became a habit for us to say in a singsong voice together when we heard or saw a train, "Oh, boy, oh boy, oh boy, oh boy. A train, a train, a train, a train." And reminiscent of Gone with the Wind, *late at night if I said, "Bedtime," Bob would respond, "You don't say bedtime, I say bedtime. Bedtime…Bedtime…" But most of all, I miss the words we said every night when we got in bed:*

"Night, Sherry Lee, I love you."

"Night, Bob, I love you, too."

"Say your prayers."

"Ok, you, too."

"Remember Kevin."

"I will."

And then in a tone of wonderment that can't be conveyed in written words, Bobby would say, "Our favorite time of day," and I would respond with a deep sigh of contentment, "I know."

I still go through the ritual each night; I just say Bob's words and mine. It's not the same, but it is the time of day I feel closest to Bob, and my heart is touched by the words just as it was when Bob said them with me.

What do I miss about Bob? Everything.

Almost three years since my husband's death, that answer has not changed.

⤣

Words from the French Impressionist artist Pierre-Auguste Renoir prompt a deeper perspective: "The pain passes, but the beauty remains."

I have learned to be grateful I had so much to lose. For most of us, even in the depths of our grief, we can acknowledge what we had was worth living for, and now it is worth the pain of missing. We can cherish the deep joy we shared, even as we suffer the anguish of absence.

In the darkness of deep grief, Alfred Lord Tennyson had the wisdom to know, "Whate'er befall, 'tis better to have loved and lost than never to have loved at all." That remains true whether our loss was of a child, a spouse, a sibling, a parent, a grandparent, or a friend. Even experiencing great sorrow, we would never have given up the years we treasure should our immense loss have been foretold. The blessing of love was worth the agony of loss. As I wrote in *Sips of Sustenance, Grieving the Loss of Your Spouse*, "The sting of sorrow smarts less with that realization. The greater our loss, the greater should be our gratefulness that we had so much to lose. It was a love worth living for — and now it is worth grieving over."

Chapter 3

FINDING YOUR WAY THROUGH THE BLIZZARD OF GRIEF

The soul's order can never be destroyed.
Parker Palmer, American educator, 1939-

Parker Palmer begins his book, *A Hidden Wholeness*, describing how, years ago, farmers on the Great Plains ran a rope from the back door out to their barn at the first sign of a blizzard. They didn't want to end up like neighbors who had wandered off and been frozen to death, a whiteout hiding their homes a few feet away.

"Today we live in a blizzard of another sort," Palmer says. Getting lost in the gales of life, whether financial, physical, or spiritual, happens all too frequently. In the whiteout, it is easy, he avers, to believe our soul "has lost all power to guide our lives." Yet he disagrees with the lyrics of Leonard Cohen's song that "The blizzard of the world...has overturned the order of the soul."

In the midst of grief, when a whiteout veils our view, we need a line from the kitchen to the barn—a rope to cling to until we can see the life that awaits us after the storm subsides. That lifeline resides in our soul.

The order of the soul, Palmer maintains, can never be destroyed, though it may be obscured by a blizzard—by our despair over the death of one so dear to us. If we hold onto the aura of our loved one—if we know in the depth of our soul our spirits remain connected and will someday be reunited, we can survive the fierceness of the storm.

~

The storm that struck Julia when her only son was killed as he stepped on a land mine in Iraq was worse than any blizzard—far stronger than the sandstorms her son had endured in the sweltering heat of the desert. Blinded by the gale, Julia could not see how her life could be whole again. Each day, she forced

29

herself to go to work, but the blank look in her eyes told her co-workers she wasn't really seeing them. Withdrawn and silent, her heart broken, Julia's soul felt dead. "Gone…gone…never to return," she moaned as she drove home each day. Like the singsong children's rhyme, "All the king's horses, and all the king's men, couldn't put [her] back together again."

Today, almost a year after her son's death, the smile on her face still seems painted, not real. And, although she no longer says the words as she drives home each day, "Gone…gone" still rings in her head like a mallet striking a gong twice in slow but sure succession.

Marcia+ felt a similar reverberation in her head after her daughter Tira's death. When grief finally penetrated her numbness and anger, she recalls, "I thought I was going to die. It was the most terrifying feeling I had ever had. My mind was racing; my chest hurt. I just walked around repeating the 23rd Psalm. I took Tira's pictures off the wall, because it hurt so much to look at them. I cried all the time; I screamed some. God, I missed her! I felt like I had a knife in my heart. I thought I was going crazy."

⤶

Thomas Merton, a Trappist monk of Gethsemani, Ky., proclaimed, "There is in all things…a hidden wholeness." Yet, when death rips a hole in our heart, we think the pieces of our being can never be mended together into a whole vessel and that the waters of life will forever flow through the fissures.

As I mindlessly watched television months after my husband's sudden death, an actor's voice penetrated my stupor: "I don't know how to exist without my beloved." Struck by this thought, I wrote it down and mulled over it for days. And then, it hit me, I knew how to *exist* without Bob, I just didn't know how to *live* without him. I could get up every morning and go through the routines of life, but I wasn't living. I only existed. My life was not whole without Bob.

Later, when I read Palmer's words, "Wholeness does not mean perfection: it means embracing brokenness as an integral part of life," I realized I could be broken and still live.

So much of who and what we are comes from those with whom we share our lives. And losing that person is like tearing an orchid blossom from its stalk. The plant remains alive, growing, but that which made the plant strikingly beautiful is gone. Will the naked stalk produce blooms again? With luck, water, and nourishment, the orchid can indeed flower once more. Yet, even if it doesn't, the leaves and stalk, stark and straight, have their own beauty and strength. Different, but lovely still.

Palmer tells how American naturalist Douglas Wood described such splendor in a jack pine. Not elegant enough to win a beauty contest, the distorted tree displays a different kind of loveliness. "In the calligraphy of its shape against the sky is written strength of character and perseverance, survival of wind, drought, cold, heat, disease."

It is that same hardiness we must find to rediscover the beauty and joy in our lives. It will be different — perhaps more stark than before — but we can find wholeness again.

Do we find the toughness we need by pulling ourselves up by our bootstraps? I tried that, and it didn't work. The hidden wholeness Merton described was truly hidden — I couldn't find it. As American religious author Brennan Manning says, it didn't take faith for me to know God existed; almost everyone takes that for granted. Rather, what I needed was to trust that His master design included my loved one's death at the time it occurred. It took time and grace for me to accept that wisdom not only in my head, but also in my heart.

As Paul Tillich described in *The Shaking of the Foundations*, "Grace strikes us when we are in great pain and restlessness. It strikes us when we walk through the dark valley of a meaningless and empty life...."

That's where we are when death unleashes a blizzard far greater than any we have ever experienced before. Grace is that lifeline to the security of the soul where hope resides.

Chapter 4

SORROW KNOWS NO SCHEDULE

If there is no struggle, there is no progress.
Frederick Douglass, abolitionist and writer, 1817-1895

Some people move through grief gradually, slowly and sorrowfully, while others seemingly take sorrow in stride, safely making the passage through grief with grace. Is it that those who struggle less loved the departed less? Or, was death the last step in a painful struggle, a welcome release more than a regretted departure? Do some have more resilience and stamina to deal with death? Or are some just more tender hearted? Is the faith of some stronger than others?

The answers as to why one flows with the tide of sorrow and another gets sucked down by the undertow are as varied as the mourners.

Elizabeth Kübler-Ross, who wrote extensively on death and dying and introduced a model for the five stages of grief, believed all men are basically the same, fearful and frightened by death. It matters not whether you are the one dying, the one watching the death, or the one dealing with its finality. None of us, Kübler-Ross says, has mastered death. Euphemisms don't change the reality, and lying to others or ourselves merely postpones the inevitable.

Saying a loved one has "passed away," "moved on to the next life," or "gone to heaven," doesn't change the undeniable truth of death. The bell tolls each hour of grief despite any attempt we make to soften the sounds with stories. Thus, it is unwise, Kübler-Ross advises, to tell a small child who has lost a brother that God loved Johnny so much he took him to heaven. Likewise, she advises us that pretending to a child his mother has gone on a long trip or making up another unbelievable yarn doesn't delude for long. The child intuitively senses the untruth, knowing something is decidedly wrong.

If it is wrong to mislead children, is it also wrong to deceive others or ourselves? When my husband first died, I wanted to scream when someone sanctimoniously told me, "He's in a better place" or offered something else I considered a pitiful platitude. My heart cried out in agony, and though I believed the truth behind the clichés in saner moments, hearing them didn't satisfy my soul. I needed to feel the pain of loss, to face the finality of his bodily life, to rail against the heavens. Unlike Atlantic salmon that return to the freshwater streams of their youth, my husband won't revisit the place of his birth when the seasons change, and that realization cuts cruelly.

In the throes of grief, we should not repress our feelings of loss. Whether through weeping or shrieks of shock, through moans or stifled silence, mourners need to express grief in their own ways. Even so, we all go through stages of sorrow that bear similarities. We may progress through the phases at our own pace, but pass through them we must. Kübler-Ross studied those steps in hundreds of patients, and her work has profoundly influenced not only how the dying are treated but also how families deal with the death of loved ones.

The first stage described by Kübler-Ross is **denial**, which can be short-lived or long. We say to ourselves, "This can't be happening." "I will wake up in the morning and he will be right here beside me, laughing and mischievous." "If I close my eyes long enough, this will become a horrible nightmare."

Linda+ recalls planning how she could repay the insurance check she received if her husband came back. She knew it was irrational, but her mind played the game with her, letting her pretend death might reverse its trip to her house.

Muffin+, shocked by her brother's death even though he had been sick for many years, remembers thinking in the days after the funeral, "The hospital is going to call telling us Charlie is through with dialysis and is back in his room for us to visit." She admits, "It makes no sense; I knew he was dead, but my mind still held out that hope." Muffin believes it may be "God's way of allowing you to absorb it all slowly, a little bit at a time, so you can endure the loss and the grief without coming apart."

Such denials may last an instant and be gone, or they may recur. Just as we can't look directly into the sun for long, sometimes we can only bear to stare at the face of death for brief moments. But, in the end, denials are temporary, because we live in a real world where burials or cremations aren't symbols but concrete, irrefutable ends for earthly existence. Harsh, but true.

When denials drift back into the realm of unreality, **anger** may move in. In this phase, the origination of our frenzy is undeniable, for as author Frank Herbert notes, "How often it is that the angry man rages denial of what his inner self is telling him?" Denial meets reality, and thunderous rolls of fury fill the air, voiceless or boisterous.

Sometimes the anger is directed at God for his unthinkable choice of victims — Why me? Why my loved one? Envy that others remain alive can eat at us like a vampire. At times, our rage is misplaced, aimed at anyone and everything. Sometimes we chastise ourselves that we didn't prevent the death. And at other times we are simply resentful we have been left alone.

I'm a fixer, a caregiver, and a controller. Faced with death, I find I can't fix it; I can't give enough love and compassion to make it all right; I can't control what has happened and what is happening. If I could, I would barter, do anything to bring my beloved back, make outrageous promises if this dastardly deed could be undone. This third stage, **bargaining**, is more helpful to our psyche when the person is still alive, but even after death, we lapse for moments into the bargaining position, temporarily returning to the denial phase.

Bouncing from one step of the grieving process to another is common. Sorrow is not a straight-line progression from shock to acceptance. Consider a woman who has fought with her husband for years, perhaps even being abused by him. Kübler-Ross avows this widow may pull her hair, cry out in anguish, and whine for her loss, then beat her chest in anger at the life she shared with her partner. Later, this same grieving spouse may struggle with remorse that she didn't love her husband more, turning her anger inward.

Remorse often leads to **depression**, although this stage can occur without regret. Kübler-Ross describes the depression that comes before death, as the patient prepares to lose everything and everyone he loves, as preparatory, and the despair that follows death as reactive for those left behind.

While dying patients withdraw themselves from life and its relationships to accept death, those remaining may also find respite in silence and solitude. Family and friends observing the dying and the grieving may find wordless times difficult, but to those in the throes of death, silently sitting together is enough. In that stillness, **acceptance**, the final stage, eases its way into the room. And so it can be for those that remain.

Acknowledging that death is the victor—final and irrevocable—enables us to move on. An inscription on a cathedral wall in Amsterdam affirms such an acceptance: "It is so. It cannot be otherwise."

Kübler-Ross warns acceptance doesn't equate to happiness. Rather, it is a period "almost devoid of feeling," without fear and anxiety. We may be tired and weak, but in absolute acceptance; if we are the survivors, we have passed through the journey of denial, anger, regret, and depression with at least some modicum of hope. It is this glimpse of hope that enables us to endure the worst times. From the hope we will wake up and find it was all a nightmare, to the more realistic hope we will unearth some meaning in our loss, we are nourished by our hopefulness.

Shakespeare wrote, "The miserable have no medicine but hope," and which of us would refuse medicine if it would ease our pain, if it would make us feel better?

Chapter 5

WEEPING AND WAILING

*There is a sacredness in tears. They are not the mark of
weakness, but of power. They speak more eloquently than ten
thousand tongues. They are the messengers of overwhelming
grief, of deep contrition, and of unspeakable love.*
Washington Irving, American novelist, 1783-1859

Some people tell us we need to let our emotions flow freely. Others become concerned with our incessant crying. To cry or not to cry? Only you can answer that question.

What is right for you may not be right for someone else. You may have no choice—your throat trembles and tears well up, filling your heart, until they force their own escape. Or you may have shed a sea of tears watching a loved one suffer; even immersed in the dark shadow of sorrow, no more tears may flow after death occurs.

Although everyone doesn't cry, and some cry more than others, most counselors and ministers avow weeping is beneficial, because it releases pent-up pressure. If we hold back tears, we can explode, like a pressure cooker with no outlet for steam. Even without an explosion, we need to be cautious about silencing tears, for as philosopher Christian Nestell Bovee wrote in the 19th century, "Tearless grief bleeds inwardly." Submerging our sorrow, remaining stalwart and silent, may cause depression or physical ailments as our body and mind struggle with grief.

⤛

Finding a place where we can let our grief flow is important. For Jayne, that place was in her husband Wayne's antique car, which he had restored and cherished. For months after his death, she sat in the car, tears flowing freely, as she tried to feel Wayne's presence and struggled to submerge guilt that she had spent so little time with him during the last days of his life. Taking care of her elderly mother had consumed her. If she had only known Wayne was going to fall dead with a heart attack at the age of 50, she would have carved out more time with him. But it was too late. Her sobs spilled over the grief and guilt like overflow from a broken levee.

Beneath silent or strident tears, pain reigns. Abandoned, deserted, the urge to cry out in umbrage grows deep within our soul. Anger—directed at our loved one, at God, at people offering platitudes, at ourselves—simmers beneath the surface, ready to emerge as a slow-burning flame or erupt in a blinding flash fire.

⤐

Even strong Christians aren't immune from anger against God. Aileen+, flooded with anger that God had taken her husband, found her prayers hitting a brick wall. Carla+ also felt betrayed by God. Both had tried to live good lives, had loved their husbands, and thus couldn't understand why God would do something "so senseless and awful." Like a thunderhead gathering on the horizon, these reactions are a part of the natural order.

Muffin+ experienced only a few small episodes of anger toward God after her brother Charlie's death, asking "Why?" Though she isn't "mad" at God, she does still wonder "why Charlie had to endure such physical pain and sickness, why the prayers for healing were not answered (at least how we had hoped to have them answered), and why I was not allowed to be a match for him to donate a kidney directly, or at least indirectly through the paired donation exchange?"

Acknowledging and venting such feelings is acceptable. If we could hear God speak aloud, he might tell us: "It's okay my child, scream at me if you wish. I'm strong enough to take it."

Honoring the sense of desolation, temporarily giving in to the urge to rail at the awfulness of what has happened, doesn't harm us. Some will discipline themselves to be strong in public, but in a quiet place, alone and grieving, we should scream if it helps. Like a ship lost at sea, sound the bullhorn, shout at the heavens. In the dark night of grief, others may not hear, but our soul's heavy weight will be lightened.

Faces of Grief

Weeping or wailing, crying softly or screeching, it matters not. What counts is the relief we feel when we give voice to our emotions. Jane Goodall, who struggled with the loss of her husband, wrote that when she went to one of his favorite places—a chimpanzee feeding station in Gombe—she cried a long time, "weeping away the anger, the sorrow—and the self-pity...I cried myself to sleep." Goodall found tears can be healing, and she awoke knowing that while she would always grieve her husband Derek's passing, and the manner of it, she could cope with her grief.

Goodall unearthed "peace that passeth understanding" in the forest, where spiritual power was so real for her.

～

Vicki+, whose 25-year-old son died suddenly from an arrthymia caused by an enlarged heart, found her way to the same place Goodall found: "My pain was huge, but my faith was stronger. I knew God would give me the strength to survive this tragedy, but I had to go through so much pain and suffering. There was and is no way around the grieving. I now know there really is a 'peace that passes all understanding,' but the peace doesn't come immediately." Vicki cried a million tears, and she advises, "You can't bypass the heavy hand of grief that seems to weigh you down with every step you take. It's a process and a journey and there is no way around it." She adds, "If you had told me the day before Jonathan died that I would lose him from this life forever, I would have said, 'Then dig two graves because I can't imagine surviving without him.'" A million tears shed; six years later, sobs still sometimes come unbidden.

～

Beyond releasing our stress, tears connect us to the world. For Goodall, that included the world of nature. This outer expression of grief also opens the door we have bolted against sharing our sorrow. Although some people are more comfortable when we contain our grief, others welcome an invitation to enter our sorrow with us. We are not alone in our sadness, and company on the uncertain journey through grief can keep us from sliding down a steep slope into a bottomless pit of gloom.

Our loved one will always be part of the warp and woof of our being, but our life's tapestry must now be patched and repaired. Fresh colors and strands must be added. Letting others see and share our sorrow may help us form these new patterns — different than the ones from our past, but with satisfying shades and dimensions. Newborn connections and relationships can be discovered when we unlock the door to our heart, allowing others in.

Kübler-Ross and Kessler remind us, "Strength and grief fit together. We must be strong to handle grief, and in the end, grief brings out strengths we never knew we had." They advise we should surrender to our grief, "allow[ing] it to wash over [us] and feel the strength return to [our] body and [our] mind." From extensive research on death and dying, they know we will discover we are much stronger than we ever imagined as we let our sorrow flow freely. "Peace lies at the center of the pain, and although it will hurt, you will move through it a lot faster than if you distracted yourself with external outings."

Avoiding the expression of grief by diverting our energies is a short-term fix. In the end, we must go through the depths of our sorrow before coming out on the other side. Friends and family can help by sensing our pain, seeing our tears, and sometimes just by being there, even in silence.

⋙

For Shelby+ and Connie+, and for innumerable others, bereavement groups form the bridge from their past to their future. Crying with others who had lost spouses, bonds were made and lasting friendships evolved. In the midst of people who had walked the same path, they found a circle of understanding that helped them express their grief without fear of judgment. There, they felt sheltered from the world's failure to stop spinning while they suffered. There, even when they were incapable of expressing their feelings, others understood. They didn't have to apologize for a trembling chin, choked back tears, or abrupt anger. Their craving for empathy instead of sympathy was fed by others who had lost spouses. Wavering words found experienced translators.

Gordon+ also found support in bereavement groups. Too much of a man to accept that a male can't shed tears, he admitted he couldn't control his crying for many months. At first it bothered him, but his pastor told him, "When you get emotional, you are honoring the person you loved."

As Gordon grasped, tears are not a measure of strength, but a tool of recovery. As we shed them, our soul processes our sense of abandonment and distress. Inside us lies the source of our survival — a spiritual power that is always available to us, even when we rebel in rage and collapse in tears. When the weeping and wailing wear down, we can tap into that source, drawing courage to face the days ahead.

Chapter 6

DEPRESSION AND GRIEF
PART 1: SELF-PITY

The late morning blazed with blue skies and the colors of fall, but none of it was for me. Sunlight and beauty were for other people now, my life stark and without song. I stared out the window at a neighbor raking leaves and felt helpless, broken, and gone.
Patricia Cornwell, American novelist, 1956-
Black Notice

When the finality of death strikes us, we may go into free fall, descending deeper and deeper, swirling into blackness, until at last, we hit with a thud. Our beloved is gone, and he or she isn't coming back. As Carolyn, the protagonist in *A Prologue to Love,* said, "It is this which is the worst…the knowing…the dead have left you, finally and for all time."

Even when we believe in our suppressed spirit that "for all time" is just for earthly time, we may sit, stunned, for weeks that stretch into months. We stare into nothingness, even though our eyes see shapes and figures as the world about us continues its usual movement. The prisms of life radiate vibrant color, but we only notice drabness. To others, our eyes look vacant and empty; our face, blank and expressionless.

Faced with losses of love greater than she thought she could bear, Carolyn "struggled for order in her mind…repeatedly overcome by an awful spiritual weariness, a repugnance, that was really despair. The soul's night of darkness was upon her."

The cold, drafty bitterness of grief has turned inside us, and we welcome its absolute authority: Left alone and bereft, we have every right to feel sorry for ourselves. Before we drown in self-pity and self-recrimination, we, like Carolyn, should be mindful of Og Guinness' observation: "The opposite of having faith is having self-pity."

Like F. Scott Fitzgerald in his introspective story, "The Crack-Up," we must recognize that, even if we wait "around for a thousand hours with the tin cup of self-pity, [we] could walk from her door, holding [ourselves] very carefully like cracked crockery, and go away into the world of bitterness, where [we] are making a home with such materials as are found there — and quote to [ourselves] after [we] leave her door: 'Ye are the salt of the earth. But if the salt lost its savour, wherewith shall it be salted?'" (Matthew 5:13 KJV)

Our existence has become bland — flat and flavorless. We crave the taste of salt in our life, and in due course, from deep within our being, the urge to live again attempts to make its way to the surface.

Yet, when we muster the will and force ourselves to make the climb out of our well of lethargy, the walls of the hole crumble and we tumble back to the bottom.

That's how depression works when we feel sorry for ourselves too long. Grieving is a normal part of giving up a loved one, but we must be cautious we don't slip so deeply into self-pity that we become comfortable in our numbness. Would we feel guilty if we edged sorrow out of its central place in our lives? Can it be that we embrace, rather than shun, our grief? Has our melancholy become a welcome companion?

Seneca spoke with truth when he said, "We are as miserable as we think we are." We might add, "We are as miserable as we consent to be."

If climbing out of the pit we fell into when our loved one died seems to take more strength than we have, we may need to take stock, evaluating ourselves to see if symptoms of severe depression are present: irregular sleep patterns, apathy, loss of appetite, unkempt appearance, numerous physical ailments, anxiety, or fear. Have we withdrawn from our friends and family? Is our sadness overwhelming us months and even years after the death of our loved one? Are we constantly discouraged and despondent? Is our despair continuous and severe?

Depression is our nation's number one emotional illness, and death of a loved one is considered the underlying cause of more depressive states than any other factor. And we need not think we are immune. Depression can strike anyone.

Following weeks of denial after her brother Charlie's death, waves of depression swallowed Muffin's+ spirit. Always strong and in control, she found, "I wanted only to pull inward and shut out the world. I did not want to burden others with my sad feelings, and I did *not* want to be around others, making small talk, or participating in activities for the sole purpose of 'cheering me up' or 'taking my mind off' the loss and feelings of grief."

"As time passes," Muffin says, "I have come to realize that the real source of the initial depression and the current intermittent bouts of sadness is 'survivor's guilt.'" She found that, "like others forced to watch a loved one struggle with a critical illness and the ensuing physical limitations it causes, you not only feel incredibly helpless but also extremely guilty for the good health you are enjoying." For Muffin, as she watched her brother's quality of life diminish, the guilt was compounded: "Here is Charlie with a wife, two sons, and three beautiful grandchildren who love him dearly and who are already missing his presence in their lives, and here I am, enjoying good health, with no children and no grandchildren to miss walking and playing with me."

Martin, a counselor, assumed he could handle whatever came his way. After all, he helped others deal with life's problems, including grief. But when a brain aneurysm suddenly took his 13-year-old son, dealing with his loss hurled Martin from social drinking into alcoholism. Depressed and desolate, he turned to a bottle to combat his depression. His knowledge, tools, and experience were as useless as the unread self-help books in his bookcase—unwilling or unable to seek help, he lacked motivation and resolve to face life without liquor.

Depression, like death, strikes the young and the old, the rich and the poor, the smart and the less so. Counselors tell us what we already know: At the root of most depression is self-pity. In grief, we feel sorry for ourselves that we have been left alone, that our loved one's life was cut short, that we didn't get to say goodbye, or that death did not take someone else. When self-pity gets a hold on us and won't let go, the battle to regain control can be fierce.

When her 18-year-old son committed suicide in his room, Sara wanted to lash out at his girlfriend, who had been on the phone with him when he shot himself. Not taking his threat to kill himself seriously, the nonchalant teenager had taunted him to go ahead and pull the trigger. Struggling with the anger deep in her heart, Sara sank into depression — unable to deal with her rage at the girlfriend for such reckless disregard; exasperated that she herself sat downstairs, unaware of the drama unfolding above her head, when she might have been able to help. No amount of reasoning helped. She just sank deeper and deeper into depression. Today, more than 10 years later, Sara has moved on with her life, but her emotions can still send her on a rollercoaster ride. She never knows when she will lose control and go down again, when the rollercoaster will crash into the bottom of the pit, forcing her to face the long climb out once again.

How can people like Martin, Muffin+, Sara, and other mourners be helped? How can we pull ourselves out of the depth of depression?

Medication is one answer. After her husband's sudden death, Shelby+ refused to talk to family and friends, who she felt could not understand since they had never lost a spouse. Exhausted from lack of sleep and the stress of grief, she spent her days feeling like a sleepwalker. Not realizing the depth of her despair, Shelby hadn't thought about taking an anti-depressant until her doctor suggested she take medication for her depression. Within days, her emotional numbness began to thaw. She still had to face her loss, but she had regained her equilibrium, her ability to process her grief.

Those who prefer not to take medication may find a change of circumstances brings temporary relief, but when depression constantly follows you, outside help to surmount the self-pity underlying the feeling may be required. We should not close our eyes to the unraveling of our lives.

The first step in overcoming our depressive state is to recognize we have let our sad thoughts become an established pattern—that it has become our habitual way of thinking. As difficult as it is to admit, we have chosen to stay sad and miserable. Helen Keller, who had every right to indulge in self-pity, saw feeling sorry for herself as her worst enemy: "...if we yield to it, we can never do anything wise in this world." Keller's example of facing the hand life dealt her is an inspiration to choose a different pattern of thought, such as finding something for which we can be thankful. Our loss was terrible—overwhelming and painful. But surely there are other aspects of our life for which we are grateful.

As challenging as it may be to force ourselves out of self-imposed exile, one of the best ways to discover how much we have to be grateful for is to help others. In our desolation, we may discover others who have lost more, who have suffered more greatly, whose agony is more acute. Not only can this help keep our grief in perspective, it has the side benefit of keeping us busy—another important factor in combating depression. When our lives are filled with activity, we have less time to dwell on our sorrow.

Muffin+, who still has bouts of sadness over the loss of her brother, tries to deal with it in her own way. She has found it helpful to visualize her brother in Heaven, his health restored and his wisdom and understanding complete. She is contemplating donating a kidney to give someone a chance for a healthy life, believing it will help lessen her remorse that she was unable to do so for Charlie.

When Laura's mother died, she found that volunteering in a hospital helped her realize losing a parent suddenly may not be as bad as watching a loved one suffer for months on end, fighting torturous pain. Serving others was emotionally therapeutic for Laura because it compelled her to think of someone else's problems instead of focusing solely on her own. She also found that when her memory triggered her to think of the loss of her mother, she could force herself to think of the good times they had shared.

Another therapeutic activity is writing. Connie+ and Shelby+ both discovered that journaling helped them deal with their bereavement. Putting feelings—both positive and negative—into writing has healing powers. When we express our emotions instead of holding them inside, we find strength and stamina to fight depression. Tears may sting our faces as we explore our innermost fears and pain, but working our way through distress, perhaps even in letters to our loved one, can be cathartic. And, as noted in a previous chapter, bereavement groups can be a place where craving for understanding finds nourishment from those who have walked the path before us.

Writing in journals, attending bereavement groups, helping others — all contribute to our healing, but it would be misleading to imply these activities take away the ache, the anguish, the absence. Depression can be strong, with tentacles long and relentless, and it can grip even the sturdiest of humans.

King Saul found himself caught in "a vexation of spirit." He, too, needed help, calling on David to play his harp. In the soothing strands of music, he found solace. And, for some of us, songs may lift our spirits, too.

On the dark streets of depression, only the one in grief can make the decision to find the path back to the light–to search for newness of spirit, for illumination in the blackest night. The urge to re-enter life resides beneath our self-pity; we must give it a foothold for the climb out.

Chapter 7

DEPRESSION AND GRIEF
PART 2: HELD HOSTAGE NO MORE

Sadness flies on the wings of the morning, and out of the heart of darkness comes light.

Jean Giraudoux, French novelist, 1882-1944

A few months ago, fragrant forsythia blooms prompted me to prop open my back door on a lazy spring day so I could suck in the sensuous aroma wafting from the tiny buds. It was a delicious moment as I breathed in the smell of spring and listened to the melodic tinkling of wind chimes just outside the door. But the silky sound and smells were interrupted by a young bird thrashing from wall to wall as it attempted to flee the prison into which it had unwittingly flown through the open door. Wanting to help, I pushed the door wide open and stepped back, hoping the winged creature would see the easy escape I had prepared. When it continued to crash into the walls of the room, I ran for a broom, hoping to gently guide the bird to the open door. Instead, it just lashed out more furiously. Finally, I closed the door from the bedroom into the den and left, hoping in time the bird would calm down and find freedom.

Depression is like that. We thrash about, battering ourselves against the walls of life, hammering our head against the ceiling, while, right there in front of us, an open door offers the way out. Friends and family try to help, using their own form of brooms to nudge us, but we continue to struggle in the confines of our mind, unable to flee from our pain.

Mired in our grief, we sit silently, staring into space, for hours on end. Not only can we not accept the help of friends and family, we don't have the will to explore our inner being for relief, for answers to our questions and strength for our sad spirits.

Dr. Allen Unruh tells of a headline in the *Chicago Tribune* years ago: "Ice Packing Plant Burns Down." Underneath the headline, Unruh notes, the story read: "The building had over 100 tons of ice inside. It had all the materials capable of putting out the fire, but it was in unavailable form." Unruh adds, "FROZEN ASSETS." The building had the water needed to extinguish the fire, but it could not be used — it was frozen. Unruh says, in the same way, we have all the material inside us to put out the fires in our lives, but we can't use it because we are "frozen by fear, doubt, anger, anxiety, and indecision."

Instead, we anesthetize ourselves, suppressing our painful feelings. If we can still our minds, perhaps the hurt will diminish. Like a hibernating bear, we want to slumber our way through the worst of the winter. After the death of her mother, Sylvia remembers saying to herself, "If I could just sleep for the next six months, I will feel better when I awaken." She wanted to fast forward the clock to bypass the most dreadful days of grief.

We can't rush our way through grief any more than we can compel an iris to stretch its self before our eyes. The flower will grow, and our depression will lessen, but progress transpires as slowly as the blossom unfolds. Even so, we can take steps to speed up the process. Support stands waiting from people around us, and as much as we want to stay in the cocoon of our depression, we should not stay isolated in our sorrow too long.

Sometimes friends and family push too hard. They want to help, but they don't know how. They think they understand, but they don't. Muffin+ tells how friends thought she should go on with life after an "appropriate" period of grief. They seemed to imply that since she and her brother were "older adults," and she had a husband and a life apart from her brother, she should not be as affected by his death as his wife and children. Telling Muffin she was grieving too much or too long was insensitive, even though her friends thought they were providing good counsel. As she notes, "Loss impacts each of us differently," and people shouldn't assume they know how we feel. American author Joseph Bayly said it simply: "Grief is grief." For each of us, loss is still loss; sorrow is still sorrow.

Tim LaHaye, in *How to Win Over Depression*, says the best support for a grieving person comes from someone who knows how to just "be there." To be present—not offering advice, not probing, not even talking at all.

Alisa and Darlene+ remember getting tired of people asking them how they were feeling after their brother's death, but then, when friends and co-workers stopped inquiring, they wanted to shout, "Don't you know we are still dealing with this?"

In the depths of depression, we don't want to hear clichés or platitudes. When people tried to tell Kay+ they understood her loss, she remembers thinking: "No, you don't. You can't understand. He was our only brother. He was the light of our lives."

Family and friends should recognize and accept that no pattern for grieving fits all individuals. And, while some people resent their faith, others turn to their beliefs to combat depression. Although it was difficult, Alisa, Darlene, and Kay accepted their father's admonition: "We've always preached His grace is sufficient, and now we have to show it."

Our sorrow doesn't need to be reinforced—we need someone to accept where we are without condemning or supporting our self-pity. We need empathy and understanding, LaHaye declares, not sympathy.

When others try to pull us from the depths of depression, we need to remember Merton's words: Despair "is reached when a person deliberately turns his back on all help from anyone else in order to taste the rotten luxury of knowing himself to be lost." He wrote, "Despair is the absolute extreme of self-love." Merton's words may seem callous to a grieving heart, but when we stay imprisoned by self-pity, we need straight talk.

Life is a series of good days and bad, tears and laughter, grief and joy. When relentlessly depressed over the loss of a dearly loved one, we forget this cycle, unable to see joy can enter our lives again. With this loss of understanding, some people turn to pills, some turn to anger, some stifle their grief, and still others bury themselves in bitterness. Some dig deep, finding inner resources, as Ardis Whitman once wrote, "imperishable treasures of mind and heart we have deposited in the bank of the spirit against this rainy day."

For me, such a moment of peace, the beginning of my escape from two-plus years of depression, came from a mid-day walk on a long stretch of beach. As I watched waves of humanity unfolding before me on the wind-swept sand, I heard the ocean whispering its eternal message: The loss of my husband was part of the wondrous cycle of life and death, and I had to accept its place in the infinite universe. Every person on the jam-packed beach that day had lost loved ones at some time. And, in turn, everyone within my sight would someday die. I was reminded, as Whitman noted, all any of us have is *le petit Bonheur* — the little happiness. The best way to pull ourselves from the deepness of depression — to break loose from the prison detaining us from life — is to welcome each minute as an "unrepeatable miracle — which is exactly what it is."

Whitman concludes, "The web of life is woven from threads like the slow straining of the sea by a pale sunrise;" the joy of watching a "row of baby ducks swimming valiantly behind a pair of mallards, stately as galleons; a branch of apple wood burning in the fireplace; the wind making silken serrations in the pines." For me, as with Whitman, peace came from nature as I sat alone later that day on the altar of the beach, the music of the waves washing over me, cleansing me. For others, peace comes from different threads in their lives.

Whitman says, "No thread alone is wide enough to encompass a sorrow, but all together, they make a shelter that tempers the chill and slows the rain and softens sadness to the point where it can be endured." We cannot escape losses, so we must store up the good times as a resource to remind us life is worth living despite its sorrows. That storehouse holds the key to unraveling the depression holding us hostage.

Like Carolyn, faced with death's reality *In a Prologue to Love*, we may find our existence is "a mass of many-colored ropes, slippery, twisting, tangled together, in which [we] are bound and beyond escape. Yet, escape [we] must, if [we] are to live, or even die, in a measure of peace."

Chapter 8

WHY IS LIFE SO UNFAIR?

It is impossible that anything so natural, so necessary, and so universal as death, should ever have been designed by Providence as an evil to mankind.

Jonathan Swift, Irish author, 1667-1745

Rabbi Harold S. Kushner offers one explanation for life's unfairness in his book, *When Bad Things Happen to Good People*: God is "limited in what He can do by laws of nature and by the evolution of human nature and human moral freedom." When God created the world, Kushner believes, He gave man free choices. With those free choices came consequences, but the consequences are not always equal for the same choices.

This sounds like a game of Russian roulette to me. My friends' parents live, and mine die. My child is taken in a freak accident, but my neighbor's child (like millions of others) takes the same chance on the playground and lives. My teenager drives sensibly, yet he becomes a fatality. My friend's child drinks, drives recklessly, but he arrives home safely. My brother has cancer, and he dies; others survive their ordeal with the dread disease. Can I just accept fate as the source of my devastating loss?

We want to cry out, as C.S. Lewis did, "Oh God, God, why did you take such trouble to force this creature out of its shell if it is now doomed to crawl back—to be sucked back—into it?" These words sound like heresy, but "This sort of honesty does not turn God away from us," Bayly asserts. Instead, he says, it "brings Him near." In that closeness, we may be able to let go of our sense of unfairness even though we may not understand the reason behind life's rhythms.

One rabbi suggests we may be better off not knowing why innocent people suffer, that enduring the unanswered question is more tolerable than the answer we might receive. If we find the answer, he maintains, we may no longer sympathize with those who suffer. We may no longer try to help them. This rabbi cites as an example hearing a woman scream in pain in her hospital room while outside her family members chatted and smiled. A passerby challenged, "What's wrong with you? Can't you hear how much pain she is in?" They responded, "This is the delivery ward. She is having a baby. Of course we are happy." Knowing the pain would end — and that it would bring new life — allowed the family to ignore the woman's cries.

When we have such an explanation, pain doesn't seem so bad anymore, the rabbi says. With answers, he adds, we might become inured to suffering. But, as long as we are troubled by pain, we work to alleviate it.

Still, nothing shakes our faith as much as the inexplicable loss of one we love. Rabbi Kushner spoke from the experience of his son's tragic illness when he wrote his book. The victim of progeria (rapid aging), Aaron Kushner became a little old man while still a child — he was never to grow beyond three feet in height; he would have no hair, and he would look like an elderly man before his death in his early teens.

Kushner struggled to accept his son's diagnosis. He was a religious man, his life committed to God and his fellowman, how could such a tragedy befall *his* child? He reasoned that even if *he* deserved punishment, it was unfair his child had to suffer physical and psychological pain his entire life. It didn't make sense to Kushner his son had been chosen to die before knowing marriage or fatherhood — that he wouldn't even grow into adolescence. An evenhanded God shouldn't allow it, he surmised. Had he, the father, done something to anger God? After struggling with his beliefs, he refused to believe in a God who would strike down a child for someone else's sin.

Gordon remembers a tragic story from a parent in his grief support group: Their little boy was wearing a superman cape while riding his scooter with his parents just a few feet away in another room. Without a warning sound, his cape became entangled and he strangled to death.

Kushner asks of this kind of freak accident: "Is it to teach parents to be more careful?"

"No," he declares. "That is too trivial a lesson to be purchased at the price of a child's life." Kushner also rejects the explanation that the tragedy occurred "to make the parents more sensitive, compassionate people." The price is too still too high, he says.

Likewise, Kushner refuses to accept that tragedies such as his child's illness and death are bestowed on people who have some special spiritual strength. Perhaps he became a more sympathetic counselor through his son's struggle, but he says he would have given up such gains in a moment to have his son back, normal and whole.

Many will quote to us that we are never given more than we can bear. Our experience shows otherwise. Marriages break up after the loss of a child. People abandon their faith, blaming God for their loss. Others embrace bitterness, angry at an oblivious world. Years ago, I watched a couple, devout church members, shut the door on God after the death of their three-year-old child. They became resentful and embittered as they watched friends and neighbors' children live in good health.

As Kushner says, "If God is testing us, he must know by now that many of us fail the test."

When death strikes, we may question how a "good" God could allow such injustice. A dear friend of mine, and her siblings, were adopted by their godparents after their biological parents died. Then, in a tragic accident when their car crashed into a river as they traveled home from a church meeting, her godparents were killed. My friend, who already had seeds of agnosticism growing in her heart, told me, "I don't want to believe in a God who would do such a thing." Having lost two sets of parents, my friend had no room for faith left in her heart. And I had no words, no wisdom, to justify or even explain why bad things happen to good people.

Years later, I still don't have an answer to that question. I do, however, believe we don't have to punish ourselves because we have caused our losses or because we deserve them.

Tragedy is indiscriminate, striking good people and bad. As Kübler-Ross and Kessler note in their book, *On Grief and Dying*, the Grand Canyon was not punished by the raging waters and wild windstorms that carved its walls over hundreds of years. Rather, they created the magnificent canyon. While our loss may feel like punishment, they write, we are not the product of a Creator who punishes us by taking our loved ones. Instead, we are created with an "unbelievable power to weather life's toughest storms."

Although many may challenge Kushner's premise that God gave up control when he created the laws of nature, they may believe God stands ready to help us cope with life's tragedies. A source outside ourselves is our only hope.

Countless people firmly believe, "All things work together for the good of those who love the Lord," even if they can't see with their worldly eyes how tragedies work for good. We can hope to have that wisdom someday, even if it is in another dimension. In the interim, when we cannot see the meaning in heartrending losses, we can shape how we respond to them.

As Rabindranath Tagore offered, let us "not pray to be sheltered from dangers but to be fearless in facing them."

Just as Carolyn found in her sorrow in *A Prologue to Love*, inside us is "something still in its hard husk but something alive and waiting." She says it was as if "her first overpowering emotions had been a crude spade which had dug into earth for the thing that had been planted a little later."

The seeds of faith, however small and whatever the hardness of the shell that surrounds them, can find fertile ground and grow, even in grief.

Chapter 9

I PRAYED FOR A MIRACLE, BUT THE ANSWER WAS "NO"

The miracles of the church seem to me to rest not so much upon faces or voices or healing power coming suddenly near to us from afar off, but upon our perceptions being made finer, so that for a moment our eyes can see and our ears can hear what is there about us always.

Willa Cather, American author, 1873-1947

I'll never forget Sharon's striking beauty, her perfectly formed head hairless from chemotherapy, as her quavering vibrato filled the sanctuary at the Nazarene Church in the community where we both lived. The picture, forever etched in my mind, graced the cover of a tape of her music. For years, until that recording was scratched and worn, I played the songs she sweetly sang, remembering the solid strength she showed in the midst of her debilitating illness. Lifting her voice in song, testifying to her trust in God, Sharon touched the hearts of friends and strangers alike. Every day, like scores of other people, I prayed for a miracle—that Sharon would be healed from the leukemia stealing her life.

But Sharon died. To the thousands who prayed for her healing, it was as if, in C.S. Lewis' words, instead of an answer, we heard only the "sound of bolting and double bolting [of the door] on the inside."

We have all had prayers answered—and answered with a resounding "yes." We can cite stories of people who have been miraculously healed. As Willa Cather tells us, "Where there is great love, there are always miracles." So why wasn't Sharon healed? She used her beautiful voice to glorify God. There was great love in her heart for Him, and great love for her abounded from everyone whose life she touched with song. Why didn't God say, "Yes," and leave her on earth to spread the good news?

Did we not pray hard enough?...Long enough?...Was our faith not sufficient?

Bernard Berenson wrote, "Miracles happen to those who believe in them. Otherwise why does not the Virgin Mary appear to Lamaists, Mohammedans, or Hindus who have never heard of her?"

Was Sharon condemned because, as an old French proverb declares, "There are no miracles for those that have no faith in them"? Sharon had undeniable faith, as did her supporters, so why was it not enough? Was Sharon's illness and death a random act of nature? Or, was there a greater purpose served through her death than her life?

Should we think as Lewis suggests, not that there is no God after all but, "So this is what God's really like"?

More than 30 years after Sharon's death, I still have more questions than answers. Lewis reminds us that numerous passages in the New Testament seem to suggest "an invariable granting of our prayers." But he quickly notes a "glaring instance to the contrary: In Gethsemane the holiest of all petitioners prayed three times that a certain cup might pass from Him. It did not."

Nonetheless, Lewis points out, petitionary prayer is not only allowed, but commanded, citing, "Give us our daily bread." Yet, on dark street corners and under busy bridges, homeless people pray for food and get none.

Despite the seeming silence or the "no's," should we give up? Should we abandon hope? Should we, as a young paraplegic writer in Minnesota did, accuse God of holding the promise of healing before us like a piece of meat before a starving dog? If we sincerely and earnestly pray for a miracle and it doesn't happen, will it be a significant impediment to our faith, as Philip Yancey asserts in *Where is God When It Hurts?*

If we receive a miracle, we thank God or celebrate our good fortune. If we don't receive the miracle for which we prayed, we may need to acknowledge, as William James did, "If the grace of God miraculously operates, it probably operates through the subliminal door." If we do not understand the answer to our prayers, Hal Borland tells us that, "for all [our] learning or sophistication, man still instinctively reaches toward that force beyond." We yearn to be filled with a spirit of faith, even when doubts descend.

In Mark 9:24, the father of a boy possessed by an unclean spirit utters a cry with which we can identify: "I believe. Help Thou my unbelief."

As paradoxical as it sounds, we believe and disbelieve at the same time. How can we expect certainty when our knowledge of creation and its complexities is so limited? Still, belief can win the battle if we move from seeking a complicated answer to why God says "no" to one specific question and shift toward a simple example that assures us life goes on, even when it ends on this earthly planet. "Miracles, in the sense of phenomena we cannot explain," George Bernard Shaw reflected, "surround us on every hand: life itself is the miracle of miracles." Many decades later, Borland expressed a similar belief: "Only arrogance can deny [their] existence, and the denial falters in the face of evidence on every hand. In every tuft of grass, in every bird, in every opening bud, there it is."

Chapter 10

PUBLIC AND PRIVATE GRIEF

The sort of taboo Victorians placed on public discussion of sex has been transferred to death in our culture.

Joseph Bayly, American author, 1920-1986

In 1981, Bayly reported one estimate that the average person can go through as many as 20 years without being exposed to death in the immediate family or circle. Although I suspect that ratio has decreased in the 21st century, and although exceptions can be readily cited, most of us don't have to deal close-up with death at its most intimate level very often.

Even though we go to funeral parlors or religious houses and express condolences to family members, facing the death of someone dearly loved is a different matter entirely. More often than not, we are absent when our loved one dies. Unless he or she has been allowed to spend the last days at home, death comes in a sterile hospital environment, often with only medical personnel present. Or a sudden accident or natural death occurs when we are not there. Even when we are present, the lifeless body is soon shrouded, swiftly stripped from our sight.

Around 3 a.m. on a dark and dismal December morning, just four days after Christmas in 1986, my sisters and I gathered around my mother's hospital bed and sang hymns — we didn't know if she could hear them as she lay there in a coma, but we wanted to believe she did. A short time later, her slow, shallow breaths faded. And then, with one last short gasp of air, she was gone. Within seconds, a nurse hustled us out of the room. Hospital personnel, oblivious to our grief, callously suggested we gather her belongings and take them as we departed rather than return later. Undoubtedly, the nurses wanted our public grief to be carried outside their presence — and did not want it returned later.

Compliant, we trudged back into the death-filled room and hurriedly loaded a hospital cart with our mother's belongings.

Shivering, we must have been a sad sight that moonless night as we walked across the frigid parking lot, pushing the cart loaded with gowns never to be worn again and fragrant flowers whose scent now smelled of death. No public watched; no one embarrassed by an outpouring of grief. Only the still night air witnessed our furrowed foreheads, lined with angst; our tear-stained faces remained hidden in the darkness. The nurses had accomplished their aim.

In a vastly different scene, my husband's nieces and nephew said their goodbyes and sent their mother into the next life in a much more caring atmosphere than what my sisters and I experienced. Doris' four girls and her son+ gathered around her bed in one of the girls' homes as the time of her death approached. In a familiar place, they read scripture and sang, just as we had done in the cold confines of a hospital, bringing comfort not only to their beloved mother but also to themselves. After releasing their mother into the arms of death, they consoled each other with the assurance she no longer suffered in the realm of the spirit she had entered with their loving send-off.

Regardless of how compassionate or impersonal the death scene is, the next acts of the play are staged in similar ways, although customs vary based on religious beliefs. Whatever our faith or lack thereof, we quickly find deeply ingrained rules for how we should act and only a few have the courage to "do it their way."

Will the body be cremated or buried? There are burial clothes and caskets, or urns, to be selected, a burial site to be secured, and memorial service details to be decided. Will we receive friends? When? It's a busy time, and many people carefully contain outward displays of grief as they make preparations for their loved one's final departure.

Like millions of others, I will never forget Jacqueline Kennedy's control after her husband fell into her arms on November 22, 1963, as an assassin's gunfire erupted from a school book depository in Dallas, Texas. I remember how she swallowed her sorrow, displaying a stoic face as Lyndon B. Johnson took the oath of office as the nation's 36th president. I remember the public mass. As described on the web site for

Kennedy's presidential library and museum, "Perhaps the most indelible images of the day were the salute to his father given by little John F. Kennedy, Jr. (whose third birthday it was), daughter Caroline kneeling next to her mother at the President's bier, and the extraordinary grace and dignity shown by Jacqueline Kennedy." The face of public grief displayed that day is permanently etched in history, but the private face of sorrow was never unveiled.

Whether a person restrains grief or lets it flow unchecked from the moment of loss, most people find getting through the first few days of grief sometimes seems easy compared to the strength needed to face the weeks, months, and years ahead. After the activities accompanying the rituals of ending a life are past, finality of loss must be faced. The healing process cannot begin until we get beyond being brave.

I had always prided myself on being strong, and even though my heart was breaking, immediately after my husband's death, I held myself together, in F. Scott Fitzgerald's words, "very carefully like cracked crockery." At Bob's memorial service, when I stood rigidly before the gathering and paid tribute to his life, and to our life together, I barely commanded authority over tears threatening to escape. When the public phase ended, my brave face shattered. As Fitzgerald said, "Sometimes ... the cracked plate has to be retained in the pantry, has to be kept in service as a household necessity." My cracked plate could be put up for a while, but the necessity of my grief put it back on my table. For the first time in my life, I didn't put up a front, submersing my feelings, hiding them from the world. Family and friends were shocked, expecting me to show the same strength I had projected in the past. But I was mortally wounded, the scraps of my life shredded, burned into dust in an urn, and I just couldn't feign peace I didn't have.

Darlene+, respecting her parents' wish that she "live her faith," sometimes visited Flavia and Ronnie, good friends, where she knew she could grieve like a wolf howling in the dark night, where she could let her tears flow unchecked, without fear or criticism. She knew there her faith was unquestioned, that her friends understood she just missed her brother more than her heart could sometimes hold inside.

Even those who face their publics with stoicism find, as Colette said, "It's so curious: one can resist tears and 'behave' very well in the hardest hours of grief. But then someone makes you a friendly sign behind a window, or one notices a flower that was in bud only yesterday has suddenly blossomed, or a letter slips from a drawer...everything collapses."

We walk on a swinging bridge of grief. Whether in public or in private, whether triggered by a word or scene or ever present, sorrow sways us back and forth. We must clutch tightly to the rope sides of the bridge to avoid falling into the cavern below.

Chapter 11

WAVES OF GRIEF

Every wave, regardless of how high and forceful it crests, must eventually collapse within itself.
Stefan Zweig, Austrian author, 1881-1942

I can sit for hours watching waves roll into shore. Sometimes they are magnificent — large and white-capped, giant mountains in a stormy sea. At other times, they are calm, swishing and swirling as they gently sway before fading away in the yawning waters. Kids and grown-ups alike revel in riding the surf, sinking into its depths and letting its buoyancy carry them toward the sand. Wave riders must be careful though, to avoid being sucked into the undertow. "There is no secret to balance," Frank Herbert wrote, "you just have to feel the waves."

Grief comes and goes in waves, like breakers surging the shoreline. Some days we weep quietly, a calm, easy undulation; at other times we sob with abandonment, our bodies shaking with despair as tears roll down our face, great whitecaps breaking the surface. On good days, we can hold our sorrow in check; a stoic face masking our inner turmoil. The ocean of tears is still — not tranquil but not erupting unbidden. For a moment, we can accept Ovid's words of wisdom, applying them to our loss: "Neither can the wave that has passed by be recalled, nor the hour which has passed return again."

Even with that realization, the triggers for emotional ambushes can be pulled unknowingly. A kind word, a couple walking hand-in-hand, a mother hugging her child, a patch of goldenrod along the side of a highway, a song lovingly shared, the smell of a freshly baked cake — anything and everything can set off a wave of grief. Gordon+ found that hearing a song his wife Anne had been emotional about would bring him to tears. Even something as simple as a television show she liked could threaten his fragile stability.

Waves of Grief

For Carla+, driving up her driveway, three-quarters of a mile long, to the log cabin home she and her husband had moved into only six months before his death, touched off a geyser of grief every afternoon when she returned home from work. Before Kelly's accident, that long drive up the farm road had been always been filled with anticipation. She knew Kelly would be waiting for her, eager to hear about her day. They might walk out to the horse barn together, laughing as the horses competed for their attention. Or, they might curl up beside a warm fire. It didn't matter—just being with Kelly was enough. Now, as she began the climb up the curving driveway each day, her grief erupted, and she choked back sobs, tears carving a path down her pale cheeks.

After my husband died, everywhere I went I saw people in pairs—holding hands, laughing together. When a friend called or e-mailed to share that she and her husband were going out for lunch or were working in the yard or whatever, I wanted to scream, "Do you not realize you strike my heart like a javelin when you tell me what you and your husband are doing?"

I knew I was being irrational, but I couldn't control my feelings. I saw others going on with their lives, seemingly oblivious to my pain, when my world had stopped, and I wanted the world to stand still with me, knowing that is not reasonable or realistic.

Sometimes, we think certain triggers affect only us. Recently, in talking with Hazel+, I found we shared that, inexplicably, sitting in church listening to hymns inevitably triggered our grief, and we would weep. Songs that should have comforted our hearts left us desolate.

In the months following my husband's death, every Sunday I sat in the church Bob and I loved, biting my tongue to hold the sobs in check. But they moved with their own volition. I couldn't control my emotions—a strange experience for me. Throughout my married life, I rarely cried. I could go years without shedding a tear. But after Bob's sudden departure from this world, I couldn't stop crying. No matter how much I willed myself to halt the flow, the tears fell like rain over the ocean, making more and larger waves.

Faces of Grief

Even now, three years after Bob's death, sometimes memories sink me into the waves. But, hearing others' reminiscences can also bring a smile. Recently, I told a friend how Bob used to grab me in an elevator, plant a big kiss on my lips and hold me there, laughing as I struggled to get away before the elevator doors opened. In response, she recalled how she viewed my marriage to Bob:

You, the pretty and polished college president, and Bob, the outgoing cut up (at least that's the side I saw), but I am sure that inside you two must have been a match made in heaven, the perfect balance. I saw him several times at the mall during the day just browsing for clothes for you. At first, I thought he was kidding me, and then I realized he really did select a lot of your gorgeous clothes! What a testament of love, to do something that personal and from a man who was truly a man's man. It was like, if he couldn't be with you, he was doing something for you.

Poignantly, as I read my friend's words, I slipped away into Bob's love for a moment before returning to the world where he no longer exists. But it was good to be able to remember him with joy, even for a fleeting flash of time. As Longfellow advised, I sat "in reverie, and watch[ed] the changing color of the waves that break upon the idle seashore of the mind."

In that translucent reverie, I remembered Bob and I were not individual waves crashing against the shore. Morrie Schwartz, in *Tuesdays with Morrie*, captured the essence of waves. He tells a story about a little wave, "bobbing in the ocean, having a grand old time." Morrie says the little wave was enjoying the wind and the fresh air, until he observed the other waves nearer the shore. Seeing them crash against the coastline, the little wave said, "'My God, this is terrible...look what's going to happen to me!'" Then, Morrie says, another wave came along and saw the grim-looking little wave. Pausing in its march to the sea, the new wave asked, "'Why do you look so sad?' Holding back tears, the little wave responded, 'You don't understand! We're all going to crash! All of us waves are going to be nothing! Isn't it terrible?'" But the older, wiser wave, who had crashed many times before, said, "'No, you don't understand. You're not a wave. You are part of the ocean.'" And so are we — we, and our loved ones.

Chapter 12

SPECIAL CIRCUMSTANCES –PART 1

DEATH OF A CHILD

DEATH CARES NOT ABOUT AGE

Death is simply a shedding of the physical body like the butterfly shedding its cocoon. It is a transition to a higher state of consciousness where you continue to perceive, to understand, to laugh, and to be able to grow.

Elizabeth Kübler-Ross, Swiss-American psychiatrist and author, 1926-2004

If you've ever watched an effervescent orange and black monarch butterfly emerge from its chrysalis, you've witnessed a miracle. After the mystical metamorphous into a full-grown butterfly, the newly-winged creature flies into the air, flitting from flower to flower, sucking the sweet nectar from each bright bloom before fluttering into the distance. Although you can no longer see the delicate, color-sewn wings, you know they have only carried the tender body away temporarily, that the butterfly will linger just out of sight before presenting its vibrant splendor once again for your viewing. But then, after flirting in and out of your range of vision, the butterfly vanishes with the breeze, never to return.

Babies and children are like those butterflies, fragile and winged, their charm and beauty brightening our lives with color and excitement. Ever so often, though, they too soon take flight beyond the bounds of the sky, long before we expect them to disappear from our lives. After they shed their cocoon, we want to confine the butterflies to this world, but sometimes we can only watch helplessly as the majestic creatures soar beyond the azure sky, making their way toward the heavens.

Parents who have lost a young child say there is no other loss that compares. Many don't know how they will get through their grief, going on autopilot to survive, planning and attending wakes, funerals, memorial services, shiva, and other mourning rituals.

Numb and inconsolable, they make decisions about where the child's body will rest, select a casket and the clothes in which their beloved will be buried, pick pallbearers, and deal with countless other details as if they are watching the action without being a part of it.

How do you make sense of something so senseless? How do you bear the unspeakable pain? Your role as a parent was to protect your child like a lion guarding a cub, to take care of him, to wipe away her tears, to prepare him for dealing with your death at some distant point in the future. You never imagined having to deal with *her* death. Nothing can prepare you for that. "A period placed before the end of the sentence" is how Carl Jung describes a child's death. Joseph Bayly, who lost three sons, adds, "...sometimes before the sentence has hardly begun."

The whole world is transformed with the loss of your child. All the hopes and dreams for their future faded into nothingness. Your universe, where they revolved in every turn of life, came crashing down, never to turn on the same axis again.

Ann Finkbeiner, who lost her college-age son in a train wreck, learned two things as she talked with other parents who had lost children: A child's death is disorienting — "children's deaths make no sense, have no precedent, are part of no pattern; their deaths are unnatural and wrong." And, she found that "...letting go of a child is impossible."

In Bayly's words, "In a way that is different from any other human relationship, a child is bone of his parents' bone, flesh of their flesh. When a child dies, part of the parents is buried."

In her book, *After the Death of a Child: Living with Loss Through the Years*, Finkbeiner expresses the profound truth she faced after the death of her son: "Our children are in our blood; the bond with them doesn't seem to break." She continues that all parents seem to find "unconscious ways of preserving that bond."

Tommy and Jenna, devoted Christians, didn't give their teenage son Jeremy his every desire, but when he begged for a red Jeep for his 16th birthday, they sacrificed to make his dream come true. Two months later, he took friends on a fun ride on a gravel road where he could show "his stuff." Gunning the engine to make the jeep spin on the loose rocks, he looked over his shoulder to grin gleefully at his friends for a second before turning back to the road ahead. Startled, he froze as the jeep spun out and flipped over. The only one not wearing a seat belt, Jeremy's body propelled to the ground where the jeep landed on him, crushing him to death.

Their tragic loss compounded by guilt they had bought their son the jeep that killed him, Tommy and Jenna tried to put up a good front, knowing others watched their faith being tested. Alone, it was a different story. Almost three years later, Tommy sometimes still finds Jenna curled up in a fetal position, crying herself to sleep when he returns home from business travels. When their son's best friend, who had remained close to them, was killed in a tragic automobile accident recently, unhealed wounds were impaled by new spears of sorrow. The bond with their son kept open by their continuing relationship with his special friend, broken again.

One man, who lost his son in a tragic industrial accident, said getting over a child's death is like pushing a wheelbarrow with a flat tire uphill through mud — a task that leaves the parent with blisters on his hands — and in his soul. Big, festering sores that break open every time the hand grips the handle of the wheelbarrow.

In *The Grieving Garden*, the authors describe how Stathi Afendoulis recalls his utter desolation after the death of his young daughter from cancer: loneliness and "isolation so profound it seemed to envelope my entire being." Afendoulis says the earliest days were "so enshrouded by grief that every moment is about the loss." He could barely stand his grief, "overcome by this feeling of helplessness, it rendered [me] mute and frozen." He vacillated from being immobilized to wanting to kick and punch anyone and everything about him. Feeling like dust himself, he wanted to crush his surroundings into dirt. He says he felt gutted, like a fish that had been cleaned out. "There was nothing inside me. I would stand with my fists clenched, thrusting them upward toward heaven, waiting for God to help me and cursing Him with every fiber of my being." Afendoulis compares it to "The Silent Scream," a physical body with no soul, just an abyss.

Nita and her husband Walter+ watched their butterfly named Hannah soar into the heavens halfway through the twelfth year of her life, but they both testify their response to God's call was never anger. Despite the devastating loss, Nita and Walter, even in their darkest moments, praised God for the time they had with Hannah. Their feelings of grief were no less than those of Afendoulis, the hole in their life no less vast and deep. And, they directed their grief in the same direction—heavenly—but their message was one of thanksgiving for the life they had been loaned.

Did God understand and accept both the anger of Afendoulis and the thankfulness of the Brunings? I have no doubt He did. He knows His children—He created us—and whatever we send His way He can handle with amazing grace. He knows both Afendoulis and the Brunings are pushing wheelbarrows up rough ground.

As days turn into weeks, weeks into months, and months into years, you wonder if you will ever recover, or will you just go on with life, broken and desolate in a world where your beloved child no longer walks? Mitchell and Volpe, writing in *Beyond Tears: Living After Losing a Child*, talk about how they moved from "relentless grief" to "shadow grief" after both faced "senseless and untimely" deaths of their children. Relentless grief, overwhelming and unending, hits you at the beginning. Shadow grief comes later and is always with you, but it is bearable. Walls of darkness become more ethereal as you re-enter the world of the living.

An aspect of your life demanding attention is your relationship with the other parent. Stressed not only by loss but also personal, and sometimes differing, reactions to that loss can fracture relationships. Even if you reach out to each other, you may find your emotional bank drained, leaving you unable to console your partner as you grapple with your own sorrow. And, one parent may blame the other, adding more tension and pain. Some counselors suggest couples force themselves to connect each day, even scheduling time to talk, to share their feelings and memories. Keeping the communication lines open is critical, even if they are strained. If one partner withdraws and refuses to talk or go places, the other partner needs to gently and lovingly understand. If one partner feels better when escaping to the outside world, the other partner needs to respect that. Compromise is essential — each must be willing to bend a little, to help the other in the way that person needs.

Sometimes men and women grieve differently, and this is usually seen in how long tears flow unbidden. Gary notes that marriages sometimes don't survive the loss of a child and pays special tribute to his wife Diane+. "I couldn't have made it without her," he says candidly. But he also concedes it sometimes bothered him when people would ask, "How's Diane?" It was like they thought he wasn't grieving as much as Diane because he didn't cry in public as much as his wife. "I don't open that door except in certain places," Gary says, but it doesn't mean he isn't aching inside. As he talked with me about Jason's death, it was evident his anguish was as deep and wide as the Amazon River.

Men often feel they aren't manly if they cry in public; but for some, like Gary, it may just be that tears don't flow as freely at any time, not just in sorrow. Gary admits only his children can bring tears to his eyes.

In situations where parents are separated or divorced, the death of a child can be even more devastating. Unlike horses yoked together, most separated parents don't pull together. In their grief, they shift the burden, adding to the heavy load of the other partner.

Together or apart, parents must realize, if there are other children in the family, they need attention, too. Some parents find it therapeutic to help their child grieve. As they focus on the surviving child[ren], they either submerge their own feelings to be dealt with later, or ideally, they work through them simultaneously with their child[ren]. If a parent is emotionally unable to help his or her child[ren], the child[ren] may feel neglected or abandoned and may even believe the parent wishes they were the one taken — that if you don't care about them, you would have preferred they were the one to die. Counselors emphasize it is important to communicate with your child[ren], letting them see both your love for them and your grief over the lost child. Honest, open grief helps everyone live through and accept the loss.

Many parents find solace in establishing some type of perpetual memorial to their child. This can range from a foundation that supports an area of personal meaning to the child or parents (such as the ones set up by the Brunings+ and the Fowlers+), a book that celebrates their life (and it doesn't have to be published — it may just be a booklet you share with family and friends), donations to charities or other organizations that have relevance to you or your child, memorial books you assemble to preserve drawings, letters, or other special items (such as the ones lovingly prepared by Muffin+). One of the more current ways to memorialize a child's life is to create a Web page where you can include pictures, videos, stories, and other remembrances. This also provides a place for friends and family to contribute their thoughts and feelings, making it therapeutic for them and touching for you as you read about the deep love others had for your child.

None of this will make the pain go away, but it may bring glimmers of joy into your darkest days. Parents who have survived the loss of a child avow it is unlikely you will ever get over the death of your child, but you will learn to live with your pain. Sometimes others, and sometimes you, will pick away the scab that covers your wound, but eventual healing will come. Scars will remain, but the unspeakable, unbearable pain gets more muted with time. Always there, but the throbbing becomes less intense, the misery more bearable. And the hope of a reunion makes all that possible.

Chapter 13

SPECIAL CIRCUMSTANCES—PART 2

SUICIDE

NO REASON TO LIVE

What makes life worth living? Better surely, to yield to the stain of suicide blood in me and seek forgetfulness in the embrace of cold dark death.

Zane Grey, American author, 1872-1939

Worldwide, each year more than one million people die of suicide, the 13th leading cause of death. In America, where suicide ranks 11th as the cause of death, one person succeeds in taking his own life every 16 minutes, more than 30,000 each year. An estimated 4.6 million Americans alive today have attempted suicide. Staggering statistics.

Pliny the Younger wrote, as related by Bayly, "Corellius has died and died by his own wish, which makes me ever sadder; for death is most tragic when it is not due to fate or natural causes. When we see men die of disease, at least we can find consolation in the knowledge that it is inevitable, but when their end is self-sought, our grief is inconsolable because we feel that their lives could have been long."

Those who choose life can't understand why anyone would opt out. According to the Centers for Disease Control and the National Institute of Mental Health, 90 percent of suicide victims suffer from mental illness at the time of their death. Chemically or genetically imbalanced, the mind says life isn't worth living...that hope is gone...that no one cares...that there's no future...that life's not worth the pain...that it's never going to get better. Karl A. Menninger noted the major weapon against the suicide impulse is lost at that point, because hope is a necessity for normal life.

Suicide becomes the only outcome a victim thinks he can control. As Bill Maher says, "Suicide is man's way of telling God, 'You can't fire me—I quit.'"

Those left behind often feel abandoned. Bayly tells us suicide is unusually hard for survivors to cope with because it is avoidable. Some feel rage against the person who selfishly removed himself from their lives, leaving them to cope with not only the death but also guilt.

Connie+ felt guilty that she couldn't "fix" her husband. She couldn't make his mind well. She was also consumed with guilt that she didn't pay close attention to signs he had reached the end of his lifeline. On the other end of the spectrum, she suddenly felt free of her husband's depression—the ups and downs of his emotional imbalance that made him unpredictable and difficult to live with at times. But even her relief could not hold the hounds of regret nipping at her heels.

Carla Fine, sharing her story in *No Time to Say Goodbye: Surviving the Suicide of a Loved One,* tells readers she was "haunted by the infinite regrets that are woven into the fabric of suicide. I would replay the chronology of events leading up to Harry's death, searching for lost opportunities to reverse the inevitable outcome." Only when she came to accept the actuality that her husband's choice to kill himself was his alone was she able to loosen the crushing grip of "what if's."

"Gradually," Fine discloses, "I came to understand that while it may be possible to help someone whose fear is death, there are no guarantees for a person whose fear is life."

Suicide completers' fear of life is greater than their compassion for those who will be left to deal with their fatal act. That doesn't mean victims did not love their family and friends, or that they were unconcerned about the impact of their actions. It's just that, in a skewed mental state, despair is greater than rationality, greater than the ability to envision the horror to be inflected on those they loved. Judy Collins, whose son committed suicide, says, "The message of a suicide survivor leaves a trail as distinct as the trail of a comet in the sky if you can read the sky."

Somehow, those left behind must grasp that their loved one was both the perpetrator and victim of the deadly decision. Robbed of their beloved and resentful the suicide victim didn't care enough about those who loved him or her, family and friends' emotions propel them on a carnival ride. Angry, longing, hurt, sad, guilty, helpless, and unjustly shamed—the flow of grief is harsh and bumpy with twists and turns strong enough to shake up and even unseat the steadiest rider.

Collins once compared suicide to cancer 50 years ago, noting that people avoid talking about it; most don't even want to know about it because they are frightened of it. And, sadly, they don't understand that the issues are medically treatable. That knowledge can help prevent suicides, but when it comes after the act has been committed, one must not attach too much self-blame.

Peter Greene said, "As anyone who has been close to someone who has committed suicide knows, there is no other pain like that felt after the incident." Pain the survivor must bear. As Collins' sister wrote in her journal, "Every day I have to choose light, to put aside darkness. I cannot let the darkness destroy me. Or the shame."

The journey through grief is excruciating, but it becomes ever so more complicated when the casualty comes at the hand of one wounded by his mind. As Kübler-Ross and Kessler say, there are no models for dealing with a suicide, although they do stress the importance of sharing the truth. To avoid talking about it, to pretend the person died a natural death, will result in increased shame and secrecy. Even if others attach stigma, you should plant your feet firmly, holding your head high. The act was one of illness—not one of dishonor.

We are all human beings struggling to survive in a world rife with problems. The suicide victim had his or her own set of issues, for whatever reason feeling cut off from help and hope. Trapped, unable to see a way out, victims choose, in John Hewett's words, not death "as much as choosing to end this unbearable pain."

Fortunately, today most religions no longer paint suicides in shades of disgrace. St. Augustine's view that suicide is a grievous sin no longer reigns, even in the Catholic Church. Instead, most religious organizations stand ready to help grievers work their way through the complicated dynamics and struggles that accompany this particular kind of death.

Collins, writing in *Singing Lessons*, dreamed of her son on the anniversary of his death. In the dream she tried to persuade Clark not to die, that he didn't have to end his life. She remembers her son looking at her with a smile and love in his eyes, saying, "'Mother, death is not an ending.'"

Somewhere along her journey through grief, Collins discovered she didn't have to stay in depression, that she had the tools to help: a spiritual book, a kind word from a friend, reminders of the good things in her life, which she often recorded in writing. "In the moment of silence, there is the sound of God bringing me strength — bringing me healing."

In addition to these sources of help, Collins discovered that only those who have lost a family member through suicide can *really* touch your innermost thoughts — two people who speak a language foreign to others but totally understandable to those whose loss has made them the same. Only someone who knows the wound that ripped your heart when a person you love decided to leave, only "...a wounded one can heal you." To teach you how to walk down a path, a person must have walked the same path.

When she talks about her son, Collins' blood stops and she lapses into shock. "I can be talking, and suddenly, I am white as a sheet emotionally. My breath comes in shorter takes. I am in it again." But if she is in the presence of another wounded survivor, she knows the secret place of her pain is understood.

Suicide dismantled Collins' life, distorting the world into her enemy: "The place where this could happen. The place where this did happen." She didn't think she would survive, "floating on this new and terrible ocean that had sprung up around us, an ocean full of storm and sorrow." Collins recalls the tears for her terrible loss kept coming not only in the days that followed, but for years, "dropping like rain from the foggy valley through which I would walk, the valley of the shadow of death." Describing the weight of her son's death as the "weight of white snow," she says it "stilled every bird, froze all life. Nature wanted to stop…time wanted to stop…life had stopped. For my son, there would be no thaw."

For a time, Collins feared there would be no thaw for her, either. But she chose to emerge victorious rather than become another victim. Before she suffered the tragic loss of her son, Collins says she had been immune to how deeply a soul could be shaken, how vulnerable and raw a spirit could become. She surmises this may be the way the wound of loss works, opening up the mourner to the depths of life so that the heights become more magnificent. After floundering in her grief for years, the introduction to her book relates Collins' heart was freed to treasure the precious moments of life and perceive the miracle that memory bestows to ease the pain of loss.

Still, there is darkness. But "as time passes," Collins acknowledges, "the dark becomes lighter.… At times, in the middle of the night, I must hold my faith before the phantom like a cross of gleaming silver. I glare back at the phantom. I dare her: she has done her worst, and she can do no more. I fear not."

Holding on to God, trusting Him more than life's illusions and death, Collins knows she will never get over her son's suicide. But she believes Clark would "understand the bittersweet poetry of having to go on living when you want to die of grief." As she moved into another season of her life, this one without him, she prayed he would understand she must continue living. For herself, and for him.

Chapter 14

SPECIAL CIRCUMSTANCES—PART 3

MULTIPLE DEATHS

RESILIENCE WHEN LOSSES COME IN LEGIONS

This is courage...to bear unflinchingly what heaven sends.
Euripides, Athenian playwright, 480-406 BC

Few alive on September 11, 2001, will ever forget the horrific image of planes commandeered by terrorists taking thousands of lives in a matter of minutes. On a smaller scale, on a more recurrent timetable, school buses crash, vans plummet over guard rails, explosions implode buildings, tornados twist and tear houses into splinters, and earthquakes erupt, dropping people into their wake. Lives lost not one by one, but in legions. Thankfully, most of us never have to experience these kinds of losses; but ever so often, our lives are touched by more than one loss in a relatively short period of time, pounding us again before we have recovered from the last collision with death.

Where do we get the strength and fortitude to go on with life in the presence of loss, especially when deaths come not in a solitary march into our lives, but in succession, one after the other?

Consider Mount St. Helens, where every living stalk and creature was burned to extinction when its volcano erupted in 1980 after being dormant for many years. Newspaper articles decried the ruination—annihilated forests, choked rivers, destruction of fish and wildlife, poisoned air, and on and on. Yet, one year later, green sprouts rose from the ashes, wildflowers bloomed, salmon had returned (even though they had to find alternate routes), and animals came to join in the rebirth of the forest. Where devastation had reigned, life returned.

The end is sometimes the beginning. Myriad examples can be found where people thought their life was over, only to discover a new life awaited them. When our son's biological parents died (his mother from terminal cancer when Kevin was five and his father from a heart attack when he was eight), he thought the gods were against him, that he was awfully unlucky — perhaps jinxed — to lose both parents when his friends hadn't lost even one. And, then, Karen (the family member who took Kevin in) decided he was too much to handle, and he was thrown into the laps of complete strangers, my husband and me. I will never forget the night we told him he would be living with us: He had been sitting beside my husband, but when he heard his frightful fate, he jumped like a jack-in-the-box to the other end of the sofa. He sat there, his little belly shaking with racking sobs, sensing he was leaving behind his previous life forever. Later that week, as we drove someplace in the car, in a pitiful, quiet voice from the back seat — as far away from us as he could get — Kevin muttered, "I have *worser* bad luck than anybody. First my mama died, then my daddy. And now Karen doesn't want me."

No amount of reasoning or cajoling helped; Kevin was desolate. Then, one night, about two weeks later, I heard him singing in the shower. He had adjusted so quickly I feared he was repressing his sorrow, but a quick trip to a counselor proved he was remarkably resilient. From that day on, although I am sure Kevin missed his mother and father enormously, he became a happy little cotton top, tow-headed boy. His life — and ours — had been evermore altered.

For Kevin, as Joseph Bayly said in his book, *The Last Thing We Talk About*, "Time heal[ed] grief; love prevent[ed] scar tissue from forming." He had learned, as had a 12-year-old child quoted in Worden's book *Children and Grief: When a Parent Dies*: "It is a struggle, but you can survive it. It gets easier as memories come in and the grief goes out."

Like Kevin, Aileen+ learned early to be resilient. She was 24-years-old when her first husband died at sea while serving in the U.S. Navy during World War II, but the need to take care of her three sons, Floyd, Johnny, and Jimmy, forced her to find the strength to go on with life. Years later, she remarried and had two more children, Donald and Barbara. But her life was not to be without further sorrow. In 1964, following in the footsteps of his father, Aileen's son Jimmy died while serving in the United States Air Force. Losing her husband had been terrible, but the death of her son hit at a profoundly deeper level. Shocked and stunned, Aileen held herself together as her son Johnny married less than two weeks later, but inside she bled from the fiery arrows that had pierced her heart.

Aileen's collisions with death were not to end. Many years later, she lost another son and her second husband in a ten-day period. After so many tragic deaths in her family, Aileen could have cried out in anger, "My God, My God, how much more can I bear?" Like Christ, she could have asked God if he had forsaken her. How she found peace and strength is conveyed in her personal story found in Section Two.

The Stone family faced death many times over the years as grandparents, aunts, uncles, and friends died. But Pam+ says, "None of that prepared us for what would happen during a short four-year period from 2001 to 2005." First, the loss of Pam's rock — her brother Butch. Then, long before she had anchored in the sea of her grief, Pam's sister Anna died, doubling her misery, filling her with unspeakable rage. Anger at the doctors who hadn't saved her siblings, fury at her brother and sister for leaving her alone to care for their aging parents, wrath at God for deserting her. "Why would God do this to my family?" she cried out in frustration.

When the third family member died, her dad, Pam could have said, as Emily Dickinson did after losing her father, her mother, her nephew (struck down by typhoid fever at the age of eight), and four close friends in a few short years, "The crisis of the sorrow of so many years is all that tires me." Unlike Dickinson, Pam did not have a nervous collapse. She still struggles, she is sometimes still morose, but she hasn't given up. Someone once said we should mimic what birds do — they sing away their grief. And that's what Pam does each time she steps into the choir loft of her church. Sad, missing her family members, she lifts her voice toward the home where she believes they are listening, awaiting her arrival.

Battered by dark waves of multiple losses, peace can be elusive. For some, like Pam, songs give interludes of solace. For others, overpowering sadness from accumulated grief relentlessly tosses their beleaguered spirits, pushing aside faith and reason. How can we bear so much loss? Bear so much grief? Bear so much loneliness? How can we go on living? Yet, repudiating life is not the answer.

In the quiet shadows of sorrow, shattered and shaken, we have to go on. What seems utterly intolerable now will become progressively endurable as the years tick by. Even with our hearts turning violently in our chests, we learn to fill the empty places, at least for periods of time. Days we dread come and go; emotions ebb and flow, until we settle into a new routine. Then, the "arrow that flieth by day" will no longer strike our souls with fear.

How can we know that? Can we become more like Corrie ten Boom and less like Elie Wiesel? Both suffered the atrocities of the Holocaust; both undoubtedly questioned God's justice in allowing six million Jews to die. But they traveled their journey through pain with different attitudes. Yancey offers the stark contrast of the two lives:

Wiesel, who relates his experiences in *Night*, describes the horrors of seeing fellow villagers pushed into cattle cars with only the clothes on their backs, babies pitchforked to death, starving men killing fellow prisoners for a ration of bread. In the unfolding nightmare, he witnessed human ovens devouring his mother, his little sister, and other family members.

"Never shall I forget that night, seven times cursed and seven times sealed. Never shall I forget that smoke. Never shall I forget the little faces of the children, whose bodies I saw turned into wreaths of smoke beneath a silent blue sky. Never shall I forget that nocturnal silence which deprived me, for all eternity, of the desire to live. Never shall I forget those moments which murdered my God and my soul and turned my dreams to dust. Never shall I forget these things, even if I am condemned to live as long as God Himself. Never."

Wiesel's words convey utter hopelessness. He describes himself as the "accuser." Overwhelmed by the atrocities he had witnessed, depressed by man's evil heart, Wiesel felt he had witnessed the death of God in the souls of children and men.

Corrie ten Boom endured the same depravities as Wiesel, including seeing her own sister die at the hands of Nazis. Aiding Jews, she ended up in a death camp herself, and at times she flailed against God in absolute anger at the atrocities unfolding before her weary eyes. But interwoven throughout her writings, threads of hope are sewn with small moments of joy, simple acts of kindness offered at great personal risk, songs of faith, and readings of scripture.

After reading about both Weisel and Corrie, Yancey confesses he was tempted to identify more with Weisel by "throwing off the confining shackles of belief." He says he was "gripped by the innate human urge to flee to despair, away from hope." But in the end, Yancey comes down on the side of Corrie: "However deep the pit, God's love is deeper still."

And so it is with the losses in our lives. If we but choose, the deepness of God's love can pull us out of the pit of hopelessness.

Chapter 15

ACKNOWLEDGING BAD MEMORIES

There is no grief like the grief that does not speak.
Henry Wadsworth Longfellow, American poet, 1807-1882

Mary didn't like admitting it, but her husband Sam was a sluggard — even though he had a job; whenever he was home, he lounged on the sofa, demanding that Mary take care of his every wish and desire. This was bad enough, but Mary was mortified at how Sam allowed their home to fall into disrepair, a neighborhood embarrassment. How it hurt that he berated her for not being a better wife when he failed miserably as a husband.

There was never any harmony in the household; Mary struggled daily with Sam's constant griping, his short fuse often leaving her in tears. Sometimes she wished he would just move on so she could have some peace.

It bothered Mary that Sam refused to go to church with her — or anywhere else for that matter. Even though they shared the same house, Mary and her husband pretty much lived separate lives.

Yet, when Sam died, one would have thought the two were the closest of companions — all thoughts of wishing him gone buried with his body. Moreover, from the way Mary talked about him, one might surmise her husband had been a saint.

Mary's reaction to her husband's death is not unusual. When a loved one dies, even if he were not perfect, the temptation to idealize the life that has now ended takes over like the urge to paint a wall of graffiti. Whitewash the sullied parts of life, covering up bad memories. It is a false kind of grieving, though, to shed tears over something that never existed. Sorrowing over a life that never was is not only unrealistic but also deepens grief.

Like Mary, when Marcy and Mike's son died in a car accident at the age of 17, they shed sad tears over the loss of Paul, their youngest. In their pain, the idealized picture they drew of him in their minds and to others bore no resemblance to the real less-than-perfect son who made their lives miserable. In truth, their son was a belligerent, angry young man who frequently disrespected his parents, refused to abide by their rules, and was in trouble with the law countless times.

Mary, Marcy, and Mike shared a common syndrome—don't say anything bad about the deceased. Forget anything wrong he ever did and pretend righteousness reigned when the departed one was alive. While this may seem noble, taking such a stance can cause conscious and subconscious problems, including suppressing our feelings and prolonging our sorrow.

Truth be known, Mary, Marcy, and Mike—and incalculable others—likely felt some relief in their loved one's absence. Fleeting thoughts of freedom from worry flow through the mind before being banished by self-reproach at having such unseemly notions. Such short-lived thoughts are not terrible. We are humans with complex emotions, stirring like sailboats heeling in the wind as grief blows through us. Thoughts ebb and flow in a current we can't control.

At some point, to make it through the mourning process, we must face both the good and bad in our loved one's life. Otherwise, the baggage secreted in our mind may weigh us down. Whether we hold the anger we feel for the way a person lived deep inside us, or rage aloud that their actions caused their death, resentment taps away at our spirit, a woodpecker in our soul.

It is important to realize, though, that condemning our loved one for the misery inflicted in our lives does not help. Rather, we should acknowledge unkind and cruel words, thoughtless actions, and unloving ways alongside the positive attributes. Every human being is a composite of both virtue and sin, bringing both joy and distress. To erase the terrible times and the trauma they caused is a temporary fix.

In *How to Say No to a Stubborn Habit*, Edwin Lutzer reminds us that suppressing feelings will not cause them to disappear. Instead, he declares, "Feelings must be dealt with honestly; they cannot be ignored." In admitting our loved one was a flawed human being (and aren't we all just that?), we need to be careful we don't lose sight of the balance in that person's life. Cataloging all of the wrongs should not wipe out the good. What we should do is to admit the truth of our feelings without painting our loved one in black or pure white for the world or for ourselves. We will then be able to grieve the person who was.

Gordon MacDonald recalls a painful past in China when its culture demanded that young girls' feet be wrapped and tightly bound to keep them small and attractive. Similarly, our refusal to face the good and bad in our loved one's life can be discomforting and deforming. MacDonald concludes it is no different with hearts that have never been unwrapped by repentance. I add that it is no different with hearts that have never faced the truth.

Our heart must be unbound.

MacDonald says it this way: "A broken heart will never be rebuilt until we learn this principle of the unbound heart. It must be unwrapped and exposed to the light. The light will show some unattractive evil, but then something wonderful will happen. The love of God will be free to flood into the dark recesses, and rebuilding will begin."

Chapter 16
FORGIVENESS – PART 1

FORGIVENESS IS A TWO-WAY STREET

To err is human; to forgive is divine.
Alexander Pope, English poet, 1688-1744

At the opposite end of pretending our loved ones were perfect is the inability to forgive any wrongs done to us. Alone, in the shadows of our soul, we may bear a grudge, resentful of their behavior. Around others, we may hold the secret inside, sharing our heart with no one, perhaps fearing the embarrassment of revealing our true home life, or feeling besieged by guilt that we can't forget the dreadful fights and harsh, angry words.

Ignoring these feelings will not make them disappear. They must be acknowledged, accepted, and confronted. We may need to weep our way through this process — or we may need to shout our rage. Only after we have sorted out our resentment, tackled our anger, and coped with our regrets can we move forward.

Then, after we have faced our bitterness, we should put it away, absolving the person who has wronged us. Our spirit may be broken — both with the life and death of the person — but if our heart is open to forgiveness, we will move more softly through our sorrow.

How do we forgive someone who isn't around to ask our forgiveness? It starts by admitting what we all are — sinners saved by grace. We need to set aside the temptation to condemn the sins we do not commit ourselves and to condone those we carry inside our own hearts. To be human is to err; to make mistakes that hurt others is part of our nature. When we acknowledge, in Brennan Manning's words, that our own halos are tilted, it becomes easier to forgive those who have left us marred and mangled by their actions.

Manning tells the story of Fiorello LaGuardia, mayor of New York City during the Great Depression. On a cold, icy night in

January of 1935, the mayor decided to dismiss the judge of a night court in the poorest ward of the city and sit on the bench himself. The first person brought before him was a shabbily dressed old woman, charged with stealing a loaf of bread. Her defense was simple: her daughter's husband had left her, her daughter was sick, and her two grandchildren were starving. The shopkeeper, saying she must be punished to teach other people in the neighborhood they couldn't get away with stealing, refused to drop the charges.

Shaking his head in dismay, LaGuardia told the woman the law gave him no choice — he had to punish her. And the law was specific — ten dollars or ten days in jail. As he issued his decision, he reached into his pocket, pulled out a ten-dollar bill, and tossed it in the big sombrero he often wore. Telling everyone in the courtroom he was paying the old woman's fine, he also issued another verdict: He fined every person in the courtroom fifty cents for living in a town where a person had to steal bread to keep her grandchildren from starving, pronouncing, "'Mr. Bailiff, collect the fines and give them to the defendant.'"

The next day New York City newspapers reported $47.50 was handed to the elderly woman, who had watched in amazement as the storekeeper, petty criminals, people with traffic violations, and city policemen each handed over their fifty cents. And then, the papers added, those who had paid the fines rose as one in a standing ovation for the mayor.

"What an extraordinary moment of grace for anyone present in that courtroom!" Manning concludes, adding, "The grace of God operates at a profound level in the life of a loving person."

At this same deep level of grace, Pope John Paul II walked into a prison and said to Mehmet Ali Agca, the hired assassin who had tried to kill him, "I forgive you." Shot as he rode in an open car across St. Peter's Square on a late spring day in 1981, the Pope took two hits to his stomach, one to his right arm, and one to his left hand. After emergency surgery saved his life, he visited Agca in Rebibbia Prison in Italy; and, in another moment of extraordinary grace, held the hand that shot him and forgave the would-be killer. In that instant, the violence of St. Peter's Square was transformed into peace and pardon.

It took her longer, but Betty Ferguson forgave the man who killed her 16-year-old daughter, Debbie. Lisa Collier Cool tells the story in a May 2004 *Reader's Digest* article:

Ferguson took her daughter's murder hard—as any mother would. She couldn't sleep, became despondent, and drank herself to sleep every night. "'I was consumed by hatred...'" But six years after her daughter's death, at her sister's funeral, a line from the Lord's Prayer awakened her slumbering soul: "Forgive us our trespasses as we forgive those who trespass against us." Like a mighty eagle scooping her up in its wings, the words lifted her anger and she looked heavenward, seeing that forgiveness might be the answer to her grief.

Visiting Debbie's grave soon after her epiphany, Ferguson paused at the tombstone and read the words inscribed there: "What the world needs now is love, sweet love." It was then she knew what she had to do. In 1986, eleven years after her daughter' murder, she visited Ray Payne at the prison where he was serving a life sentence for his crime. She told the murderer what her daughter had meant to her and how lost and brokenhearted she had been. As Ferguson talked, Payne, the man who had abducted and killed her, who had been her daughter's high school English teacher, cried with her. "I left a different person," she says. "My heart felt soft and light and warm."

If we can find the kind of grace Manning describes, the kind demonstrated by Pope Paul and Betty Ferguson, we can forgive. After all, as Ferguson said to friends who were amazed by what she had done: "Forgiveness is the greatest gift I ever gave myself..." It was, she adds, a "healing journey that's saved my life."

Lewis Smedes, author of *The Art of Forgiving*, wrote, "Forgiveness happens inside the person doing the forgiving. It heals our pain and resentment before it does anything for the person we forgive; they might never know about it."

We, too, can be healed of our hurts. As said by St. Francis of Assisi: "It is in pardoning that we are pardoned."

Chapter 17

FORGIVENESS – PART 2

I'M SO SORRY

And throughout all Eternity
I forgive you, you forgive me
William Blake, Broken Love, English poet, 1757-1827

Aristotle says we are rational men, but in the bewilderment of death's aftermath, the strong arm of irrational thoughts grips us with great force. Regrets seem to be written into the language of grief. Regrets over words not spoken, and remorse over words spoken, flash lightning in the dark sky of our souls. The "if only's" and "I wish I had's" thunder through our heads.

Early in our grieving, the memories of wrongs we committed converge in singles or in multiples. Bayly reminds us we have all, in one way or another, hurt the person we loved. Few if any of us can truthfully say we have no regrets, even those who had an opportunity to right wrongs before death struck. And if we didn't have that chance, we are haunted by actions taken...or not; words said...or not.

Sharp words were said; we behaved selfishly; we were inconsiderate; we fought, or we let our loved one leave without saying, "I love you." We sent our teenager on an errand we should have done. We didn't spend as much time with our loved one as we could have or should have. We didn't insist he go to the doctor; we didn't notice she wasn't feeling well; we didn't pay attention when he said his arm ached. For Alisa+, it was something as simple as not cooking the meal her brother requested—a decision that still troubles her thirty years later. "If I had only cooked that dumb dish," she says, still angry at herself, "Dennis would be here today."

As with any death, dealing with regrets clouds the grieving process. You blame yourself even if there was nothing you could have done. And, if you could have done something, even if it might not have made a difference, the pain stings like a quiver of arrows hitting your heart one by one, time after time.

Your head tells you to forgive yourself, but your emotions run rampant with regrets. As Kübler-Ross and Kessler note, "Intellect does not inform matters of the heart." And, they add, regrets come from the yearning to do something differently. Reminding us that regrets should belong to the past, they also candidly admit, "Death has a cruel way of giving regrets more attention than they deserve."

Yet how do you stop the regrets? In your saner moments, you realize it is impracticable and even impossible to have done everything—you aren't perfect and your relationship wasn't perfect. Doubtless you did many things right; dwell on those.

Still, the recriminations go on—the words change but the remorse doesn't. As Bayly said, death has closed the door on making amends. We are left standing on the other side of an impenetrable barrier, unable to reach out to the one we hurt.

Edwin Lutzer describes our guilt feelings as millstones around our necks, keeping us tied to our failures and actions. Troubled by our conscience, we rehearse what we did or didn't do in dramatic detail. Like a broken record, the scenes replay in our minds.

Sylvia cannot forget the words whispered by her father as he struggled to convey some message as he lay dying: "Aaaaya...Aaaya..." he uttered with his last labored breaths. As hard as she tried, Sylvia couldn't decipher the strange sounds seeping from lips tortured by pain. More than 40 years later, she is still haunted by the indistinguishable words, wondering what her father was trying to say, regretting she couldn't answer his anguished cry.

Shelby+ is sorry she wasn't kinder. Tom feels compunction for the dumb little arguments with his wife. Nita+ wishes she had paid more attention when her daughter said she couldn't breathe well after she had been outside running. Sherry laments she was emotionally distant. Connie+ is remorseful she didn't realize her husband was so despondent. Jim wishes he hadn't put off traveling with his wife. Carol can't forgive herself for not knowing her son was so depressed. Julia grieves that she supported her son's desire to join the Army. Melba feels guilty that she didn't notice her brother had stopped taking his medication.

Diane+ is haunted she didn't know Jason's death was imminent — had she known, she would have taken off work to be with him fulltime. Because she didn't know, she was saving her sick days for when he might need her later. Sooner came before later, and now she feels guilty she wasn't with him as much as she could have been. She and Gary both are also haunted by not knowing if Jason was aware he was dying. Their voices soft with pain, they wonder if he lay there with his face covered with a breathing apparatus, knowing he was about to leave his parents and siblings to cross into another dimension.

Muffin+ regrets she didn't tell her brother how much she loved him while he was still able to communicate. Knowing Charlie was a very private person, it was sometimes awkward for him to share his feelings and for others to share their feelings with him. Not wanting to make him feel uncomfortable, Muffin tried to show him how much she loved him. But the unsaid words still echo: "*Why didn't I tell him?*"

Marsha+ is stricken with remorse she didn't notice her teenage son had been drinking; that she didn't stop him from driving the car. "*If I had just been more perceptive, if I had only known, I wouldn't have let him drive.*" He wouldn't have wrecked. He wouldn't have catapulted through the windshield. "*He wouldn't be dead if I had only noticed.*"

Vicki+ always longed for more time with her boys, and she carries the weight of not being home fulltime the entire 12 years Jonathan was in school. "He was the kind of child who loved school and would call me at work wanting to share his day," Vicki recalls. It broke her heart then, and it still does that she wasn't there in person. "I realize many mothers don't have a choice and have to work, but I don't think that was our situation. It has taken me years," she laments, "not to think, 'I should have just done it.'"

As Vicki looks backward, she whispers in a wavering voice, "It was always my dream to be a stay-at-home Mom. That dream was stolen from me as is the opportunity to spend time with

Jonathan now." It is a bitter pill for her to swallow. Vicki also chastises herself she might have missed a clue that would have signaled Jonathan's heart problem. "I have relived hundreds of times I was with Jonathan," searching for any sign that escaped her mother's eye.

We can each fill in our names and our regrets. Angry with ourselves, we are filled with self-blame.

We impugn ourselves for a multitude of sins, wishing we could go back and relive yesterday, last week, or last year. But there is a limit to how much guilt we can and should feel. Time moves in only one direction, and what's past is past. Or, as Paulina said in apology after raging against King Leontes, in Shakespeare's *The Winter's Tale*, for his horrible deeds, "What's gone and what's past help should be past grief."

Paulina had attacked Leontes after the apparent death of Queen Hermine, who had been on trial for unfounded charges of treason and infidelity. Delineating Leontes's dishonorable deeds, including not only lying about his wife but also casting their son into the wild to be eaten by animals, Paulina had no mercy. Under assault, Leontes finally faced up to his faults, and Paulina momentarily regretted the harshness of her words, giving Leontes a respite from her rage when she acknowledged what's past cannot be rectified and thus should not be a source of remorse. And, yet, upon Leontes' request, she would remind him many times later of his shameful sins.

Whether presented by an accuser, like Paulina, or self-inflicted, regrets are dead-end streets. They take us nowhere, mire us in misery, and refuse to let us go. And, as long as we dwell on our regrets, our grieving process will be stifled. As Publilius Syrus, a Latin writer of mimes, declared, "How unhappy is he who cannot forgive himself."

If our loved one were alive, we could ask forgiveness. And, for most of us, pardon would be readily given. Even though he or she is not beside us, would our loved one want us to berate ourselves? More likely, they would want us to forgive ourselves as they would have forgiven us. Indeed, is it not likely that in their new state of being they have already absolved us of any wrong we committed against them? Perhaps, as Patricia

Cornwell wrote in a letter from Benton to his lover just before his presumed death in *Black Notice*, "It's time to stop dodging your pain and let me comfort you. Hold my hand in your mind and remember the many times we talked about death, never accepting that any disease or accident or act of violence has the power of absolute annihilation because our bodies are just the suits we wear. And we are so much more than that." Doubtless, our loved ones, like Benton, would want us to feel their comfort.

I recall one day, when I was expressing regrets, my son said with compassion and tenderness, "Madre, none of that matters to Padre, now." Subconsciously, in my limited human perspective, I saw my husband with a physical brain that still processed hurts. My remorse presumed he thought as he once thought, even though I knew that was not possible. Later that day, I softly touched the urn where my husband's ashes reside, and I felt the wisdom of Kevin's words. What seemed of such magnitude to me was now inconsequential to my beloved. If, in the spirit state, he remembered any of my past wrongs, I have no doubt he has wiped the slate clean. What remains is for me to forgive myself, to leave the chilly cavern of compunction.

But how can we forgive ourselves?

First, we can't dodge the pain of our regrets. To get to the other side of grief, we must walk through some dark valleys, and regrets are among the most difficult ones we will travel. We must plunge straight through them, acknowledging them and the emotions they trigger. If we just suppress our pangs of guilt, they will return to raise their ugly heads again later. The best response to regrets is to face them, to accept the piercing pain they inflict. Only then can we begin the process of forgiveness.

Forgiving ourselves requires that we accept our humanness. We are imperfect beings who make mistakes. Lutzer warns, though, we must be cautious about "false guilt, bringing torment upon [ourselves] for matters beyond [our] control." While acknowledging and accepting fault, we should also be fair with ourselves, not exaggerating our wrongs.

When we get to the point we can realistically assess our guilt, we are ready to cancel the debt we owe. We know the departed would forgive us if we asked, and in a quiet spot, perhaps beside the grave or other burial place, away from others, we should do just that. Confess our sins to our beloved and ask for forgiveness. Even though we will not hear an audible response, our hearts will feel the echo of words whispered far away.

Then, we should accept that forgiveness. We should refuse to let our regrets burden us again. Rebuff any inclination to let guilt slip back into our consciousness, reminding ourselves we have been forgiven. Tie our guilt up in an old garbage bag and toss it as far into the ocean as we can. I thought I had done that with my regrets, but I discovered I had left a rope tied to the bag; and for a while I regularly grabbed the heavy twine and towed the bag of regrets back to shore, unable to resist grappling with them again. It took a long time for me to cut the tie line and toss the weighty bag into the deep water where it would never surface again, giving it forever to my higher power.

Dealing with regrets is like that. We make it through a day or even a week without letting them slip back into our minds. Then, suddenly they reenter our consciousness. We tackle our guilt again and again, finally thinking we have mastered it. But, as Lutzer describes it, "Then WHAM! Suddenly, you're back to Square 1...Here you thought you had it licked, and then it exploded in your face." He concludes we begin to think victory isn't possible at all. "We've stood up—only to fall back on the same slippery slope. We've all wondered whether we should ever get up again."

Like learning to ride a bicycle, we must get up every time we fall. Gradually, we don't fall as often, and eventually we won't fall at all. Freedom from nagging thoughts of regret is possible. It just takes time and grace.

Chapter 18

STRENGTH AND BALM—INSIDE AND OUTSIDE OURSELVES

No man is an island, entire of itself…
John Donne, English poet, 1573-1631

A few months after Sally's two children died in a fire, the sight of two young girls, their backs turned, would explode her fragile feelings into flames. Tom fought back tears as he attended a football game at the local high school, where he once loved watching his son. Mary had to switch television channels any time news of the war in Iraq began, unable to listen, knowing her son's life had exploded with the grenade thrown so casually by a drive-by insurgent.

We can be as hard as an elephant tusk until a trigger explodes the ivory and we crumble.

Hazel+ held her tears inside every time she visited her daughter-in-law Carla, but when she left the tears flowed unchecked. A Christmas cantata unleashed submerged emotions for Kay+ long after she thought she had her emotions under control. For 13 weeks, Walter and Nita+ held each other and sobbed at 6:50 p.m. every Wednesday, the time their daughter Hannah died.

These are all normal reactions to the loss of a person deeply loved. But they roll over us with hurricane force, sometimes stripping us of our desire to live. We are tempted to board up the storm shutters, isolating ourselves in darkness… Alone… Silent.

And, for a time, being alone may be good for us. In private, we can cry as long and loud as needed. Some may even question God's wisdom — his plan for our lives. In isolation, we can allow ourselves to work our way through many emotions — anger, resentment, loneliness, doubt, regret, sadness, despair. Then healing can begin; we can start our search for strength.

Within every person lies a reservoir, a wellspring of life. For many, it comes from faith and hope that life does not end when the last breath is drawn. In the words of Nita, who lost her precocious 11-year-old child, "Hannah's address just changed from Georgia to Glory." Longfellow expressed this belief when he wrote, "Life is real! Life is earnest. And the grave is not its goal. Dust thou art, to dust returneth was not spoken of the soul."

If we can hold onto that belief, we will find a powerful force for recovery. Some days it may be more difficult than others, but we shouldn't berate ourselves when we struggle. As Alfred Lord Tennyson wrote in *In Memoriam*, "There lives more faith in honest doubt, than in half the creeds." Even faith as small as a mustard seed can grow. In the depth of our sorrow, we may feel the seed will lie dormant forever, but in time, it will emerge from the ground, once again growing in our soul. For Carla+, remembering that God gave her horses because He knew she would need them for comfort fertilized her dormant faith.

Letting beliefs undergird grief can take time. After her husband died, Linda+ realized that talking about God's comfort is easier than having to live it. "If this is God's will, why am I not at peace?" she pondered. Gordon+ allowed his faith to buttress him, but he has a list of questions for God when he meets him face-to-face. But neither closed the door on God.

The first great Christian theologian, Origen, taught us prayer is just an opening up of ourselves to God. We don't even necessarily have to say words. Since God is omniscient, he knows what we desire to say even if we can't articulate our feelings; he knows what we are thinking. In the stillness of our hearts, we just have to open ourselves to his presence, much like we have to watch a rose unfold. We can't rush it and we can't assist it. We just have to wait and watch until the beauty of God's creation lifts us into His presence.

In that aura, we can then view our lives from within. Denis Waitley reminds us that how we see life makes all the difference. He says his grandmother taught him "how to pull out the weeds, while reveling in and savoring the splendor and the fragrance of the flowers." In the biggest field of weeds we have ever encountered, in sorrows that sting like thorns, we can find the beauty in the flower we once held in our hands. Erich Fromm's words remind us that even briefly shared lives make life meaningful: "Who will tell whether one happy moment of love or the joy of breathing or walking on a bright morning and smelling the fresh air, is not worth all the suffering and effort which life implies."

Grief is grueling, but most of us would agree that the time we spent with our beloved was worth the pain of our loss. With that conviction, our inner strength renewed, we can then open our hearts to those who want to help.

From insight gained through the loss of three sons, Bayly advises, "An arm about the shoulder, a firm grip of the hand, a kiss: these are the proofs grief needs, not logical reasoning." What we don't need is someone to tell us what we already know.

Bayly describes a time when he was sitting, torn by grief. "Someone came and talked to me of God's dealings, of why it happened, of hope beyond the grave. He talked constantly, he said things I knew were true." Unmoved, the words irritated Bayly, and he wished the man would go away.

Another man came and sat beside Bayly. "He didn't talk," Bayly said. "He didn't ask leading questions. He just sat beside me for an hour and more, listened when I said something, answered briefly, prayed simply, left."

In contrast to his reaction to the first visitor, Bayly says the second one moved him. Calmed, he hated to see the man leave.

After the busyness of the first few days following death, we are comforted by those who recognize our "grief is not silenced, only muted." Although we may not display public grief, weeping in front of others, our grief remains grave. Written on our face, heartache and anguish color our countenance pale and ashen. Having a friend or family member sit with us at that time conveys more love than ten casseroles, hundreds of flowers, or a thousand pious platitudes.

In the company of those who speak fondly and openly of the one who died, we are comforted. Unfortunately, many people are hesitant to speak the name of the deceased, fearful it will cause fresh grief. Gary and Diane+ tell how many of their friends avoided their son Jason's name and how grateful they were when someone spoke his name with ease, talking about his life. Gary says that while hearing Jason's name may make him cry, it is still a good feeling. Speaking about his son's brave struggle, his love of friends and family, and his humorous approach to the script written for his life, stirs up both sad and happy memories, but all are welcome as they attest to the special son the couple cherished.

For months after my husband died, it seemed I was the only one who evoked his name. Undoubtedly, others thought talking about Bob would reopen raw wounds. Now, perhaps because I refused to stop talking about him, many of my friends and family flow his name into conversations just as I do.

What we need in our grief is as varied as a garden of wildflowers. One person may respond to an invitation to dinner, while another may prefer a short phone call. A child who has lost a parent may appreciate being invited to go shopping with a friend and her mother or camping with another family. When a friend asked me what he could do, I knew his desire was to do something that would be meaningful to me, and I asked that a tree be planted in memory of my beloved. Now, whenever I see that tree, it reaffirms my belief that from death comes life.

When we are most desolate, we often push people away, preferring to dwell on an island of mourning. When we can, we should accept the aid and support of those who want to comfort us, but we should also feel free to tell them with clarity what we need and don't need. Our friends and family want to help us move through the grief journey; we must help them know how.

Chapter 19

MOVING AND GROWING THROUGH GRIEF

Every piece of the universe, even the tiniest little snow crystal,
matters somehow. I have a place in the pattern, and so do you.
Thomas Archibald (T.A.) Barron, American novelist, 1952-

The calendar of the year moves on, ignoring our grief, as days drift and months mount. The pages turn with a rhythm of their own, and birthdays, holidays, anniversaries, and other special days can't be postponed or cancelled. We dread them, knowing our feeling of aloneness will intensify, our smoldering grief apt to spark into flames again. Once eagerly anticipated days of joy, filled with family and friends, become reminders of those not present.

Ready or not, we have to confront special days, move through them, and be ready to face another day.

Kübler-Ross and Kessler remind us, "Holidays mark the passage of time in our lives. They are part of the milestones we share...they bring meaning to certain days and we bring much meaning back to them." So, they ask, how can mourners be expected to cope with holidays, to celebrate the togetherness they inevitably bring, when the one with whom we were "together" no longer lives?

Our reaction to special days depends on how they were observed, the traditions we shared, and the meaning they brought to our lives, leading us to ask whether to continue our established rituals or replace them. For some, keeping old customs signifies that life goes on. For others, the empty chair at the table is too much to contemplate.

Berry Perkins, Anthony Perkins' widow, tried keeping Christmas the same for her sons, even though a void filled the air. The first year, Kübler-Ross and Kessler recount, the family "kind of glided through, because we thought, 'Okay, we are going to do this.'" When the tree went up the second year, though, it hung naked as the family unconsciously found reasons to avoid dressing it. It took a week for the decorations to get hung. It was then Berry realized she and her boys needed a reprieve — a break from pretending to celebrate when they were still grieving. When they felt like observing Christmas again, the Perkins' family created new ways to take pleasure in the holidays. Aware of her sons' sensitivities, Berry helped them move through special days without focusing on the one who was not present. Hopefully the lessons she taught her sons held them in good stead when they faced the loss of their other parent: Berry died on the one of the hijacked planes that hit the World Trade Center on 9/11.

Some days, like anniversaries — of births, deaths, weddings, and other special days — can't be changed or recreated. We must decide how to spend those days — quietly in remembrance, visiting the grave, lighting a candle in a church, doing something special for ourselves, or planning a memorial ritual to celebrate our loved one's life. Though we should be prepared to be sad on such days, days that once brought such joy to our lives, we need to remember, as Connie+ wisely reminded me: Each of those days is only 24 hours. And those hours pass, however slowly and painfully. We don't have to pretend we are happy, but we need to let them go when they are past.

Gary+ had a difficult time letting go of the memories of his son. The first couple of Christmases after his death, Gary spent hours putting together an elaborate video of Jason's life. It was Gary's gift to his family, but his daughter Staci would become so emotional when the video started, she would flee the room. Diane and Casey would be sobbing, and Gary himself struggled with tears. Finally, Diane told Gary that as much as he wanted to help the family remember Jason, it was too painful — just more than they could bear.

Gary also tried to start another family tradition. On Jason's birthday and on the anniversary of his death, Gary would gather the family around the dining room table and ask each person to tell God what was going on in their lives, requesting that God tell Jason. But this, too, was too hard on family members, and eventually Gary stopped the ritual. What he hasn't stopped, though, is something the whole family finds beautiful. When

Gary blesses the food each day, at the end, he adds, "And, God, give Jason a great big hug for us." Eight years after Jason's death, it reminds everyone how much they love Jason.

Accepting these days as they are—sad times we must travel through—is a beginning for our growth through grief. When we realize the past life we shared will never be restored, we can search for a new norm for our lives. Otherwise, as Jim Rohn averred, "The walls we build around us to keep sadness out also keep out the joy." Hence, we must live the day of the holiday or special occasion, surviving the best we can, and then as years pass we can work toward enjoying them. This does not mean we are turning away from our loved one; it is just that a new spirit-based relationship grows within our heart to replace the old one that resided in the physical world.

Our beloved doesn't have to be absent on special days—he or she just occupies a new place as we rearrange the pieces of our lives. The picture on life's puzzle is now different, but as we put the jigsaw back together, some of the colors and designs can be the same as they were in the old scene. The sky still turns from cloudy to blue; flowers still grow in the undergrowth of the forest, and the sun still rises each day. One figure is missing from the scene, but the image is indelibly engraved in our heart. Holding tightly to the love we once shared, we can move on, knowing our loved one would want us to take pleasure in our reshuffled life.

As Barren notes in the quote at the beginning of this chapter, just as the tiniest snowflake has a place in the universe, so does our loved one. The physical presence may be missing at the table on special days, but the spirit of love we shared can permeate our being to help fill the void.

Chapter 20

REMNANTS OF LIFE

A strange thing is memory, and hope; one looks backward, and the other looks forward.

Anna Mary Robertson ("Grandma") Moses, American folk artist 1860-1961

When the last shovel of dirt has been tossed, the last ash scattered, the final song sung, or the eulogy delivered, we return home. Sometimes it is alone to shadows in our home and sometimes surrounded by family and friends.

All around us lay reminders of life — the life we loved, shared, and treasured. That now exists only in pictures or in possessions held dear. For most of us, pictures are comforting because they keep our loved one's image ever close. As Moses declares in the quote above, memory looks backward. Does that mean we should turn the pictures facing downward or put them in a hall closet? What should we do with the other remnants of life — the clothes, the books, the paintings, or anything that belonged to our loved one or was special to him or her?

Some keep the rooms of their beloved intact, refusing to move a doll or a pair of shoes. Subconsciously, it is as if they expect the departed to return and occupy the room. Or, they just can't bear touching the possessions that once held such meaning and delight. The room becomes a shrine, to be entered for meditation or comfort. The place we feel closest to the one who is now gone. Even if the room threatens tears, we console ourselves by picking up the relics, leafing through scrapbooks or gently touching a dress she once wore.

After seven months, Linda+ still hasn't been able to touch Mike's clothes — they hang in the closet just as they were on the day he died. His books are still stacked on the shelf where he left them.

Only recently, nine years after her son Kelly died in a plane crash, was Hazel+ able to throw his fire department cap away.

"One day," she says, "I picked it and smelled it and smelled it again, but there was nothing, not even the hint of his shaving lotion." She tenderly took the emblem off the cap and placed it in her jewelry box. With a heavy heart, she put the cap in the trash.

Even though Hazel finally let go of Kelly's cap, in her guest bedroom she keeps a shrine for him: a picture of a memorial at the landing strip dedicated and named for Kelly; other photos of him by his airplane and one of Kelly playing his guitar; a picture of him in his helmet and bunker suit; and one of her most prized relics—a statute she found at Hallmark a couple of weeks after Kelly died: two firefighters—one holding up the other. When Hazel saw it, she envisioned Kelly's brother Alan (who is also a firefighter) holding his little brother. "Maybe I should take these things down," Hazel ponders, "but I still look at them, and I still pick up the fireman statute; and I still rub my fingers across Kelly's face in all of the pictures. It gives me another connection once again to Kelly."

Other mourners quickly strip the home of clothes and odds and ends that remind them of the person no longer present. The week after my husband died, with my heart aching, I forced myself to sort through a walk-in closet we shared, pulling clothes from hangars and boxing up shoes. I knew I could not go into the closet daily and see the traces of his life without an intolerable missing coming over me like a heavy fog. Instinctively, I knew I could not face the truth that my husband was gone as long as I saw the shirts, pants, and jackets I had so carefully selected for him. Touching the fabrics that smelled of his cologne wouldn't help me accept that he was never coming back. So I wanted what he had worn out of the house—right then. I gave articles of clothing and relics to family members, and the rest I loaded up and took to the Salvation Army. But there were things I will never part with—his glasses, his watches, his rings, his library of books on religion and World War II, his Tiffany lamps, and his collection of dog figurines. Those things stir up happy memories, but the clothes and shoes were like shadows on my soul, reminders of the physical absence I felt so keenly.

For me, these decisions were choices. For others, like Vicki+, circumstances dictate timing. Because her son Jonathan lived in an apartment, the family had to remove his possessions two weeks after his funeral. An emotional time, decisions were made to give clothes and furniture to some of Jonathan's friends and to charities, but Vicki kept a few T-shirts to sleep in — an effort to keep her son close. But the possession she most treasures is a writing Jonathan composed a few months earlier after one of his best friends was hospitalized with a brain aneurysm. Titled "My Thoughts," Jonathan explores how a traumatic event opens the mind to more clarity, discovering "how we really need people who love and care for us in our lives. We need the person who takes time to make us laugh, who calls us just to talk, who tells us they are glad to see us. We need people who listen to our sad stories, remind us of our good stories, and break our falls when we stumble." Vicki treasures these lines Jonathan wrote because they epitomize who he was. "Everyone in the family has those words beautifully framed and hung in a place of honor to serve as a constant reminder of the depth of his character."

Vicki also got Jonathan's books, scrapbooks, CDs, and the Bible from his apartment. She would like to have other relics and mementos from his childhood, but those are at his dad's house where the family once lived. Even without those precious items, Vicki can still cherish Jonathan's profound words and the thousands of memories of him in her heart and mind.

Hazel+, although she kept mementos of Kelly's life, including old license tags he had collected, an album of his cars, trucks and motorcycles, and a stuffed dog he gave her many years ago on Easter, stripped her entire house of prized belongings — beautiful cut crystal vases and dishes, her living room furniture, Christmas decorations, and numerous other things. She doesn't know if she was removing from every part of her house except one room anything she could associate with Kelly — where he sat, where they decorated a tree, where they had dinners, etc. — or whether she wanted to get rid of anything of value. "Maybe I don't want to take a chance of losing anything else of importance, so I'd rather give it away," she surmises.

Connie+ didn't touch her husband's clothes for 13 months, but she knew instinctively that, for her, she couldn't leave the rooms in her house like they were. And, long before she disposed of his clothes, she put away her husband's pictures. "It was like he was watching me, and I resented that. He had left me behind, and in my resentment, I didn't want him looking over my shoulder." Within a year or so, Connie moved to another house, buying new furniture and accessories—all in an effort to put the past behind her and move on. Like Hazel, creating a whole new environment helped keep unwanted memories at bay.

As in most phases of grief, our responses are as different as we are. While she was in shock from Tira's death, Marcia+ boxed up all of the traces of her daughter's life except her clothes. Pictures and other items she could remove, but her clothes she couldn't discard. Only when her granddaughter Brooke said it was time did she take Tira's clothes from the house. Some time later, though, Marcia slowly put Tira's pictures back up and says she can now watch her in a video—her grief still simmering but less sharp.

Melissa's+ mother died at her house, and it was months before she could clean her room. "I could walk in the room, but I couldn't clean it. I can't explain that, since I am a 'cleaning freak.'" When they could, Melissa's four siblings each came to her house, first taking anything they had given their mother. Five boxes sat around the room, and slowly they filled up with those gifts now being reclaimed. Then, starting with the eldest, they each picked in turn what they wanted from the shadows of their mother's life. Thirty-five years of treasures and junk, piece-by-piece, they chose what they wanted and disposed of the rest.

Decisions about their sister Anna's possessions a few years later didn't create an emotional upheaval, but it took a bit of time. Anna was a pack rack, addicted to hoarding things. Once again, the siblings repossessed gifts and then took special remembrances. Suzanne+ took a stuffed green frog; Melissa took one of Anna's hats. Debbie took jewelry, which she enjoys wearing. Bo doesn't remember taking anything—except the tales he relishes telling about Anna. More lingering shadows added to their collection of remembrances. And, like they fondly poked fun at Anna while she was alive, they had a bit of fun at her expense: "If one of us doesn't take this thing, Anna will never forgive us" was said more than once that afternoon.

What should we do with the traces of a life? There is no right or wrong answer. We should do what our heart tells us to do, especially during the early stages of grief. Starting the task before we are ready, before we are strong enough, can be brutal emotionally, emphasizing the physical absence of our loved one. We should not feel rushed, and if it is comforting to see the familiar shoes sitting near the door, the sweater folded over the recliner, or the glasses sitting by the bedside, we should leave them there while we adjust to the harsh reality of our loss.

After a time, we may need to examine our reasons for holding on to life's remnants. Is it because they help us or because we fear letting them go will force us to accept the reality of our loss? Do they keep us looking backward or help us look forward? Moses tell us, "Memory is history recorded in our brain," so it may not be essential to keep physical objects to remind us of the one now departed.

Seneca asks, "What difference does it make how much you have? What you do not have amounts to much more."

Few, if any, of us who mourn the death of a dearly loved family member or friend would disagree. The pictures and possessions don't amount to much compared to what we lost, so keeping them ever present and visible won't affect the truth or finality of our loss. As long as we realize this, what we do with the remaining evidence of life doesn't really matter. What counts is whether we can embrace life at a level that enables us to look forward.

Chapter 21

WHY CAN SOME LET GO OF GRIEF MORE EASILY?

To whom then will you liken Me…? Lift up your eyes on high,
and see who has created these things.
Isaiah 40:25-26

Life inflicts slings and sorrows on the strong and the weak, the prepared and the unprepared, the Christian and the pagan. While it is easy to assume the strong take sorrow in stride, and the weak weep and fall apart, experience has little guidance for how we will respond to death. Should the forewarned be more accepting of the death they've known was coming than those faced with a life stolen, unexpectedly, in the dead of the night? Does the Christian tower, holding tight to faith, while the pagan crumbles, believing he will never see his beloved again?

Like observing a game of checkers, we think we can anticipate who will be jumped and who will not, who will be crowned and who will lose their colored chips. Who will show stalwart strength and who will be pitifully weak.

It isn't that simple. Sometimes those of great strength in other facets of their lives struggle mightily against surrendering their spirit to sorrow. If a weak person fails to display outward signs of grief, does that mean he or she didn't love the departed? When a Christian can't bear to go to church after the death of a child, is weak faith the cause? Should a person who watched her loved one suffer for months on end grieve less than one whose family member's life was taken in a freak accident?

The bottom line is there is no "right" way to grieve.

Wanda+ lost her mother and went back to work the day after the funeral. She had used all of her sick days in the weeks before her mother's death, and she had no choice. Jane's mother had been valiantly fighting terminal cancer before her death, but two years later Jane still can't talk about her without a furrowed forehead and a tear-streaked face. Did one love her mother more than the other? Knowing both women, I can answer that question unequivocally: "No." Some people seem to be able to box up their grief, opening it up at times but keeping it closed at others. These individuals can go about their lives even when one significant aspect is in grave pain. Others wear their sorrow like a cloak, wrapped tightly around them, protecting them against the wintry night of grief. Everyone can see how mournful they are.

My sister Flavia, though thankful our mother no longer existed in a body that had already died, remembers thinking she felt utterly empty for a long time after her death. Later, in talking with someone who had lost both parents at the same time, she understood the emptiness came from the realization that for the first time in her life she was without a parent. She didn't grieve Mother's death; she grieved not having a parent.

Bo+ took the death of his sister Anna in stride, remembering the times they had shared. His other three sisters have moved on, but memories sometimes unexpectedly awaken latent sorrow. Pam+ felt broken by the death of her brother Butch, and when her sister Anna died, too, it was almost more than she could bear. Like Pam, Muffin+ still struggles with the loss of her brother Charlie, fighting sadness and regret.

No one response to grief fits everyone, and there are many paths to help us through our sorrow, to weather the waves of grief that wash over us. Those paths start and end with how we think. Do we see the loss as permanent or temporary? Permanence leaves us helpless, while temporary leaves us with hope of a future reunion. Finding the will to go on becomes more achievable if we anticipate seeing our loved one again. Just as we watch autumn mums die and disintegrate yet await their brilliant blooms the next autumn, we can look forward to our loved one's rebirth.

Another dimension in dealing with grief is self-talk. How we talk to ourselves will make a critical difference in how we grieve. Carolyn, in *A Prologue to Love*, made it clear she didn't believe in happy endings, but her cousin Amy's philosophy shook her certainty when she declared, "Cousin Caroline, I don't believe in endings at all." When Caroline questioned what she meant, Amy explained, "Every day is different, and in some ways we change every day." As days drift by, as we change, we can see the future without our loved one even through eyes clouded by grief.

When thoughts of the future without our precious one paint bleak images in our mind, we can substitute happy memories from the past, being thankful for the good times we shared. Instead of saying, "Without Cary, my life is over, we can say, with Cary, my life was fulfilled." We can think, "I should have been kinder," or we can think, "I wasn't perfect, but I stayed by her side when she needed me." It takes a powerful effort, but we *can* choose what we think.

Before Taylor Caldwell's novel ends, despite Caroline's decrying there are no happy endings for anyone in the world, she concludes: "But when we repent and try to make amends, there is hope, not for a happy ending, but for peace. And some small understanding."

With the discernment that life goes on, that it won't wait for us, we begin to emerge from our cocoon of grief. Sad thoughts are normal, and we must learn to distract them when they occur and, whenever possible, dispute them. Whether dealing with loneliness or regrets, we can turn our minds away or provide counter arguments. Flavia remembers at our father's death she felt it was unfair he had died at the age of 64. Later, she learned to give thanks we had had a good father longer than many people.

Robert Schuller uses an analogy to illustrate how we can rise above our depressing thoughts: "Think of the locks that enable a boat to rise and proceed up a stream that otherwise would be impossible to navigate. When ships travel upstream they are 'locked' into an enclosed area which is then filled with water. Ships weighing tens of thousands of tons are lifted easily through the floatation power of water. The lock system enables ships to sail on and on through higher bodies of water."

Schuller continues that we can lock in our mental attitude with positive thoughts, allowing our mind "to float upward by the invisible, silent, escalating flow of the spirit of faith which only the eternal God can give." He concludes that when we think we are stuck, we can move forward again by "rising above the shoals that would have grounded [us]."

Chapter 22

MENDING YOUR BROKEN HEART

A saint is not someone who is good but who experiences the goodness of God.

Thomas Merton, American theological writer, Trappist monk, 1915-1968

St. Augustine, the 4th century philosopher and theologian from Roman Africa Province, had a profound influence on the development of Western Christianity, but his conversion to Christianity came after years of hedonistic behavior and rebellion. In his *Confessions*, he often wrote of the perpetual life of brokenness, and the above quote pinpoints him perfectly.

Like St. Augustine, Brennan Manning penned words for "the sorely burdened who are still shifting the heavy suitcase from one hand to the other; for earthen vessels who shuffle along on feet of clay." For St. Augustine, for Manning, and for us as we try to mend our broken hearts, the only hope is the goodness of God.

We don't have to feel guilty about our brokenness, our anger, or our questioning God's goodness at the depths of our desolation. Even the holiest men and women have doubts, and our life while grieving can be compared to a bird with a broken wing. We may be grounded for the short term, a time when our trust and convictions no longer lift us into the security of God's nest. For a while, we may feel betrayed and abandoned, unable to accept comfort from the one who took our loved one.

While death can tear at the very fabric of our faith, deep within our soul a shimmer of light will eventually break into the shadows of our grief. It may start as a flickering candle, but the flame will grow as tenets of faith that have sustained us in the past rise above our anguish and heartache. Even when we are too weak and hurt to pray, God hears our need.

An old song reminds us, "His eye is on the sparrow, and I know He watches me." In our inability to voice our petition, in our silence, God can still speak to our hearts. As Carla's+ mother told her, "You don't have to worry about praying right now; there are others doing that for you." Similarly, when Diane's+ heartache was so deep just before Jason's lung transplant, she could not find words to submit her deepest fears to God.

We may be poor in spirit, we may be broken, but we are not alone. Because of God's grace, nothing can ever separate us from the love of God. It is stronger than death, and it is greater than our grief. Even when Diane couldn't pray, she felt the prayers of others.

Manning tells us, "God wants us back even more than we could possibly want to be back. We don't have to go into great detail about our sorrow." As in the parable of the prodigal son, all we have to do "is appear on the scene, and before we get a chance to run away again, the Father grabs us and pulls us into the banquet so we can't get away."

Even if we are so lost we can't find our way to the banquet table, discovering God's loving presence is as simple as looking around us — a sparkling waterfall, cumulous clouds drawing pictures in the sky, a mother dog protecting her pups, lightning flashing across a summer sky, a tender shoot of life rising from beneath dead leaves in the forest, surreal streaks of color creating a magnificent rainbow, wheat whispering in the wind, a father cradling his newborn son, a horse nuzzling its head against our shoulder.

On my office wall hangs a picture my husband loved. It depicts a giant shepherd dog beside the ocean, its forelegs lovingly holding a young girl. Dark clouds smother the sky, and one knows instinctively the dog has pulled the child from the storm-driven waves. The child lies outstretched on the big dog's paws, pale and still. The dog looks heavenward, knowing his silent plea will be answered.

In our grief, we are like the little girl, helpless and unable to ask for help. Whether we were close to God or distant from Him when death struck, He wants to help heal our broken heart. He wants to build a bridge over the troubled waters that separate us from His grace.

Brennan Manning reminds us, "Jesus has journeyed to the far reaches of loneliness. In His broken body He has carried...every separation and loss, every heart broken, every wound of the spirit that refuses to close, all the riven experiences of men, women, and children across the bands of time."

We just have to let go and let Him heal us.

Chapter 23

DREAMS, SIGNS, SPIRITS, AND CONVERSATIONS

Six weeks after his death, my father appeared to me in a dream...
It was an unforgettable experience, and it forced me for the first
time to think about life after death.
Carl G. Jung, Swiss psychiatrist, 1875-1961

Regardless of the strength of religious beliefs, most mourners eagerly seize any indication our loved ones are all right—that they have made it to the "other side." Desperate to feel their presence just one more time, our subconscious—and sometimes our conscious—minds may be open to dreams, signs, and other phenomena. Often, afraid others will think us crazy, we silently shelter strange happenings inside. And too, we are unsure whether they are real or imagined. Yet, desperate for contact and reassurance, we willingly grasp what might have been inconceivable only days ago, however shadowy or disguised it may be, and take from it any hope and refuge it may bring.

DREAMS

Not everyone dreams of loved ones—or remembers them if they do. Still, dreams of the deceased are the most frequently reported ways people feel connected, and they can be comforting if we see our beloved in a state of contentment—whether from a past time together or one we have never seen previously.

Three siblings shared their experience with dreams and other phenomena after the deaths of their mother and sister: Debbie+ dreamed about her mother every night for a couple of months. Bo could remember no dreams and began to think he was abnormal after Debbie continually updated him about her dreams. Pragmatic, he thinks he shrugged off any visitation or sign that may have been intended for him. Suzanne also didn't have nighttime visions of her mother or her sister, but she wasn't expecting them. She had told both her mother and sister, "I will see you in the morning," and was content to wait for that reunion. Until that happens, she's satisfied to have thoughts surface about her loved ones: When she hears a special song on the radio, she thinks, "Mother would have loved that." Or, when one of her mother's favorite football teams fumbles the ball she hears her mother's voice in her head, "Bad play!" As for her sister Anna, she never hesitates to say while shopping, "I would never buy that, but Anna would..." continuing to affectionately poke fun.

Connie+ dreamed of a night when she and others were playing Trivial Pursuit—a game she had often played with her husband. In her nighttime vision, the game is being played at church, and her husband David is in the balcony looking down at the players with a smile on his face. Connie says it was as if David were giving her his approval—not just for playing the game without him, but also for enjoying life.

Gary and Diane+ are both thankful they have good dreams about their son Jason—in their night visions, he no longer suffers as he did for so many years. Gary says he frequently sees himself hugging Jason in dreams, and Diane always sees Jason with a healthy glow, something she seldom saw during the last 10 years of his life.

Recently, Jason's brother Casey told his parents about a dream that helped dissolve the anger he had held toward God as he watched Jason endure repeated battles. In the dream, a beautiful, calm lake with a long dock extending out over the water created the backdrop for a picturesque field of emerald green grass where Jason and Casey were throwing a football back and forth. No words were spoken, but Casey's spirit filled with sheer happiness at doing something so ordinary with his brother, a poster model for good health in the dream. Casey believes God gave him the dream to help him know Jason is happy, Jason is healthy, and Jason is waiting to throw a football with him again.

In some dreams, we see the deceased with loved ones who have also died, and it is heartening to see joyous reunions of family members and friends. In others, they speak to us, telling us not to worry about them. In still other nocturnal fantasies, we see the departed in the life he or she once lived, letting us temporarily escape into the past. In our emotional turmoil, it helps to visualize our loved one in these ways.

Dreams can also be troublesome. Nightmarish, the vision may show our loved one struggling or in pain. Or, we may dream of being in conflict with the one who is now gone. Such dreams may be triggered by the circumstance of death or by feelings of guilt, or they may be caused by medications taken for sleepless nights or for depression.

Connie not only had the reassuring dream about the trivia game, she also has a cheerless recurring dream that distresses her — she and her husband David are trying to get in touch with one another by phone, but their attempts are always frustrated: a phone is out of service, a busy signal sounds over the line, or the call is out of cell tower range. Since Connie tried to reach David 15 times the afternoon he died, the source of her dream is evident, but it doesn't stop its occurrence or dull the pain.

Like Connie, Vicki+ dreams of her loved one, and the dream is frequently a variation of the same scene: Jonathan is a little boy and is lost. Vicki frantically calls out for him, but she is powerless to help. In another version of the dream, Jonathan again needs her and she can't get to him: He is in a hospital room behind a locked door, and no one will let Vicki inside. Feeling frustrated and anxious, "I always wake up in a panic and the sadness lingers for a few days," Vicki says sorrowfully.

When our night musings are depressing, one way to try to shape the tenor of dreams is to think of the loved one in happy situations just before going to sleep. Or, it may be helpful to work our way through what happens in the dream, attempting to understand what in our conscious or subconscious mind may have prompted the upsetting dreams.

Carl Jung, who studied and wrote prolifically about dreams, believed the subconscious mind communicates with the conscious mind through dream imagery. In his view, certain associations — ideas or feelings that arise in the mind — are connected to the images when the dream is considered. It is through these associations meanings can be discovered.

Unlike Freud, who believed the dream should be interpreted using "free association," Jung advocated focusing on specific images in the dream. He advised we should be open to many different meanings based on our associations, stressing we should not strip down the meaning of the dream to fit some narrow dogma. Regardless of the varying interpretations, Jung maintained we should not doubt the significance of subconscious happenings any more than we question the importance of conscious experiences. We should accept, he says, that dreams emanate from disharmony between our conscious and subconscious. The dream portrays our inner situation, even when our conscious mind wants to deny truth and reality, or only admit it grudgingly.

SIGNS

Sharing special rituals, appreciating particular beauty in nature, and knowing things about our loved one that others don't—all are ways that make our connection unique. From these distinctive aspects of our relationship often come signs— signals our loved one is okay. Inanimate objects and creations of nature become pathways for messages.

Sonja Puopola, whose mother perished on American Airlines flight 11, the first of the two hijacked planes to hit the Twin Towers on September 11, 2001, relates that her father's mournful wish was to hold once again the ring he had given her mother 40 years earlier. After almost 11 months, both Sonja and her father had almost given up hope the ring would ever be found. Then, in an inexplicable miracle, her mother's left hand was found in the rubble—her wedding band perfectly intact. A message of love and survival from her mother to her father? Sonja tells the story of this "symbol of human strength in the face of crisis, a gracious sign that love leaves an indelible import on the mind and soul and heart forever," in her book, *Sonja's Ring: 11 Ways to Heal Your Heart.*

Linda+ knows something extraordinary kept a single rose alive. She and her son Dusty had gone to the cemetery to remove the dead floral arrangements from her husband's grave several weeks after his burial. A typical cold, wintry day in North

Georgia— their hands were freezing as they tossed the last of the dead flowers into their truck. They watched, amazed, as a single, beautiful, red rose fell to the ground at their feet. Every other flower was dead, frozen in the midst of that winter's worst weather. Tenderly, Linda picked up the life-filled rose, and cradled it in her hands. And she knew…just as the rose had survived the dank, cold weather, Mike, too, had survived and was living still.

Debbie+ had several signs after her mother's death. The first signal she had that her mother was all right was hearing "If I Had a Hammer" on the radio two days after her mother died. Gathered around their mother's bed, Debbie and her siblings had sung that song, along with "Michael, Row the Boat Ashore." The coincidence was remarkable. "I'd never heard that song on the radio before," she recalls, "and I knew it was mother sending me a message. And," she adds, "that wasn't all. I had a Christmas cactus I had never been able to make bloom. But after mother died on November 15, that thing began to bloom—the first time in four years." Debbie knew it as another sign from her mother.

Debbie's third and final sign came as she and her husband Phil stood in their yard beside a hummingbird feeder. "Why can't we attract a hummingbird?" Debbie brooded aloud. Almost immediately, a brilliant red hummingbird came to the feeder. Another piece of evidence Debbie refused to chalk up to coincidence. And she still doesn't understand how a message from months before her mother died stayed on her voice mail recorder. Hitting the play button one day, she heard her mother's voice, asking how Phil was feeling following a bike wreck. Debbie hadn't saved the message; she didn't know it was still there. But hearing her mother's voice one more time is something she will forever treasure.

Melissa+ hoped for signs from her sister Anna—she even told Anna in their last goodbye, "You know we both believe in this stuff [signs and messages from the dead], so I'll be expecting to hear from you." So far, Anna has remained silent. But her mother was more forthcoming. Melissa had always wanted a horse, and shortly after her mother's death when she decided to save a horse headed for the slaughterhouse, she walked into her bedroom and saw a brilliant ray of sunshine illuminating a picture of her mother that sat on her dresser. "It was like Mother was saying, 'You finally got your horse.' I knew she was happy for me," Melissa says, the memory lighting her face as if it were yesterday, even though more than 10 years have passed.

My own mother had prayed incessantly for healing and at one point had even felt God told her she would be made well on a specific day. But healing eluded her, and on the day she believed she would be restored to good health, all we could do was play a recording of "In His Time," a song that tells us God does just what He says He will do—in His time—not ours. "In His time," the song asserts, "God makes all things beautiful." For my mother, being made beautiful again—being made whole—was a healing that would have to wait until His time. Parkinson's disease complicated by the remnants of an old stroke left our mother unable to lift her head alone, unable to feed herself or form words of communication—until the day she left this world.

In the wee hours of the morning after mother had died at a local hospital, rather than awaken each of our husbands and children, my sisters and I decided to go to my house to await the dawn and share the news. As we drove the short distance words from a song floating through the air caught our attention. Not even realizing the radio was on, we were stunned to hear a melodious voice lyrically express words that seemed just for us: Healing may not come in answer to our prayers in the way we want, but heaven's healing is a promise secure. The words reminded us of "In His Time." As we listened to the song, we rejoiced and even laughed that Mother was probably talking God's head off, giving voice to words trapped inside her for more than two years.

Later, we called the radio station to get the name of the song we heard on the way home from the hospital, but strangely, they had no record of having played it. It was the first and only time any of us ever heard that song, but its message profoundly affected us that night. Even stranger, and perhaps another sign, when Flavia left my house to go home later that morning, she heard "In His Time" on the radio — again, the first and only time she ever heard it on the air.

In one final sign, when a light rain began to fall at the cemetery where we were burying our mother, my sister Sylvia looked at Flavia and me, saying, "Mother always liked the rain." The mist lasted only a few moments, but it was enough to let us know Mother was telling us she was dancing in heaven.

Marcia+ had more than one experience in which she felt she was receiving a message that her daughter Tira was happy. The first Mothers' Day after Tira died, Marcia relates she asked God to tell her how Tira was doing. Into her mind a flash: "She's having a blast." Exactly the kind of language Marcia would have expected to describe her spirited daughter. But it wasn't enough; she wanted a sign. Then, it was as if she heard words telling her to look in her middle dresser drawer. There, among a stack of old papers, Marcia found the last Mother's Day card Tira had given her. On the outside, it read, "Mom be glad." On the inside, again typical of Tira, it said, "I could have been twins." With a laugh, Marcia says she and Tira could have been twins instead of mother and daughter — they shared the same sense of humor and several other traits.

Carla+ and Kelly had reveled in watching a great blue heron fly around their pond, so when Carla saw a heron swoop down and touch the water near her feet one day after Kelly's accident, she felt he was telling her not to worry — that he was all right. Later, after Carla's marriage to Richie, as they stood by the pond one day, not one, but two herons circled above their heads. Was it Kelly again, this time blessing Carla's new marriage, letting her know he wanted her to be happy?

Hazel+ also had a special sense of her son Kelly's presence: "Several times I would be almost asleep when I would feel something at the end of my bed. I felt it was Kelly coming to see me, and I would get up and rub my hand on the foot of the bed." She believes Kelly was trying to tell her he was fine.

Two events signaled Marsha+ that her son Daniel might be trying to communicate with her. The first was when she entered his room to look for something in his closet and a pamphlet fell on her head. The title? "One you loved has died." Another time, as Marsha was walking away from Daniel's gravesite, she heard a pleading voice: "Mom, Mom." In her mind she knew it was foolish, but her heart propelled her to turn back and look for Daniel.

In still another sign, on a trip to New York one of Daniel's friends entered a cathedral where Daniel had once visited. Seating himself at a distance from his mother and girlfriend, who had accompanied him, he meditated alone for a while. Then, he asserts, a monk came up to talk with him about Daniel, and they chatted for almost two hours. His mother and friend never saw a monk as they watched from across the cathedral.

Diane+ says a windmill her mother-in-law placed beside Jason's grave whirls around every time she visits the grave — even when no breeze is stirring nearby leaves. She believes it may be Jason spinning the windmill's arms, letting her know he is well again.

In their writings, well-educated individuals like Jane Goodman and Elizabeth Kübler-Ross tell of their own experiences in communicating with the dead. Despite this, I remained skeptical — that is, until after my husband's death. My own experiences — with a train whistle and a star — convinced me my spouse was sending me a message that he had made the transition into the next life. I recounted these experiences in my book, *Sips of Sustenance: Grieving the Loss of Your Spouse*, and even now, almost three years since Bob's death, I continue to see his bright star and on rare occasions hear the train whistle I believe he sends to remind me he's watching over me.

Although most signs come after our loss, we can also have signs that death is coming. Sometimes they are obvious to us at the time, but usually we find meaning in retrospect as we relive our last days with our beloved. Jane Goodall tells how, suspended between sleep and waking after the death of her husband, circling thoughts took her back to the night her uncle died. She remembered how she "had heard the haunting call of a barn owl, the bird that summons the souls of the dead." She didn't mention it at the time, she says, for no barn owls had been heard there [in Bournemouth] for at least fifteen years. And just before Audrey, another family member, died, she had told her that her dog Cida had been sitting beside her bed, staring up at her for a long time. Cida never went into Audrey's bedroom, but on the day of her death, her faithful dog held vigil, as if he knew her spirit was departing.

SPIRITS

History is replete with examples of visitations from the dead. It would be easy to dismiss such stories by saying the people were weird or prone to make up tales. But many well-known historical figures and well-educated people have adamantly told of sightings. Hans Holzer reported Abraham Lincoln declared his two dead sons, Pat and Willie, regularly visited him. Mrs. Franklin Delano Roosevelt admitted she often felt a ghostly sort of presence when working late in the White House. And, her servant, Mary Evan, claimed she saw Lincoln on the bed in the northwest bedroom, pulling on his boots. Other servants vowed they saw him standing at the oval window over the main entrance to the White House.

Holzer also professes the late Queen Wilhelmina of the Netherlands had paranormal experiences when she visited the White House. While asleep in the Queen's Bedroom, she heard a knock at her door. Arising from her bed and opening the door, she said she saw the ghost of President Lincoln standing there looking at her. Holzer reports she fainted, and the ghost was gone by the time she had been revived.

The ghost of Lincoln is but one of those reported in Holzer's book, *Ghosts: True Encounters with the World Beyond*. And beyond that, books abound on visitations from beyond this realm. Among those, one by Bill and Judy Guggenheim involved collecting more than 3300 accounts of after-death communications (ADCs) in 2000 interviews across the United States. Their book, *Hello from Heaven*, is filled with amazing stories of not only oral communications but also communications through touch and smell, during sleep, via telephone, partial and full visualizations, and many other forms of ADCs.

Had I not experienced a supernatural incident myself, I might be skeptical of ADCs. When my mother, my sisters, and I walked down the hall of the hospital moments after my father died, we felt his spirit floating in the air above us, telling us he was ready to go. A sense of inexplicable peace fell over us, even in our sorrow.

Weeks after our mother's the funeral, my sister Flavia walked through the den, looking with sorrow at the chair where mother had sat slumped for the past two years because she could not hold herself upright, and murmured, "Oh, Mother, I am so sad you had to go through so much." Almost audibly, she heard Mother's voice, "Oh, Flavia, it wasn't anything at all." Like the star lighting the East, which Mother had sung about every Christmas, the light in Flavia's head suddenly shined brightly: Looking back from heaven, what had happened on earth was inconsequential.

TALKING TO OUR LOVED ONES

A way we stay connected is to have regular conversations with our loved one. When they were with us, we shared thoughts and concerns, talked about our daily routines, and made note of special beauty. There is no reason we cannot continue to do this. Granted, it is a one-sided conversation, but for me, it is a wonderful way to feel close to the person who is no longer at my side. Like Shelby+, I often point out beautiful wildflowers along the sides of highways to my husband. And, I tell him when I am sad or frustrated. He doesn't answer, but I feel better for having shared my thoughts, just as I would have done if he were by my side.

Marcia+ says she talks to Tira now and then, telling her, "Tira, [or whatever your name is now," Marcia adds with zany humor], "I miss you so much."

Gordon+ talks about decisions, big and small, with Anne; it was something he did regularly for 22 years, so it seems natural to articulate his thoughts out loud.

Marsha+ talks to her son Daniel, usually silently, but sometimes she entreats him aloud. When her middle son Josh was having difficulty, not knowing where he was going with life, she walked onto her back porch and looked up at the dark, cloudy sky. "Daniel, you are right up there with God. We need your help with Josh," she pleaded. Suddenly, stars sparkled across the sky, and Marsha knew Daniel had heard. That was on a Saturday night, Marsha relates. "The next day a girl Daniel had dated came to the door and asked Josh to go to church with her. They became close and she was a positive influence for five years. I think that was an answer to prayer."

When one of Daniel's close friends took her own life, Josh, believing suicide was an impediment to getting in heaven, asked Daniel to plead his friend's case with God. "You're in heaven; talk to the big man; ask God to take Natalie into His arms." His little brother had always helped people in need; Josh had no doubt he could convince God to take his friend.

Some choose not to talk with their loved ones. After weeks of angrily telling David what she thought about his leaving her, Connie+ began talking to God about David, rather than talking to David. She still occasionally asks God to tell David something—perhaps to ask David to watch over their son, but she doesn't talk to him directly. For her, the straight line has been irreparably severed.

Pam+ fusses at her brother and sister, frustrated they left her alone to care for their aging parents.

Kay, Darlene, and Alisa+ don't talk to their brother Dennis, but they talk *about* him to their children—they want them to know their uncle, who would have enriched their lives with his love, his compassion, and his humor.

To talk or not to talk? We should do what we feel comfortable with—no more and no less.

NORMAL OR ABNORMAL?

Not everyone has dreams; not everyone has signs; and, not everyone wants to talk with their loved one. If paranormal experiences happen and are comforting, that's fine. If they don't, that is also all right. If we talk to our loved one, that is acceptable. If we choose not to, that is our choice. Each response is normal and as unique as the relationships we shared.

Our world becomes dreamlike after a death. As we make our way through the fog that envelops us, we may be prone to attach meaning where others think no meaning exists. In our disconnected state, we grasp at any indication that our loved one is okay. Are our imaginations running amok? Are we engaged in wishful thinking and grasping meanings where none exist? Perhaps. Perhaps not.

Who is to say whether the communication or signs we encounter are real or interpretations? Does it really matter? If we can hold tightly to anything — actual or imagined — that will comfort our heart by keeping the presence and love of the deceased close, then why question that experience? Why try to rationalize when our lives have been torn asunder? Why not just accept the signs or communications as gifts that warm our spirit in the cold dark of our loss?

Chapter 24

FILLING OUR DAYS WITH MEANING

If a man is to live, he must be all alive,
body, soul, heart, mind, spirit.
Thomas Merton, American writer, Trappist monk, 1915-1968

We lived for the person now gone. We cared for her, talked with her, and cried with her. We changed his diapers, rubbed his fevered brow, and watched his wobbling first steps. We cooked for him, lovingly put out the clothes he would wear, and welcomed him home in the evenings. We packed her lunch, took her to dance lessons, and helped her with her homework. We gardened with him, watched movies with him, and held his hand as we sat on the front porch swing watching a sleek sliver of the moon slip across the sky. We played together on the long stretch of beach as the sultry sun cast our shadows on the sand.

Inconsequential routines, but they formed the center of our universe. With death, our whole purpose vanished. We have outside interests and other people we love, but this one, this unique one, was different. Without him or her, life is empty. We continue to breathe, we get up each morning, and we eat what we can tolerate. But the reason for our existence has been buried six feet under the ground or has been scattered, wafting with the dried fragments of falling winter leaves, carried away by cheerless winds.

We exist, but we do not live. Thomas Merton spoke with truth, but we don't know if we can ever be "all alive" again — whether our body, soul, heart, mind, and spirit can be reunited into wholeness. Life stands still, and we are at a loss how to start it again. Like dying embers in a wood where silvery sleet has begun to fall, reigniting our desire to live seems impossible. The icy shards take hold, sucking the breath out of the fire — and out of us.

Benedict De Spinoza writes in *Ethics* that "Emotion, which is suffering, ceases to be suffering as soon as we form a clear and precise picture of it." In these words, we can find the hidden passage to the rest of our life. We cannot live again until we fully embrace our suffering, turning it round and round like a kaleidoscope, watching the prisms of dark and light turn into vibrant colors. Hundreds of hues spin before our eyes, tempting us to look beyond our blindness, to see their brilliance, lighting the path we must travel. If we fail to spend adequate time with our grief, the luminous prisms stand still; but if we examine our loss, acknowledge it, and accept it, we can then begin the journey to the other side where peace and joy are illuminated with soft lights that grow brighter and richer with time. We can once again see meaning in our lives.

Finding meaning requires a fundamental change in our attitude toward life. It demands we look forward, not backward. Viktor Frankl, who survived three years in the death camp at Auschwitz and other concentration camps, believed we should turn the tables on our thought process: Instead of saying we have "nothing to expect from life anymore," we must learn "it [does] not really matter what we expected from life, but rather what life expected from us."

In the loss of our loved one, life expected our grief. But that's not all. Life expected us to find meaning and purpose not only in the death of that person but also in the life left to us. Frankl stresses "life" doesn't mean something vague, but something very concrete and real. And it differs for every person.

Marsha+ found meaning and purpose when she presented her son Daniel's story during *Say No to Drugs and Alcohol* week, telling students that he was a great young man who thought having something to drink wouldn't hurt him. As she showed pictures of the mangled car that claimed the life of her son and one of his friends, she stressed, "No one is safe from the effects of alcohol." And, she reminded her audience, "Every person is precious cargo and has the *choice* as to whether he or she rides with someone who has been drinking or is under the influence of drugs."

Some find speaking out helps them deal with their grief, while others find different ways to use their tragedy to help others. Mary found solace in working with Hospice, helping others through the suffering she survived when her mother died of kidney disease. Gary and Diane+ set up a memorial foundation for Jason through their church to help needy young people attend church-sponsored youth trips. Henry committed himself to being a Big Brother. The list goes on and on—and it is important to note the purpose and meaning doesn't have to be newsworthy or of great magnitude. It simply has to be something fulfilling and worthwhile to us.

Denis Waitley, in *Seeds of Greatness*, recounts an analogy taught him by his friend, the late Dr. Maxwell Maltz, plastic surgeon and best-selling author of *Psycho-Cybernetics*. The mind, according to Dr. Maltz, is like a homing system in a torpedo or an automatic pilot. Once the target is set, the self-adjusting system continuously monitors feedback signals from the target area. The system then uses that data to fine-tune the course setting, making adjustments as needed. If the homing torpedo is programmed incompletely or not specifically, or even aimed at a target too distant, it will wander randomly around until its propulsion system fails or self-destructs.

Waitley says human behavior is like that—once a goal is set, the "mind constantly monitors self-talk and environmental feedback about the goal or target." Both negative and positive feedback is used to adjust decisions along the way. If we program our lives without enough detail or with goals that are unrealistic and too far away, we may wander around, often going in the wrong direction or being stalled altogether. Instead, we should plan for today and the next day, not for all our tomorrows.

Fredrich Nietzsche wrote, "He who has a *why* to live for can bear with almost any *how*." For the moment, our future has a veil drawn over it, but we can still look for the "why"—not why a bad thing happened to us but why we should find a specific aim for our lives. This "why" or "aim," Frankl says, strengthens us to get through the "how" of our existence—how we get through our loss and grief becomes less tumultuous if we can find a purpose for living. When we flounder in our sorrow, our automatic pilot directs us toward that goal, pointing us in the right direction.

Filling Our Days With Meaning

After my husband's death, after weeks of aimless wandering, unable to focus on my future, I decided to write his life's story — something we had talked about just before he died. Within days, I had moved from mindlessly staring into space to working 10-14 hours every day researching and writing *A Matter of Conscience: Redemption of a hometown hero, Bobby Hoppe.* Concentrating on telling what had happened to my husband during the most traumatic days of his life forced me to set aside my grief for long periods of time each day. Even though I sank back into my sorrow late in the evenings, my homing device corrected my faltering path and set me in the right direction the next morning.

Albert Einstein once said, "The tragedy of life is what dies inside a man while he lives." If we choose to die emotionally when our loved one departs this life, how tragic our lives will be. Does it help our loved one for us to stop living? Is that what he or she would have wanted for us?

If our answer to those questions is "No," then we must reenter life. If we can find the will to take pleasure in the sight of a newly bloomed peace rose, a melodic bluebird singing to the wind, or fragile snowflakes clinging to our windowsill, then we have taken the first step back to life. The warmth of a winter fire, the feel of icy surf against our bare feet, the sight of a young child playing in mud puddles — each reminds us life goes on. All around us nature and ordinary events await us if we are but open to their call.

In time, the hopes and plans we had for the future with our beloved will fade in the gleaming newness of each day. If we lost a child, we may forever be reminded of what we missed — the little things in life that mean so much. If we lost a parent in old age, we may think of our own mortality. If we lost a sister, we may think, as Cokie Roberts did, that we never imagined growing old without her in the next rocker. Yes, the future would have been very different if death had not stolen our loved one, but we can still see each day as a gift.

Dr. Nell Mohney, noted religious writer, talked with me one evening after my husband's death. With the sweet spirit of one who has met her own loss with faith, she suggested I begin each day with words from the little song, "This is the day that the Lord has made. I will rejoice and be glad in it." It made a difference—starting the day with a grateful heart rather than a sorrowful one.

If we can accept each new day as a gift, if we are thankful for what we have, we can let the future unfold, a day at a time. The meaning and purpose for the rest of our life may come in a flash, or it may come more slowly. Either way, if we are open to living in a world where the one we cherished no longer resides, we can find a reason for seeking worthwhile endeavors to fill our days. As G. L. Banks wrote in "My Aim," it may be "a cause that needs assistance" or "a wrong that needs resistance." It will be a cause in which we can invest our lives, "for the future in the distance, and the good that [we] can do." Our goal is to end our lives satisfied we left the world a little better than we found it.

We should accept the aspiration in Mary Oliver's poem, "When Death Comes," as our own. She concludes her verse with these lines:

When it's over, I don't want to wonder
if I have made of my life something particular, and real...
I don't want to end up simply having visited this world.

Grief is not fatal. Only the failure to rejoin life is. The journey from loss to life is steep and rocky, but we can emerge on the other side of the mountain with a new purpose—different than we had planned, but meaningful and worth the passage.

Chapter 25

GOODBYE, MY LOVE

*Goodbye isn't painful, unless you are never
going to say hello again.*
Author unknown

Saying goodbye is never easy. We send a child off to camp, a son off to college, a young man off to war. Thousands of times we kiss our husband, wife, parent, grandparent, child, brother, sister, or friend goodbye, sad at the parting but confident we will soon see our loved one again. We wait with eager anticipation for the person to walk back through the door and into our arms. And, almost always, that's how it happens. But we all live on borrowed time, and as David Friedman's song supposed, "No one can be sure when the loan will finally come due."

Even though we believe that when our own loan comes due we will be reunited, letting go, as another old song goes, is hard to do. Temporary goodbyes are just that; but when we see our loved one's body still and silent, or when we sift their ashes through our hands, the finality of death chokes our will to live. Grounded by grief, we cling to the memories of the life now ended. We see other people going on with their lives, like geese flying south for the winter, but we can't find our place in the formation. The gap created by our loved one leaves a void we cannot fill alone, so we stay on the ground.

Like the wisdom found in *The Music Man*, finding the good in goodbye is like searching for a needle in a haystack. It cannot be found.

Instead, we must simply let go. If we forever ride the breeze down memory lane, refusing to look toward the future, we risk missing the rest of our lives. As George Will avows, "The future has a way of arriving unannounced." The future is coming, as certain as a full moon, and we can choose to embrace it or let it pass us by.

Faces of Grief

We are held back by the guilt of letting go and moving on with the currents of life. We feel compelled to prove our grief to ourselves, to our beloved, and to the world. If we don't dwell on our grief, if we let go of our misery, are we betraying our cherished one? To do otherwise, we worry, would diminish our loved one's life.

I remember thinking my husband wouldn't know how much I loved him if I stopped grieving. But then I read the ancient Greek writer Xenophon's words: "Excess of grief for the dead is madness; for it is an injury to the living, and the dead know it not." Struck by an epiphany, I mused if heaven is all we believe it to be—no tears, no sorrow—could my husband watch me grieving so brokenheartedly and still be joyous? Perhaps, just perhaps, he can't see me, or if he can, he sees with wisdom beyond my earthly understanding. Logically, I knew my insistent sorrow was not helping Bob, and it was hurting me, but saying farewell was still hard.

It was easier to wallow in self-pity, drowning myself in daily despair. Like R. M. Grenon, I hate the word "goodbye." I found, as Grenon had, that "solitude has long since turned brown and withered, sitting bitter in my mouth and heavy in my veins." Despite the acid taste of aloneness, I began to feel, if not comfortable, at least "normal" in my self-imposed isolation, my regret, and my distress.

Our self-enforced sentence of suffering doesn't help our loved one and holds us back. Still, jumping headlong from grief to joy just isn't possible. Truth be known, we don't want to bid our beloved adieu. The memory of our loved one, even painted in pain, is better than nothing. If we let go, what do we have left? For most of us, if we will set ourselves free for just a moment, a multitude of blessings can be counted. There are other family members and friends to be loved, and if not, there are strangers needing support. Like walking a tightrope, most of us must have a lifeline—and we must move slowly, putting one foot at a time in front of us.

As I wrote in *Sips of Sustenance: Grieving the Loss of Your Spouse*, "Until we are ready to let go, Havelock Ellis' wisdom may be a bridge between our past and our future: 'All the art of living lies in a fine mingling of letting go and holding on.' If we aren't ready to let go of our memories, we can still bait the line to fish in unknown waters. We don't know what we will catch, but at least the line has been cast."

To fish in the waters of the future, we must begin to let go of the life we thought we would have with our loved one. Otherwise we will, as Jan Glidewell warned, "clutch the past so tightly to [our] chest that it leaves [our] arms too full to embrace the present."

The present is here, and the future is coming. Our loved one would want us to let go, to say goodbye, knowing we will meet again. Even when our hearts want to hold tightly to the past, our heads must decide to move forward.

We must weed the worst of our grief out of our lives, nurturing the new seeds ready to sprout if we give them room to grow in our hearts. We can then find in scriptures and nature a source of renewal. As Merton predicts, we'll soon stumble on a "sky [that] seems to be a pure, a cooler blue, the trees a deeper green. The whole world is charged with the glory of God and [we] feel fire and music under [our] feet."

With renewed footing, we can dance the rumba of life again; we can laugh again, honoring the life of living as we honored the life of the one now waiting for us in another realm. Letting go is hard, saying goodbye is sad, but as an unknown author once wrote, "Missing someone gets easier every day because even though it's one day further from the last time you saw each other, it's one day closer to the next time you will."

Chapter 26

ON THE OTHER SIDE OF GRIEF

...I will comfort them and turn their mourning into joy, their sorrow into gladness.
Jeremiah 31: 13 (Good News Bible)

When grief grips us so viciously we think we will explode into a thousand pieces, envisioning a day when we will sorrow no more seems implausible. But we must hold tight to that hope; otherwise our anguish will destroy us, slaying our spirit, leaving us crushed, unable to put our lives back together. Like a broken vase, we need some way to bond the shattered fragments back into a vessel that can hold beauty again.

In our brokenness, we can't see the way ahead to a day when our mourning will be turned into joy. Our human mind seeks an explicit picture, date-stamped and timed, but Thomas Merton tells us we don't have "to know precisely what is happening, or exactly where it is all going." Our earthly eyes and our limited wisdom prevent us from grasping the possibilities of the future. Realizing this, we should not be troubled by our obscure vision. Instead, Merton says we need to "recognize the possibilities and challenges offered by the present moment, and to embrace them with courage, faith, and hope."

Merton comprehended that "Every moment and every event of everyman's life on earth plants something in his soul. For just as the wind carries thousands of winged seeds, so each moment brings with it germs of spiritual vitality that come to rest imperceptibly in the minds and wills of men."

Or, as Toby Talbot said, "Piece by piece, [we] reenter the world." Expanding that wisdom, Martha Hickman encourages us to "take pleasure in the small ordinary events of life." When the "sharp teeth of our loss no longer bite[s] into our consciousness all the time...we're aware of the wonderful life-sustaining things going on around us—like red cardinals against a winter snow or the warmth of fire when we have come in from the cold."

At a time when we think our world has ended, if we can seize Julian of Norwich's words—"All shall be well...and all manner of thing shall be well"—we can begin the journey back to joyous living. And, even when we struggle with this hope, we can perhaps find peace in the psalmist's words: "For he shall give his angels charge over thee, to keep thee in all thy ways." (Psalms 91:11, KJV)

In the well-known poem penned by Mary Stephenson in 1936, "Footprints in the Sand," the poet questions why she can see God's footprints in the sand beside hers except during the darkest days of her life. The answer: When she needed God most, he picked her up and carried her. Even when we can't see evidence of his presence, He is there.

If we can but "relinquish our loved one into the loving care of a Creator," Hickman reminds us, "we will find a peace coming into our lives, a trust in the order of things, and a willingness to cherish one day at a time."

Believing a master plan exists for this world—indeed for the universe and the larger infinity we cannot comprehend—gives us the comfort that the journey we walk through grief has meaning and purpose, though we struggle to sense them. Even when we acknowledge we cannot see the path ahead.

As Merton admitted, "My Lord God, [we] have no idea where [we are] going; [we] do not see the road ahead of [us]; [we] cannot know for certain where it will end. Nor do [we] really know [ourselves] and the fact that [we] think [we are] following [His] will does not mean that [we are] actually doing it." Even with this candor, Merton insists, "The desire to please You does in fact please You." The desire alone, even if it is misguided, even if it is abandoned at times as we grapple with our grief, is enough, Merton says. We can be confident a higher power is worthy of our trust, "though [we] may seem to be lost and in the shadow of death." As the psalmist wrote, "I shall not fear, for thou art with me." He will "never leave [us] to face [our] perils alone."

Beyond our fear, sometimes just out of sight, help waits patiently for our call. Even when we are too troubled to see it, we can be assured it is there.

Like a ship concealed in fog, we can sail from darkness into sunlight again.

We should not let the dull haze of our grief obscure the glimpse of blue that resides behind the clouds. Mists will hang low over our hearts after the storms of our sorrow, but patches of shallow fog won't depress us forever. They always burn off, and an azure sky awaits us. And, just over the horizon a safe harbor will welcome us, restoring our spirit and hope for a glorious reunion with the one who has traveled ahead of us.

Chapter 27

AFTER DEATH, THEN WHAT?

Now faith is being sure of what we hope for and certain of what we do not see.

Hebrews 11:1 NIV

What happens after death?

I don't know, and despite what learned men and theologians say, they don't either. Yes, the Bible and other tomes offer predictions and signs, but no one living on earth today has made the journey through death back to life, and thus none can unequivocally say they know exactly what happens after death. Even "near death" experiences are just that—a person was *near* death but did not cross the threshold to another life.

Explanations for apparent contradictions ("This day thou shalt be with me in Paradise" vs. "The dead in Christ shall rise in the final days") help, but they fall short of telling us precisely what our loved one experienced after the final breath of life on earth. What is certain, though, is that a master plan is in place.

Brennan Manning, author of *The Ragamuffin Gospel*, points out that in "contemplating the order of the earth, the solar system, and the stellar universe, scholars and scientists have concluded that the master Planner left nothing to chance."

Manning cites several examples, including how the slant of the earth, tilted at an angle of 23 degrees both north and south, is not only perfect, but the earth's six sextillion ton weight is flawlessly balanced, revolving on its axis at more than 25,000 miles per day. Simultaneously, it revolves in its own orbit around the sun, traveling more than six hundred million miles each year. And it never gets off course!

Not only do the sun and earth move in synchronization, but the eight planets in our solar system also stay on predictable orbits. Another fact puts our insignificant place on earth in perspective: The sun is only one star of the 100 billion that comprise the Milky Way galaxy.

Manning also notes the moon's distance from the earth, 50,000 miles, prevents the tides from submerging the continents under water. And had the earth's crust been ten feet thicker, there would be no oxygen, and therefore no animal life. Likewise, the oceans' depth, had they been a few feet deeper, would have precluded carbon dioxide and no plants would survive.

If that is not enough, consider how the bodies of a man and a woman were designed to fit perfectly together, providing the place where new life is created in the union of the two forms.

Such design, such complexity and exactness, surely means He has a plan for our eternity. We wish we could describe it. We want to know whether the brilliant tunnel of light so many people have been drawn toward in near-death experiences is what our loved one saw. We yearn for assurance it was a glorious moment and not a frightful one. We long to prove "signs" or "visitations" are really messages and messengers from loved ones. We wish we could see beyond earth into eternity, whether streets of gold or something grander than we could ever envision awaits us. But we only have human eyes, and they can only see as far as the sky.

Someday, as John Gillespie Magee, the World War II Royal Canadian Air Force pilot, wrote on the back of a letter to his parents, we will not only see but touch eternity, just as our loved one has done:

Oh, I have slipped
The surly bonds of Earth…
And while with silent lifting mind I've trod,
The high, untrespassed sanctity of space
Put out my hand and touched the face of God.

Magee started the verse at 30,000 feet and finished it after he landed. Soon afterward, at the age of nineteen, he was tragically killed during a training flight, traveling a longer journey than his Spitfire had ever carried him, to a destination he had only glimpsed in his sonnet.

We live in an age where certainty is expected. After all, we can Google almost anything and get myriad answers. Nebulous explanations no longer suffice. Religious beliefs we once accepted without question come under closer scrutiny when we lose a dearly beloved. Our human mind demands proof of the destination and the map followed to get there. We want to accept the rationalization that the soul flies swiftly into the presence of God while the body remains in the ground to be reunited in the final days, but we know that man's interpretation of the scriptures may be flawed. God's plan may be infinitely more palatable and beautiful.

Gordon+, like many others, wants to know what's going to happen when he sees his wife Anne again. "I want to know," he says, "on what level I will co-exist with her." For now, he doesn't think we are meant to comprehend exactly how it will be, but he does believe he and Anne will know each other in a different dimension.

Hazel+ relates she has a clearer picture of heaven now than she did before Kelly died. "After his plane crashed," she recalls, "I pictured what his 'life' was like there. I wondered what he was doing? And I thought, 'God's really glad to have Kelly; he's probably making everyone smile, spreading joy among the saints.'" With a question mark still in her voice, she adds, "I wanted to know if Kelly is happy. Is he glad he left earth to be in heaven?" In her heart she believes he is, but concrete evidence would make her grief so much more manageable.

Does life continue after death? What is the nature of our existence in the realm of the unknown? To know the answers would bring peace and comfort, but to know the answers requires our own death. Until we make that journey, we can move from skepticism to belief that one far wiser than we has a grand plan not drawn by human hand, not envisioned by earthly eyes. If that plan keeps the universe in perfect balance, if it raises a dead iris back to life each spring, then surely that magnificent design includes the survival of souls beyond death.

I may be more skeptical about the details than others with greater faith or religious knowledge than I, but I am certain of that survival. Such a belief is rooted deeply in the signs of nature — evidence that life can be raised from the dead. Hostas die and are cut to the ground, but they magically reappear the next year. Fields of wildflowers fade away, but their seeds, scattered by winged creatures and whispering winds, fall on fertile ground, their beauty to resurface after winter snows have melted. Trees shed their wilted leaves and sprout new green ones to welcome spring. Everything that dies will live again. The questions are only how and when.

Our belief in an afterlife affects how we grieve. There are those who believe death is the end. Others believe, as Kübler-Ross and Kessler describe, that our bodies are just the clothes we wear while on earth. Like these well-known authors, we can have confidence that in some form or fashion our lives continue after death, believing the death moment separates only the mortal from the immortal. Our loved one departs from the temporary house, the body we held so dearly, and moves solely into the realm of the spirit and soul.

If we believe in heaven, even though we grieve our loss, we find comfort that our loved one has entered a different dimension. As Emily Dickinson wrote, she never spoke with God; she never visited heaven. Yet, she avers she was as certain of the spot as if she had a map.

Unbelievers travel the journey through grief without the certainty Dickinson avows so forcefully. Believers know beyond the walls of death's darkness life picks up again in a different form and dimension.

Kübler-Ross and Kessler use the analogy of a ship that "exists on the ocean, even if it sails out beyond the limits of our sight. The people in the ship have not vanished, they are simply moving to another shore."

Someday we will travel to that distant shore, but the difficulty is that in grief, it seems we are the ones in eternity, not just our loved ones. It is a different eternity—on earth where times move slowly like melting icebergs as we await the hoped-for reunion with our loved one. When time seems eternal, we may find solace in Phoebe Cary's words in *Nearer Home*:

One sweetly solemn thought
Comes to me o'er and o'er;
I am nearer home today
Than I ever have been before.

SECTION TWO

STORIES OF SURVIVING LOSS
AND FINDING HOPE

Chapter 28

DIANE AND GARY

LOSS OF A CHILD

"God had healed Jason once; we knew he could do it again. So we prayed continuously for complete healing."

Riding down the narrow country road on the way to meet Gary and Diane, vibrant crimson and golden leaves carved a path of beauty for my eyes, reminding me once again of the miracle nature exhibits in its annual cycle. But as I opened the door of my car and heard the rustle of dead leaves being swept away by a gust of wind, I was saddened knowing that the last miracle this loving couple prayed for had been denied, the body of their young son, like the leaves, fallen.

Jason Andrew Fowler, first-born son of Gary and Diane; first-born grandson to James and Norma Wofford and Alvin and Joyce Fowler; big brother to Casey and Staci. A real cutie with big brown eyes, he stole the hearts of family and friends.

The picture of an all-American family, the Fowlers played together and prayed together. The kids were handsome and good, loving and fun—what every parent dreamed of. All in all, a storybook family, evidenced by pictures and the life they lived. But the story doesn't have a happy ending, at least for now.

On August 1, 1992, the five Fowlers began a journey—a journey they thought was taking them on a family vacation to Gulf Shores, Ala.; but, as Diane explains, "The journey was much more than we expected and lasted nine years, 10 months, and 27 days."

A car accident on route to their destination landed all members of the family in an emergency room in Montgomery, Ala. "By all appearances," Diane says, "Jason was the least injured, but on closer examination, he was the most critical—his blood would not clot. And so began an unplanned journey of doctor visits, hospital stays, and a scary sounding disease called aplastic anemia."

Diane and Gary

For the next two years, doctors in Chattanooga and at Vanderbilt Hospital in Nashville monitored Jason closely. "God was our source of strength as we prayed continuously that He would give Jason complete healing," Diane recalls, her unvarnished faith flowing forth.

At the two-year benchmark following Jason's diagnosis, his blood count dropped to the most dangerous level yet. The doctors advised a bone marrow transplant, the only known cure at that time. Both Casey and Staci were tested in hopes one would be a match, and they all celebrated when they heard the news that Casey was a perfect match. Excited at the possibility of a permanent cure, plans were quickly made to schedule the transplant. Then, out of the blue, a call from their insurance company sent the family into another tailspin. Their insurance would pay for the transplant only if the procedure were done at Emory Hospital in Atlanta, Ga. A new hospital and new doctors jarred the family out of its comfort zone with their medical providers who had brought Jason so far.

With no choice, plans changed swiftly, and the family made the trek to Emory. "At age 17, on November 17, 1994, after chemotherapy drugs and massive doses of radiation, Jason was infused with the life-saving bone marrow of his brother," Diane relates. Ecstatic, the family rejoiced when God answered their prayers—the transplant was successful. Jason began improving quickly, gaining energy and weight. Over the next two years, he completed high school and entered college. A miracle—Jason could live normally again.

"But before he could finish college, Jason began suffering a nagging cough and unexpected weight loss that sent fear to our hearts," Diane recalls with a voice struggling not to quiver. "Graft vs. host disease—that was the name this time." Although they had been told this possibility existed after the transplant, Jason had felt so good they didn't want to think about it.

For the next six years, Jason gradually deteriorated. Finally, the Emory doctors urged Diane and Gary to get Jason on the list for a double lung transplant. "God had healed Jason once; we knew he could do it again. So we prayed continuously for complete healing."

Jason continued to struggle; he suffered a stroke at home, but Diane and Gary believed he would be alright, never losing hope, refusing to let themselves admit Jason might die. At the hospital, watching Jason breathe through an oxygen apparatus, the family prayed for another miracle. But what happened wasn't the miracle they so desperately wanted, and even today Gary and Diane wonder if Jason's death could have been prevented.

Speaking so softly I can barely hear from across the room, Gary begins talking about his painful memory of the last hours before Jason's death. When Jason left the emergency room for an MRI, Gary says Jason knew his family. Without warning, when he returned, he was silent and didn't recognize his mother and father. His voice breaking, Gary says he has always wondered if Jason might have fallen off the MRI table and that caused the sudden change in his condition.

Listening to Gary, Diane tenderly turns to him, touching his hand. "I don't think he fell off the table, Gary." Hesitating, Diane looks troubled, and then tells Gary, "I have never told you this before, but when Jason came out of the MRI, he didn't have his oxygen tube in his nose. I started screaming at the nurse, 'Why isn't his oxygen in his nose? Get it back in there.' I've always believed the reason Jason didn't recognize us anymore was because he was off his oxygen too long."

Two parents with separate nightmares. Each not knowing the other is haunted by what might have happened. A stranger may wonder why Gary and Diane hadn't talked about their fears, their questions about what happened to Jason while he was having the MRI, but Gary has an answer: "There are certain doors you can go in, but there are certain doors you can't enter — the pain is too great. Once you go in one of those doors, you're going to be there a while in pain."

Diane adds there were also prayers she couldn't utter, especially during the bone marrow transplant. At one point, she wrote her prayers in a journal; she could write her deepest fears, her pleading for Jason to be healed, but she couldn't say them aloud. Her voice silenced by heartache and fear, by the horror of watching her oldest child go through so much pain, Diane penned the unbridled thoughts that flowed like hot coals bouncing from the belly of a volcano. Burning inside from the flames, Diane had to find an outlet.

Diane and Gary still ponder how Jason must have felt; even surmising he may not have wanted the double lung transplant. That he agreed to it for them, not for himself. He refused to read materials they provided about it, but in the end, he agreed to go forward. But it was not to be—after the MRI, he never had a chance.

When Diane and Gary finally accepted that Jason might not survive to have the transplant, they called their daughter Staci home from the Dominican Republic, where she had just landed to begin a mission trip. She wrote a poem about her big brother as she made the long, lonely journey home, her heart in anguish. When she arrived at the hospital and her parents told her and her brother Casey that Jason was not going to make it, they confirmed what Staci had known in her broken heart. But Casey wasn't prepared, and he lashed out in anger. Why would God take Jason, the kindest, most caring brother anyone could ever have? It wasn't fair. Jason had been through so much. Diane and Gary wonder if part of Casey's anger was founded in his remorse that the bone marrow transplant he had so willingly given wasn't enough to save his beloved brother.

Knowing they could not hold onto Jason in the strongest wind of his life, Diane and Gary gathered their children around Jason's bed and asked the nurse to remove Jason's breathing apparatus so they could see his face one more time before his facial expression would be forever frozen.

In the somber stillness, Gary spoke, telling Jason who was in the room with him and that they all loved him. Holding hands, tears flowing unchecked, the family sang "Amazing Grace" as the nurse took the moon mask off and they touched his face, his hair. "For the last time," Gary recalls with heartbreak streaking through his words, "we loved on him in a real way."

Spirits broken, the family let go. In Diane's words, "On June 27, 2002, God gave Jason his complete healing—he sent his angels to bring Jason home." Simultaneously, when Jason took his last breath, Diane and Gary whispered, "To be absent from the body is to be present with the Lord."

When Jason died, it was as if, in Tennyson's words, "God's finger touched him, and he slept." But Gary, Diane, Staci, and Casey, fully awake in the world Jason had left behind, now had a gaping hole in their daily lives. As George Eliot said, it was the certainty—the finality—of Jason's departure that they had to transform into hope—hope that Jason had been made whole again and that they would someday be reunited with him.

Were the Fowlers angry with God despite their firm faith that God is in control of their lives? They admit feeling rage at times. Gary remembers only one time he became utterly furious with God. In the year before Jason died, there wasn't much he could do except play cards and watch television. When his medication caused the loss of his eyesight, taking away the only ways he could fill long, lonely days, for Gary, it was too much for God to put on his son. Diane was angry about Jason's loss of vision too, but her resentment was deeper and longer: "I saw the pain and the heartache daily, and it about killed me for Jason to miss out on so much other kids were doing." More than once Diane tried to bargain with God: "Take *me* right now, God! Let Jason be well." She would have willingly given her life in exchange for her son's health to be restored. He was too young to have his life stripped from him.

Diane and Gary have let go of much of their anger, and the bitterness Casey harbored against God for what his brother had to go through has also dissipated. It was difficult to get beyond the resentment that cloaked him as he watched his good-hearted older brother, his hero, suffer while others enjoyed their days of youth, but a dream (described in a previous chapter) helped restore his faith. Today, Casey's love for Jason is exhibited in positive ways. Jason loved riding in the red BMW convertible his dad bought just months before his death, and seeing Jason, even on the passenger side with an oxygen mask, with the wind in his face, acting like a normal 22-year-old, filled his father's heart with joy. Knowing this, after Jason's death, Casey took a picture of Jason to an artist and had him draw Jason in the convertible with clouds around him, his head tilted upward toward heaven. He gave it to his mom and dad for Christmas, and the gift lifted their broken spirits. Casey also has a small tattoo on his chest that connects his hands to Jason's, with Jason's initials above the drawing. Gary absolutely abhors tattoos, but with a lopsided smile, he confesses he tolerates this one because it shows the immense love between Casey and his brother.

Almost ten years later, Gary and Diane concede grieving is still ongoing—it's a road they expect to travel the rest of their lives. They took baby steps after Jason's death, Gary says. After he and Diane went back to work, every day they would come home to a mailbox filled with sympathy cards—usually with special notes. And every day they went outside, sat on a swing, and read the cards together, tears pouring like big fat raindrops.

It took almost two years before Diane and Gary could face the selection of a tombstone for Jason's grave, but when they did, it was distinctively fitting. In memory of Jason's love for golf, Diane sketched a mountain behind a picture of Jason in a golf swing and added a church—this scene was etched on the back of his tombstone...another baby step.

The next step was the hardest, and like a toddler, Diane kept falling down. For four or five years, she would go in Jason's room, thinking, "This is the day." But when she pulled out his clothes, all she could do was hold them to her face, smell them, and put them back. She couldn't even change the sheets on Jason's bed. And no one dared to go in there and lay on them.

The world spins, and the Fowlers go on with their lives, but the pain, "the physical pain in my heart," Diane murmurs with tears filling her eyes, "I carry with me and will until the end of my life." Words by John Scalzi explain more fully: "When you lose someone you love, you die too, and you wait around for your body to catch up."

Gary feels the same. Sometimes it hits him so hard he can barely speak. Despite his anguish, he can smile again; but sometimes he catches himself, asking, "Why am I smiling? I shouldn't be having fun. I've lost a son." When Gary said that, I thought of Rose Kennedy's words, "Birds sing after a storm; why shouldn't people feel as free to delight in whatever remains to them?" But when your world has stopped spinning, those kinds of words don't mean much, so I left them unsaid.

Gary and Diane say they are still learning to put one foot in front of the other. They are thankful for dear friends who were with them every mile they traveled. The void left by Jason's death is a forever hole in their lives, but by God's grace, they are living for their other two children and their grandchildren.

As Diane wrote in a letter to one of Jason's best friends, losing their son was like being "thrown by a huge wave to the depths of despair and it was hard to breathe, think, or even function for a while." But Diane continues that she is thankful to God that the waves come fewer and farther apart with time. Acknowledging she has come to the conclusion it is okay to get thrown to the bottom of the ocean floor, she knows she can't stay there forever because Jason wouldn't want her to remain so low. He would want her to remember the wonderful times they shared. And so, Diane concludes her letter by asking Jason's friend to "Talk about his life, say his name, tell those funny stories, laugh, cry, and don't be mad with God...not for very long anyway."

Remembering Jason's sense of humor, his uncomplaining spirit, and his compassion for others evokes happy memories. Even as he struggled during the last days of his life, Jason made a list of people who had been kind and helpful throughout his illness. He gave the names to his "Papaw" and in great detail described the individual bluebird houses he wanted him to build for each person, even specifying the colors each was to be painted. And, the day before his death, he remembered his mother's birthday and asked her sister to purchase a gift for him to give her. That Jason was thinking of others when his own death was imminent epitomizes why he was so special.

Jason died before the bluebird houses could be completed, but Gary and Diane, on his behalf, later delivered them to friends who meant so much to him, along with a note that included these thoughts:

When you observe the beautiful bluebirds, we hope it will be a reminder of the beautiful life Jason lived and the freedom he now enjoys with his heavenly Father.

Even during the most stressful times Jason maintained a positive outlook and "insisted" we do the same. We chose a quote to be inscribed on the birdhouses that we think reflected his life:

"*Keep your face always turned toward the sunshine, and the shadows will fall behind you.*"

Perhaps Jason's extraordinary love for others, in Oscar Wilde's words, propelled him to "trod the sunlit heights, and from life's dissonance struck one clear chord to reach the ears of God." Maybe God needed Jason's compassion and love in heaven, and that's why He called him home.

Chapter 29

MARSHA AND CURTIS

LOSS OF A CHILD

"I don't think you let go of grief – you just deal with it."

Sapped by sweltering August heat after a day of campaigning for her husband Curtis in his bid for state representative, the usually energetic Marsha turned in early. Almost immediately, she was deep in the land of slumber, her tired body lapping up energy for the next day. When the persistent ringing of her phone penetrated her consciousness around 1 a.m., at first she thought it was her alarm clock. "It can't be morning already," she moaned inwardly. Then she realized it was her phone jangling. Still in a sleepy stupor, she fumbled for the receiver and said sleepily, "Hello?"

"Mom, what are you doing?"

"I'm sleeping, Daniel," Marsha replied to her son with a weary sigh.

"I need a favor, Mom. Come to the Brary (a nearby restaurant/bar) and bring me a copy of my dealer tag and proof of insurance. Some cops pulled me over, and I have to show it to them. And bring it right now. I've already been here 30 minutes."

What does a mother do? "Of course, I had no choice," Marsha later penned in a poem about Daniel's death. That night, fighting her tired body, Marsha scrambled into clothes and jumped in her car, the sultry night air as thick as fog. As she drove, she became concerned she might not be able to find Daniel at the Brary and dialed his cell phone, but his voice mail picked up. After a greeting, Daniel's voice came through with a perplexing sense of urgency: "Think before you leap into a situation; be true to yourself; make sure you stay true to your friends." Strange, even absurd, Marsha thought. Not like Daniel at all, whose voice mail message was usually humorous. Later, she would remember this odd message and wonder if Daniel had a premonition

148

something was about to happen to him. Had he felt compelled to leave behind those words of advice?

Marsha needn't have worried about finding Daniel—he was in the middle of three cop cars, lights flashing like carnival rides. When she handed him the tag and other documents, Daniel took them and uttered a quick, "Thanks."

"Whoa, buddy," Marsha said, faking irritation, "you owe me more than that. I got out of bed to bring you this."

With a quick smile, Daniel turned back to his mom, gently kissed her, and whispered, "Thank you, Mom. I love you."

As Daniel handed the items to a sheriff's deputy, Marsha began talking to Mike Alexander, a police officer at the scene. He explained Daniel had been pulled over because an officer saw a girl in the car trying to knock a sombrero off Daniel's head and thought they were fighting. It was all in fun and all would have been well except Daniel did not have the right tag on his car.

Thinking everything had been resolved with the new tag, Marsha was surprised when one of the sheriff's deputies started yelling confrontationally at Daniel as he knelt to put the tag on his car.

"Young man, weren't you stopped earlier in the day for the wrong tag? Weren't you told to take this car to your house? Why are you out in it again? You need to get this vehicle off the road," he exclaimed angrily.

Exasperated, Daniel turned to his mom and told her, "These guys are just messing with me." Seeing his frustration, Marsha told Daniel to head for home and she would stay to get the ticket.

At his friends' urging, Daniel did as his mother asked and got in the car, but his annoyance was unmistakable as he backed up his vehicle and stared at the sheriff's deputy with a belligerent look that conveyed what he wanted to say but couldn't. As soon as he pulled his car past Marsha, he took off like a cannon shot, almost as if he was daring the deputy to come after him. With a cragged grin, Marsha turned to Mike Alexander and said, "Well, he won't be going anywhere else tonight." When she spoke the words, Marsha had no idea how prophetic they were as she watched Mike jump in his car and take off after Daniel.

Finally getting the ticket in hand, Marsha drove home. As she approached, blue lights twirled and twinkled against the dark sky, and Marsha's spirit sank, thinking the police were there to arrest Daniel for speeding off. "Will this night never end?" she thought wearily. Then, her heart gripped by dread, she saw Daniel's mangled car in the ditch. Despite the hot air sucking the breath out of her, Marsha turned ice cold as she fearfully took in the scary scene in front of her. "Stay in the car," Mike Alexander warned ominously. Mike was the first officer at the scene; in pursuit of Daniel, he had taken another route and didn't arrive until after the wreck.

Dazed, Marsha doesn't remember what she did, later asking Mike, "Did I stay in the car?"

"You did until Curt arrived," he responded gently.

Hearing the crash, Curt came sprinting down the driveway. Together, he and Marsha started toward Daniel's car, but strong burly arms held them back. With a trembling voice, Marsha recounts the words whispered by the EMT, a friend of Curt's: "I've tried my hardest to save him. He's hurt really, really bad — major head trauma. He has a heartbeat, but he's not breathing. We're going to have to do a trach."

Bewildered and frightened, Curtis and Marsha stood helplessly; their hearts clutched by fear and disbelief as the blue lights eerily strobed the sky. Another officer approached them, asking if they knew the names of the other boys in the car.

"Laney Hodges." Marsha spoke so softly the officer could barely hear her. But his own voice was harsh and loud as he responded, "We won't have to worry about *him* going to court." Marsha's thoughts were kinder as she recalled how Daniel had pooled money from friends just days ago to get Laney out of jail, even lining up a job for him. More importantly, he had talked with his friend about getting his life right with God — and he had.

"The boy in the back seat," Marsha said, her voice trembling as she watched the EMTs using paddles on him, "is Dustin Brake." She held her breath until she saw Dustin's chest rise and fall as he came back to life. Only then did she let her own breath begin its in and out rhythm, though it still shuddered with trepidation for Daniel.

And on the ground was Brad Wise, seemingly the least injured. "What happened? What happened?" he gasped in a state of bewilderment.

As if they were looking through the wrong end of a telescope, Marsha and Curtis watched Daniel be loaded in an ambulance for transport to a Life Flight helicopter and then raced to their car. Distraught, Marsha tried to pray, but "I couldn't get the words to feel like they were coming from my heart." Then, reflecting on the head injury, she brokenly told God, "If he is not going to be right, please take him home." Today, even knowing Daniel would not have wanted to live in a vegetative state, Marsha says with tears choking her words, "Now I would take him back any way."

At the hospital, they begged to see their precious son, but the answer was, "Not now." Curt turned to Marsha with pain snaking across his face: "I don't feel good about this at all."

Shortly, a doctor told them surgery had been performed on Daniel's spleen and liver. When the doctors told Curt and Marsha that Daniel's heart was failing, they desperately pleaded to see him, to touch him one more time while his body was still warm with life. Even that tender moment was denied the anguished parents. The doctor told them he wasn't sure Daniel would live long enough for the attendants to get him cleaned up so they could go in to see him. And sadly, he didn't. By the time Marsha and Curt were allowed in, their beloved son Daniel was gone. Curt walked woodenly to his son's broken body and kissed his head, swollen twice the normal size, but Marsha couldn't. "I wanted to remember him as he was just an hour before when he kissed me," she says in a strangled sigh, daggers of despair twisting in her heart.

And then the task of telling their other two sons. Curt Jr. took the news so hard he had to ask a cousin to drive him home. Josh, who was devoted to his younger brother, was stunned, unable to comprehend Daniel was gone. He felt like he was going to suffocate, his heart beating so hard he thought it was going to rip his chest open. In a split second, the three brothers had become two. Life would never be the same without Daniel.

Almost immediately, the Curtis home filled with young and old friends, all devastated but eager to share stories of the intelligent, good-looking, kind-hearted young man whose life had been cut short. Having graduated from high school with honors, Daniel was ready to start college, eager to begin the next stage of his life. The one just ended had been filled with good times — sports, fishing, caving, and most everything else an outgoing, fun-loving young man could have desired.

Story after story lit the bleak black night. Marsha remembered one time in a soccer game when Daniel, the goalie, had failed to stop a point. Coaching her son, Marsha yelled at him from the sidelines to get out of the box, not to play so far in. With a catch in her voice, she remembers Daniel turning to her with big crocodile tears, admonishing, "Go watch *Josh* play." And then there was the time when he had a broken collarbone but stayed in a football game for one more tackle–big, tough, fearless Daniel.

On and on the stories went. And, in between, a few friends slipped into Daniel's bedroom and came back with shirts, tennis shoes, and other items, desperate to have a remnant of his life. "They wanted a piece of their friend," Marsha says with a small smile and a big heart, "and I didn't mind what they took."

Feeling helpless but keen on showing their love, Josh and several of Daniel's friends had tattoos etched on their chests or backs that week in memory of Daniel. Josh's had his younger brother's name and date of birth and death. He also had a gold cross made with Daniel's name on it that he still wears. All efforts to keep Daniel's memory alive; to keep him close to hearts that loved him.

Daniel's funeral is a blur to Marsha and Curt — they just remember lines and lines of people. And they recall how difficult it was to select pallbearers because Daniel had so many close friends. Marsha also recollects being adamant with her pastor when he suggested the soloist sing "Amazing Grace." "Absolutely not," she said emphatically, "I would never be able to hear the song again without sobbing."

Later, trying to reconstruct what happened the night Daniel was killed, Marsha talked to the man driving the truck that pulled in front of Daniel. On his way home, the man turned onto the narrow, winding road. Abruptly, he saw Daniel's car behind him. Traveling 80-85 mph, Daniel must have been as shocked to see the truck in front of him as the man had been to see Daniel's car. Trying to avoid hitting the truck, Daniel jerked his steering wheel hard to the left, veering to the wrong side of the road. Unable to control the car at such a high rate of speed, Daniel was helpless as it spun out of control, cascading into a telephone pole in a thunderous, deafening crash. The air was left flavored with steel, smoke, and muted aftershave lotion.

Dustin's girlfriend, who had been talking with him at the time on her cell phone, heard laughing and joking in the background — then suddenly stark silence. Maybe, Marsha thinks, they were laughing about outrunning the cops. Or maybe they were just being joyful about the college life that lay ahead. Gloriously happy one second, and then: BAM. A crash that took two lives and forever changed countless others.

Not even one of the boys was wearing a seatbelt. Daniel was propelled through the front windshield. The other boy who was killed, Laney, was slung headlong into the back of Daniel's seat, breaking his neck, his eyes immediately lifeless and still. Later, Marsha and Curt learned the boys had been drinking, though neither Marsha nor the cops had noticed anything to suggest the boys were inebriated when they were in the Brary parking lot.

Not detecting that, not stopping Daniel from driving, are relentless regrets from which Marsha cannot escape. But she's not angry — at Daniel or at God. "I never questioned God; I was always grateful for the years I had with Daniel. He believed in God. I wonder if God saw things coming in Daniel's life that he wanted to save him from. Do I believe in predestination? I don't know. I know what happened to Daniel was an accident, but God may have played a hand in it."

Today, Curt, Marsha and their two sons still struggle, even though Daniel has been gone almost six years. Not surprisingly, the two parents grieve differently. Curt holds most of his pain inside, rarely crying. Not overly affectionate in a demonstrative way, it's typical for him to hide his feelings, retreating into silence. In contrast, Marsha is open with her sorrow. She still sheds sad tears every day. "Not a day goes by that I don't think about him." Talking about Daniel's death is hard; in fact, Marsha said thinking about sharing her grief for this book was one of the most difficult times she has experienced since Daniel's death. Reliving the night he died, revisiting the awful anguish and loss, colored Marsha's voice with a silver mist as memories of pain flowed like acid over her soul.

But Marsha wanted to tell Daniel's story, as torturous as the experience would be. She wanted to warn others about the danger of drinking and driving, using Daniel's death as a teaching tool to encourage other young people not to drink and drive. She shares how a judge, talking with Daniel after he was caught with an open container in his car the night of his girlfriend's senior prom, required him to go to Cumberland Heights for rehabilitation, admonishing him, "I don't want to see you in a body bag someday." Words that no one saw as Daniel's destiny. Words Marsha hopes will deter teenagers from following Daniel's path to death.

Beyond the warnings to others, Martha also wanted to share how Daniel's death had changed her life. "I want to do something every day so that if I die tomorrow, I have made someone's life better; or set an example, helped someone understand life is what you make it. You strive to do the best you can and give God the credit."

Even though she considered not going back to her position as a teacher after Daniel's death, Marsha reentered the classroom with a new vision: She put Daniel's face on every student and tried to be the teacher she would want him to have. Despite her devastation, it was her best year ever—her students' scores skyrocketed. Keeping busy probably kept Marsha sane—and her students benefitted. It was a tough year, though. Marsha cried on the way to school every day, went in and taught her classes, and then sobbed all the way home.

"I don't think you let go of grief," Marsha concedes. "You just deal with it." She adds, "I can still smile because of memories imbedded in my heart. Daniel was always the one who made people laugh. So to be down…Yes, I hurt; I cried; I still cry. But I laugh and enjoy life because that's what he did; he would want me to." But Marsha confesses smiling is not always easy. "Is it fake sometimes? Sure. But that's because you don't want to bring others into your realm of grief."

Today, she goes to Daniel's gravesite regularly. On the footstone is an epitaph Daniel had written as part of a class assignment. On Daniel's 21st birthday, three years after his death, she was speechless when a group of Daniel's friends showed up at the cemetery to have a birthday party for him. Strange, she thought, but her heart was touched that his friends still cared. And they do; just recently, she found a letter his friend Slayden Johnson had written, six pages full of memories, expressing how much he misses Daniel. How he wished he had listened to Daniel's advice about doing the right thing, about being the best he could be. A lasting impression, only one of many Daniel made. He burrowed his way into the hearts of friends and family, leaving footprints on their souls, indelibly etched impressions that continue to lead them on paths of goodness and love. Inexorably, Daniel lives on in their lives.

Chapter 30

NITA AND WALTER

LOSS OF A CHILD

"You feel like a giant balloon — one minute your life is full and you have purpose, and the next minute your whole life is deflated. All that's left are the remnants of the burst balloon."

Hannah, energetic and exuberant, frolicked at Camp Lookout with her fifth-grade classmates at their end-of-the-school year trip. Running, playing, turning cartwheels, laughing all day with not a care in the world. Not a cloud in her blue sky, not a thunderstorm on the horizon.

As the sunset colored the sky with flames of scarlet and topaz that evening, tranquility hung over the chapel where the children and teachers gathered for evening prayers, tired from their day of fun and ready to settle down for the night after thanking their Maker for their day. In the stillness of that time, the storm that struck Hannah with one swift stroke came without warning. One moment she was sitting in chapel, and the next she fell over into her teacher's arms. The storm didn't come from outside — it came from within. A heart defect no one knew was there.

Later, Nita would describe the image she tries to hold in her mind, saying the words so lyrically they almost become a song: "As Hannah took her seat in the chapel, I like to think that God said to her, 'Hannah, we're closer to my house right now than yours. Why don't you come home with me?'" Nita adds with both joy and sadness tempering her voice, "In an instant, Hannah's address changed from Georgia to Glory."

Although staff and paramedics performed CPR on Hannah for more than an hour, she couldn't be revived. An urgent call sent Nita and her husband Walter rushing to the hospital, their hearts in their throats but never imagining the worst. It was too late. Their beautiful, blond-haired, hazel-eyed Hannah, just eleven and one-half years old, was gone.

Crushed, disbelieving, heartbroken, empty, confused, lifeless—that's how Walter tries to describe the indescribable. "How do you comprehend that one minute she is smiling with you and the next minute she is dancing with Jesus? You can't lift your arms...you look around and see nothing...words don't register. You feel like a giant balloon—one minute your life is full and you have purpose, and the next minute your whole life is deflated. All that's left are the remnants of the burst balloon. At 6:49 p.m. our hearts beat strong; at 6:50 p.m. death had brutally ripped a large piece of our hearts away, leaving us to survive or waste away."

Walter, Nita, Jody, and Hannah had a near perfect life; an all-American family; good looking and smart. A family full of love for one another and others. Kids who were happy and well, active, and good at school. For Nita and Walter, their kids made their lives whole. Hannah, like her brother Jody, had a soft spot for animals, especially dogs and horses, but she also had a place in her heart for those less fortunate than she. One day in the third grade she came home crying because one of her classmates didn't have money for lunch or clothes. That was Hannah.

Hannah's teacher dubbed her and five of her friends the "Six Pack" because they spent so much time together. Whether encircled by her friends, working out as a gymnast (something she wasn't particularly suited for but worked so hard at she won medals to prove to herself she could do it), or walking between the legs and under the bellies of her horses, Hannah was a character. Always playful, always caring. Always Hannah. And always with a big smile lighting up her face morning, noon, and night.

That smile was so bright it could have replaced the sun the day Hannah's cousin Tom gave her a three-year-old yellow Labrador Retriever. Hannah and the big dog bonded in an instant, and she chuckled with delight as Kiawah hung her head out the truck window, her tail beating Hannah in the face. Nita says she still remembers Hannah coming home with Kiawah and the two of them running around the pond with the family's other Lab, Missy. "Kiawah barked, Hannah giggled, and all was well with the world," Nita says with a poignant smile, then adds, her voice threatening to crack, "Hannah would move to Heaven three days later on Wednesday night."

Even knowing Hannah was now robed in white, living with God's angels, Nita remembers thinking as she woodenly went through requisite preparations for her daughter's funeral, "I'm supposed to be buying tennis shoes and shorts, not clothes for a casket." Nita also recalls her mind being absolutely blank, almost as if she were watching from afar, when the funeral director asked what song the family wanted sung. She was astounded when "Then Came the Morning" unexpectedly popped out of her mouth. At the time, she "had absolutely no idea how the words so completely spoke to Hannah's death."

When the soloist at the service began singing the words from the song Nita had selected, she suddenly discerned what God had done. A rapturous smile spread across her face as she began singing right along. "I guess folks thought I was crazy or something," she says with a grin twitching at the corner of her mouth. And it wasn't the song's words about a son being taken, "wasted before his time," that brought unfathomable joy. It was the line that the mother knew "deep in her heart...somehow her son would live again."

The final words of the lyrics assured more than 1,000 people gathered at Hannah's service that there is indeed hope beyond the grave. Death loses and life wins when morning comes. Death is not the end. Nita believes God sent that specific song to remind those listening of His promises—He had promised to welcome Hannah, and He had promised to comfort those who were hurting. If that wasn't cause for a celebration, hearing 1,000 voices singing "When We All Get to Heaven" was enough to make people want to shout.

Even with such a victorious homecoming someday, losing Hannah to life on this earth was heartrending. Reflecting how he made it through the first few days after Hannah died, Walter poses a thoughtful question: "With friends, family, and God's love, what other way is there?" People were there constantly, helping Nita, Walter, and Jody cope. From back rubs to suppers to answering the phone, friends and family didn't ask what they could do to help—they just did something. Without them, Nita wonders how they could ever have come to grips with the hole inside them.

Friends didn't take the place of Hannah, but they helped fill the empty spot temporarily, with prayer—and laughter. "Hannah was a hoot to be around—we were blessed to have had her in our family." Over the coming months and years, many hours were spent just "laughing and remembering her antics."

Levity didn't wipe away the sadness, but it helped bring momentary respites from the deep grief. It was more than that, though, that kept the Brunings sane. Stalwart Christians, they grasped the loss of Hannah as a way to live their faith. They still had another child in the house, and they knew they couldn't expect him or anyone else to believe in a loving God if they didn't trust Him themselves. In an amazing way, even in their desolation, Nita and Walter—and their tightly knit family—were still able to witness. At least eight people came to a saving knowledge of Christ within the two weeks after Hannah died, they acknowledge with grateful hearts. With strength beyond what most can pull from the deepness of despair, Nita asks quietly, "That's what we're here for, isn't it?"

Walter and Nita don't blame God for taking Hannah when she had so many unrealized dreams, including being a veterinarian, when she had so much of life ahead of her. They don't speak of the wedding they will never plan, the grandchildren they will never hold in their arms. They talk about God's perfect plan. Walter observes softly, "We didn't create Hannah and we did nothing to earn her."

Acknowledging their sadness lasted a long time and will probably never dissipate, Walter and Nita believe God gave them Hannah as an eleven-year gift—"We cherish our time we had with her and can't wait to see her again. We've told many people over the years, Hannah isn't 'gone,' she's just moved to a new home, and we'll be so glad when our list of chores is done down here so we can move to where she is." Nita concludes, "Heaven is real, and God doesn't make mistakes. God is taking great care of her, and of us, and if we'll be patient, we will see her again."

Straightforward and candid, Nita admits the "in control by faith" face she showed the world sometimes broke down. It wasn't that her faith crumbled; it was that the splinters in her shattered heart sometimes pierced so deeply she couldn't hold back the wellspring of tears. "It was thirteen weeks after Hannah died before Walter and I stopped looking at the clock at 6:50 p.m. every Wednesday night, holding each other and crying. And," she says, "it may have been two or three years before we stopped crying during a random conversation about Hannah."

But they knew they couldn't stop living. They had to go on with life for their son, and they were committed to "walking the talk." They buried Hannah, but they refused to be buried by their grief. They had been given a new job, and as painful as it was at times, they used their grief to bring others to God's grace. From their faith, they drew "unexplainable strength." Amazingly (and admirably), Walter and Nita continued to teach the junior high class at their church, missing only the Sunday after Hannah's Saturday burial, even though each class meeting was a starkly sharp reminder of their missing daughter.

Heaven is so much closer now, Walter and Nita feel. "Up until that time, Heaven had been a place that we'd see when we were seventy or eighty years old — not much to ponder on at that time. Once Hannah 'moved' there it became a real place, just as if Hannah had moved far away, say, to California. Heaven is right within our grasp; it's as close as one step away."

While they wait out their time on earth, Nita, Walter, and Jody feel "unmatched." Where there were four, now there are three. After spending several days at Nita's parents the week following Hannah's death, Walter, Nita, and Jody headed for home, stopping at a Cracker Barrel along the way. When the hostess unwittingly asked how many, after a long pause, Walter whispered miserably, "Three." It was the first time the family had asked for a table without Hannah, and it broke their hearts. It's still hard today, Nita confesses. "We go out to eat and there is an empty chair. We ride a carnival ride and someone rides alone. We play a game and someone has to referee. We're 'uneven,' like having a broken leg—we can't be comfortable; we're not settled, content, satisfied." It's getting better. They're working on building their lives around a "threesome," and it's beginning to feel more normal.

The Brunings have learned to live with Hannah's loss, but "there's always that 'awkward' moment when you see the 'hole,' and you remember what was." Still, they believe it is easier to cope "if you're content with where Hannah is and how she arrived."

Still sad but excited. Looking forward to seeing Hannah again one day.

In English, the Biblical name Hannah means "favor or grace." Hannah Bruning was indisputably a favor bestowed by the grace of God on her family; grace was granted in sufficient measure in the middle of their darkest night; and by that grace, they will be joyously reunited with her. Like the old hymn declares, it is amazing grace. The Bruning family has come "through many dangers, toils, and snares." They give thanks grace "brought [them] safe thus far," and they are confident "grace will lead [them] home" to be forever with Hannah and the Savior they love. The sweet sound of amazing grace.

Chapter 31

VICKI

LOSS OF A CHILD

"If you had told me the day before Jonathan died that I would lose him from this life forever, I would have said, 'Then dig two graves because I can't imagine surviving without him.'"

At 6'3", with light brown hair and sapphire blue eyes, Jonathan Wyatt stood out in a crowd—not just because he was handsome and charming, athletic and toned, but because his physical presence exuded character and compassion.

In high school, Jonathan looked out for others. Every day when the bell rang, he managed to be the last one out, shuffling papers, rearranging books, and in general just procrastinating while everyone else was running out the door. But Jonathan hung back to be sure he could hold the door open for a young girl with multiple sclerosis. A kind gesture the girl on crutches never forgot. At Jonathan's funeral, she stood in line three hours so she could tell Vicki how Jonathan had helped her—"so you would know what kind of son you had."

But Vicki knew. Jonathan had always shown kindness and concern for others, and it continued in college. He often left Beale Street to walk young ladies back to their dorm so they wouldn't have to walk alone at night in Memphis, while others, including their boyfriends, stayed behind and partied. A true gentlemen. After seeing the young ladies safely home, Jonathan would head back to join his friends.

At the University of Memphis, Jonathan excelled in academics, graduating magna cum laude and presiding as University Man of the Year and president or Grand Master of his fraternity, Kappa Sigma Phi. A born leader, Jonathan led by example, inspiring his fraternity brothers. Even after graduation, when Jonathan had returned to Nashville to accept a position in the banking industry, his fraternity brothers turned to him for strength and support when another brother died in a car accident.

Returning to Memphis for the memorial service, Jonathan stood before the crowd of mourners and spoke eloquently of his friend whose life had been cut tragically short. He never once showed anger toward God for the great loss they were all feeling—he simply spoke of Matt's unique and special qualities and ended the eulogy by counseling, "Let's not leave today asking why or being angry that this happened; let's just remember the tremendous blessing Matt was in each of our lives."

Three short weeks later, Jonathan's words would hit his mother Vicki like a boomerang straight from heaven.

"The night I found out Jonathan died was surreal in many ways," Vicki recalls, her voice like a silky wind whispering from afar. "I felt disbelief, as well as an uncanny sense of 'I knew it.'"

Vicki had tried to reach Jonathan several times that unusually warm February day, wanting to invite him to dinner on Valentine's Day. Although she had no basis or reason to have such a morbid thought, she recalls with a tremor in her voice, "My first instinct was that he was dead." A mother's intuition? With every passing hour and no return call, "I became more convinced of that horrible thought." Jonathan always called her right back, and by late afternoon, when his voicemail was full, Vicki admits, "I became unglued."

With fear clutching her throat, Vicki tried to reach Jonathan's friends but couldn't. And, since he had been working at Capital Bank and Trust in Hendersonville, Tennessee, only a couple of months, she didn't know how to contact anyone after business hours. Calls to Jonathan's apartment manager went to voice mail. Finally, at 9 p.m., Vicki was so distraught she decided to drive to Hendersonville to try to find out what had happened. Just as she was walking out the door, the call came that confirmed her worst fears—her beloved son had died alone at the age of 25. A cardiac arrhythmia caused by an undetected heart condition called hypertropic cardiomyopathy had claimed his life. Like a stealthy tiger, it had pounced unseen, taking Jonathan and ripping Vicki's heart out with its fangs.

Faces of Grief

Later, Vicki would find the apartment manager had known since 1 p.m. when she let the bank manager into Jonathan's apartment to check on him after he had not shown up for work and wasn't returning phone calls. Jonathan's dad, who was also in banking and was known to the president of the bank, was immediately notified; but, inexplicably he didn't call Vicki for many hours. Could he just not bear telling the mother of his son that she would never see him alive again? Vicki wants to believe that was the case, but having an estranged relationship with Jonathan's dad at the time, she did wonder on the worst day of her life if it was another way of punishing her for the divorce. Regardless of the reason, the failure to tell her first, before friends and other relatives knew, added to the trauma Vicki lived through that night when slivers of ice were slashing her soul.

"The moment I heard Jonathan was dead changed my life forever," Vicki murmurs, misery swathing her words. In the shock and sorrow that threatened to overwhelm her, Vicki knows she could "have easily asked why someone who had so much to offer this world would be taken so suddenly and just as he was beginning his adult journey into this life." But in the darkest abyss of her grief, Jonathan's words wove their way into her thoughts: "Don't ask why. Just remember the tremendous blessing he was in our lives." Words Jonathan had spoken a short three weeks earlier about his friend–words that returned to comfort and strengthen Vicki. Words that sent her back to Philippians 3:1 for recalibration of her soul: "I thank my God every day I remember you." (NIV)

In retrospect, Vicki feels the words Jonathan spoke at his friend's funeral were another gift from the divine—words she would remember when the "light of her life" was extinguished. Those words helped Vicki not to feel angry toward God—not to blame him for the tragic loss she endured. "I don't look at life as 'fair' or 'unfair,' nor do I believe God took Jonathan because it was 'his time.' I believe we live in a world where good and bad things randomly happen. Sickness, death, accidents, natural disasters, and other heartrending events occur without reason. I

164

Vicki

never felt immune from the possibility of something 'bad' happening to me."

Vicki adds, "My frame of thinking made me especially appreciate the very special times I had with both my sons. Even before Jonathan's death, it also made me look at life like someone with a terminal illness. I just always felt that time was limited, and I needed to take advantage of every moment with my boys."

Thankfulness for the time she had with Jonathan, buttressed by her faith, family, and close friends, sustained Vicki during her darkest hours. "But," she concedes with a heart of rare love, "my Cavalier King Charles Spaniels, Brinkley and Claire, have been the constant source of comfort that has probably done the most to keep me sane. They have been like guardian angels since Jonathan died...one always on my left and one on my right. I know their need to stay close is the nature of this breed, but it seems uncanny how much consolation they have provided just by always being there and expecting nothing in return. They have seen me cry until my eyes were swollen together and have been with me during most of my happier moments."

Vicki acknowledges part of the comfort is that she can bestow on her dearly loved dogs the nurturing she misses giving as a mom. Like others who have the "dog gene," Vicki finds therapeutic value in having pets. Instead of anti-anxiety drugs and anti-depressants, she claims Brinkley and Claire have proven to be her "drug of choice."

The solace Vicki found in her dogs, the strength she didn't know she had, the faith that was stronger than she ever imagined, the ability to withstand so much pain, and the unexpected moments of joy and happiness—all are divine gifts from above, Vicki says with immense gratitude.

Despite her positive attitude and unquestionable appreciation for the time she had with Jonathan, Vicki knows her life will never be the same. A professional career woman, she always knew her highest calling was to be a mother. And even though she loves her other son Christopher with absolute devotion, one-half of her motherhood is gone and will never return.

Her life has been switch-backed — its direction dramatically changed — and sometimes the uphill climb seems too steep for steps shattered by pain. "To some extent," Vicki says softly, "I have let go of parts of the grief, but honestly, it is still a part of who I am. Some days it feels like a heavy burden I am carrying on my back. It's a little like being handicapped. If you lost your leg, you might be able to walk again, but it wouldn't be the same. You would walk with a limp. I guess I will always walk with a limp that you can't see, but every day I wish I had my leg back."

One tangible remnant of Vicki's changed being is that she cannot ride an elevator alone. "I've always been somewhat claustrophobic, but now I will wait 15 minutes for someone going to the same floor as me and ride with them rather than get on the elevator alone." She adds that she knows it seems strange to others and confesses her sister chides her, "This should be a piece of cake after what you have been through." But Vicki knows it is just one of the ways she is weak and vulnerable. "Maybe," she ponders, "it is because I know the worst can happen, and I expect the elevator to get stuck every time I get on it."

Forthright in her self-analysis, Vicki concedes, "No need for anyone to tell me the odds of that happening, because I was also told that the odds of my son suddenly dying at 25 of an arrthymia caused by an enlarged heart were about the same as winning the lottery." Vicki concludes her phobia is a strange phenomenon, and "hopefully with time, I will get past this stumbling block."

A self-proclaimed "positive thinking" advocate, Vicki has turned part of her tragic loss to change in positive ways, too. "I tend to live in the moment now and get pleasure and enjoyment from the simplest of things; I let go of grudges, don't take things personally, and try on a daily basis to do whatever I can to make someone else's life better. Like the author of *Don't Sweat the Small Stuff — and Everything is Small Stuff*, Vicki realizes the "real" little things in life are actually the big things.

Vicki seizes every moment she has, as her son once advised in a fraternity initiation speech. In Jonathan's words,

"Participate. Make your voice heard. Leave your mark. When Jackie Robinson was asked how he wanted to be remembered, he said life is not about accomplishments that can be etched into stone or written in a book somewhere but about the positive effects and lasting marks one can make in others' lives. He knew it was far better to carve your name into hearts than into marble." That's what Vicki tries to do. It's her way of honoring Jonathan's memory.

Vicki also has a new appreciation for the wonders of nature. "I get comfort from a beautiful sunset, a hike in the woods, a rainy day, watching the snow fall, dancing, seeing an old couple hold hands, and a good hearty laugh. I try to be kinder and gentler to myself, accepting I am a fallible human being doing the best I can. I realize more every day I still have many things to be thankful for."

Even when she doesn't feel like smiling, Vicki says, with a tiny twinkle in her eyes, she fakes it. Jonathan wrote her a note when he was in junior high saying she was always at his games, and he always knew she had a smile on her face for him as he played. "That has been my motivation to wear a smile, even with a broken heart. You give a smile and nine out of ten times you will get one back, and I need all the smiles I can get. Maybe my smile can brighten the day of others who are bearing their own burdens."

Moving back into the grief zone, Vicki reminisces about the first day she truly felt joyful after Jonathan's death: "I will never forget that moment. I was driving on a beautiful spring day and had the windows down so I could feel the fresh air on my face when one of my favorite songs, 'Brown-Eyed Girl,' came on the radio. Turning the volume up, I started singing along—and for a brief moment I forgot I was sad. I suddenly remembered and thought, 'What am I doing? I have lost my son and I'm singing and feeling joyful!' I almost lost that feeling immediately with the harsh reality of my life, but something inside of me said, 'Don't stop. Don't let go of this moment. Hold on to this feeling. You deserve to be happy again.' I tried and although the feeling didn't last very long, I began to have other moments of unexpected happiness. I tried to not shoo those moments away any more. I began to embrace them as little reminders that life could be good again. Never the same, but at least good. I will never live another day without missing Jonathan, but I must accept the little joys in life whenever and wherever they appear."

Baby steps, Vicki declares with conviction. "I just took baby steps, one step at a time, one day at a time, some days one hour at a time." That's her advice to others: "Take whatever size step you can and be kind to yourself—and let others be kind to you."

She knows each journey is as different as the child a parent loses, but she thinks all parents need to let their grief out. "Cry until there are no tears left. Cry every time you feel like it. There's no way around the grief. You have to go right through it. Your grief is a gift of love to your child, but there will be a time, maybe months or years later, when the grief won't be your whole life. It will always be a part, but not the all-consuming part it is right now."

To those still in the early throes of grief, Vicki says with compassion, "You, too, can find your smile again for your child and for yourself and for all those other 'walking wounded' people we encounter on a daily basis." With the intensity of one who speaks from a broken heart, Vicki concludes, "Life isn't easy for any of us, but the pain of a parent who has lost a child seems to be the most unnatural of all. The one we never expect to endure in our lifetime." The end result of losing a child before his time should not be withdrawing from the world forever, and although Vicki acknowledges her way may not be the right way for someone else, she thinks we can all benefit from the words of Ralph Waldo Emerson: "If you can cause one life to breathe easier, then your life has been a success." And so it is that Vicki believes, "We must help each other in order to help ourselves through this pain." When death pummels us to the ground, we can't give up, Vicki gently declares. "There are too many other people who still need us."

An amazingly positive woman of deep conviction and unfathomable love, Vicki, vivacious even in grief, still never expected to do as well as she has. And she certainly doesn't want to come off as a "Pollyanna."

Vicki

"If you had told me the day before Jonathan died that I would lose him from this life forever, I would have said, 'Then dig two graves because I can't imagine surviving without him.'" While Vicki found strength within and from God to remain alive without Jonathan, she has had many hard days "when the reality of how much I had lost became even more apparent as I slowly came out of the fog, the shock, and the disbelief." It's not a battle that is ever won, but the fight goes on. Vicki is a valiant soldier who wills herself to live—and as much as possible, to live joyously. Even if she did eulogize and bury her son on Valentine's Day when she had hoped to have dinner with him on that day of love.

Chapter 32

MARCIA

LOSS OF A CHILD

"Losing a child is a life sentence."

When I think of Marcia, two pictures fall before my eyes: Gorgeous, flaming-red hair cascading around her lively face and a scene where we stood in a circle with other little girls at Vacation Bible School. Having romped and played in the churchyard, we had gathered to say prayers before lunch, each girl in the circle taking a turn. When it was Marcia's time, her petition was short and sweet: "Lord, please make everyone's prayers be short so we can hurry up and eat." Typically Marcia — precocious, impetuous, and funny.

I lost track of Marcia over the years but reconnected with her while writing this book. She's had lots of experience with prayer since that day in the churchyard, and her entreaties to God haven't been short. Losing her 35-year-old daughter Tira has kept her on her knees many times.

When she talks about Tira, Marcia's thoughts ramble a bit, moving from funny stories that brighten her memories to the tragic loss she endured. When she was in the second grade, Tira stepped off the school bus one day and lay down on the ground, immobilized. Marcia thinks it was the first sign of the health problems that would haunt Tira the rest of her life. At the age of 13, she fainted at the church altar while reading a poem. When her doctor told Marcia Tira might have had a religious experience, Marcia's humorous side rose to the occasion, telling the doctor, "We're Baptists, not Holy Rollers."

Over the years, Tira had a number of fainting spells, but it was only after her marriage that she was diagnosed as being bipolar. After that, she went through counseling and tried numerous medications, but she didn't get better, telling Marcia one day, "I feel like my brain is moving round and round." Suicidal, she cried a lot and was compulsive, moving furniture around, shopping a lot, constantly changing her hair color. No one ever knew how all of this related to the occasional seizures.

On the evening of December 19, 2004, walking down the hall in her home, Marcia says the Lord came to her and said, "Give me Tira." Comfortable with talking to Him, Marcia replied breezily, "You know she already belongs to You." Later that evening, Marcia realized she had not fully understood the message. About midnight, she saw her message light blinking and clicked to hear the voice mail. Her ex-husband, crying, told her to call him. When she returned the call, in broken words, Jim Nation told Marcia that Tira had died during a seizure.

"My heart raced," Marcia recalls, "but then the Lord came to me and said, 'I have her; she is safe and you won't have to worry about her anymore.'" Awakening Brooke, Tira's daughter who was staying with Marcia, she told her what had happened. Crying, Brooke wondered how her "maw maw" could be so calm. Later, Marcia realized she was in shock. "I was numb. It's something the Lord puts in you until you can really deal with your loss." She wasn't so numb she didn't go into denial, calling the hospital, hoping it was a bad joke. "But it was real. It hurt me for a long time I wasn't with her. I felt guilty, but the Lord did not want me with her; it would have been too much for me."

For a while, Marcia couldn't cry. "I just sat there." She tried to protect Tira's two children as much as possible, even hiding the paper containing Tira's obituary so they wouldn't have to see the reality of their mother's death in black and white print. Tira was buried the day before Christmas. Marcia recalls it was like a bad dream, "but the Lord was in the shadows." Even though Marcia had some relief that "Tira was at last with Jesus," she grieved because "I was without her."

Marcia had lost her mother thirty years earlier, and she remembers "The Lord was over me like a bright light." But this was different, she says, "I couldn't feel anything." She just wanted to be alone. The only peace she had was when she first woke up each day. "And then, it would hit me, 'My daughter is gone' and the pain would start. It was a living hell!"

Soon anger took the place of numbness. She wasn't upset with God, though, she was "real mad at people who had hurt

Tira." Laughing about it now, Marcia says she made out a hit list and held it toward heaven, telling God to kill them! Her daughter had been so good-hearted she had often let people mistreat her, and it infuriated Marcia. It took her a long time to let go of her rage. "I finally came out of that," Marcia says, adding with a little girl giggle, "God didn't kill anybody and I repented what I had said."

Marcia says she didn't really blame God, "Although I fussed at him a little because he wouldn't give me a vision of Tira in heaven," like he had her mom.

When Marcia's grief finally penetrated her numbness and anger, "I thought I was going to die. It was the most terrifying feeling I had ever had. My mind was racing; my chest hurt. I would just walk around repeating the 23rd Psalm. I took Tira's pictures off the wall because it hurt so much to look at them. I cried all the time; I screamed some. God, I missed her! I felt like I had a knife in my heart. I thought I was going crazy."

Believing she was having a heart attack, Marcia went to the emergency room, expecting the doctor to tell her she was dying. "Hallelujah, I am going to heaven and be with Tira," she recalls thinking. When the doctor told Marcia her heart was as strong as steel, Marcia's sense of humor kicked in: "I told him on my daddy's side of the family people don't die. They finally turn into skeletons and we bury them." Then she bemoaned, "I guess I'm stuck here on earth."

Marcia struggled with medication for depression and sleep, not wanting to take it but knowing she needed it to survive. "A few people told me to get over it; life goes on. How dumb!" Enraged when one man compared losing a friend to losing a child, saying he got over his loss, Marcia lashed back: "Well, look in a coffin and see your child there and then come and tell me to get over it!"

Some people told Marcia to pretend Tira had gone on vacation. Marcia's reaction: "Guess what, they are, but they aren't coming back!" One lady told her to pretend it never happened — more mindless words, Marcia says. She advises people to say nothing rather than saying they've been there or some other inane words. It did help when people said, "I don't know how you feel and I hope I never do," to which she responded with compassion, "It's for certain you don't want to join this club."

How did she get through her grief? "My body just went through the stages it had to go through and I had to bear it. You can't hide from it or it will kill you."

Marcia says she had been through a lot (losing her mom early, having cancer, her house burning, Christian counseling for co-dependency, divorce), but "Nothing in this world is worse than losing a child. Part of me is gone and always will be 'til I get to the other side. Until I can hold her once more in my arms." In the interim, Marcia has learned to accept grace, and that has helped keep her going. She's not sure why she didn't let God comfort her when she was so grieved but suspects it just comes with His own timing. "He slowly shows you what to pray for to get through each day."

Life goes on for Marcia, but there will always be a sense of sadness surrounding her. She no longer wants to sink into some dark place and hide, but the permanence of her loss never totally leaves her. Sometimes it swims back unbidden like a shark threatening to kill her.

She concedes, "Time does help some" but has also accepted that "losing a child is a life sentence."

It helps that Marcia believes, "The Lord knows what he is doing. I trust his heart, though mine will always be broken. I've learned to pray for grace every day, and it helps; I can feel His love." And she's comforted by the presence and love of her other child, Frankie, and Tira's other child, Brooke—and more recently, the birth of Brooke's first child, Tyree. They call him Ty, after Tira.

Chapter 33

AILEEN

LOSS OF CHILDREN AND SPOUSES

"I've never felt strong going through a death. Knowing my husbands and sons were Christians and that they were in heaven made it easier, but the losses were still powerful and heartbreaking."

Speaking with wisdom that comes from age and multiple grief experiences, Aileen's down-to-earth candor comes forth softly but assuredly. She's been tested more than once, and like a diamond, she sparkles, no longer the rough, black coal from which the iridescent jewel is transformed. Just as it is difficult to believe any relationship exists between dismal, brownish-black lumps of coal and shimmering diamonds, the transition Aileen has made from an angry, disillusioned Christian in the aftermath of her first husband's death into a person who shines with inner peace is amazing. Like the clumps of coal, she had to go through a long period of time under extreme pressure and heat, but she came out glistening, reflecting the goodness of God as she shares her experiences with grief.

Although Aileen now knows God never puts more on a person than he or she can bear, she wasn't so sure the first time death turned her world upside down.

In 1945, the young mother of three boys, ages five, three, and 10 months, worried about her husband, Grover Phillips, knowing he served in a dangerous war zone as World War II raged in the Western Theater. But, busy with her active boys, trying to keep their lives as normal as possible, kept her from dwelling on her fears. After all, she was a faithful Christian, and she prayed daily for Grover's safe return from the Navy to his waiting family.

Out shopping for groceries at the local Ransom's Store one glorious day, she thanked God for the warm sunshine chasing away April's spring rains. She warmly greeted a neighbor as she walked in the store, but her words torpedoed Aileen like the blast from the German warship that sank her husband's ship.

"I listened in shock," the 24-year-old mother recalls, "as my neighbor told me Grover was dead." Devastated, Aileen somehow drove to the home of family members to break the news.

"No body, no casket, no funeral," Aileen murmurs quietly, her eyes misting with memories of her misery. Without these "normal" accompaniments to death, Aileen couldn't find closure. One man wrote her he had seen Grover being eaten by sharks, a gruesome scene haunting Aileen for years.

Months later, the Navy notified Aileen Grover's body had been recovered and buried at sea. A belated memorial service was held in their church, but it was void of any tangible evidence of the man with whom she had planned to spend the rest of her life. Now, not only was he gone, she had to find a way to raise three young boys alone.

Aileen says Grover's death threatened her faith, bringing her the closest she ever came to giving up on God. "I had been faithful to God and tried to do what was right, and I blamed Him for taking Grover's life." Anger flooded her soul, shutting out prayers. When she did manage to utter a plea to God, "It was like I was praying to a brick wall." Shell shocked, she walked around in a daze, functioning but in a state of stupor. An uncle died and she went to the funeral, but later she didn't remember he had died. She doesn't even recall much about the fire that destroyed the home where she lived with her parents four months after Grover's death. Everything she had was destroyed; she somehow survived that, but it is all a blur to her.

Pretense protected her children — "I tried to act brave and not cry much in front of my boys." Back then, the only private place she could find to let her tears flow unchecked was in the family's outhouse, a hundred yards from the house. There she could be herself, could let the grief exploding in her chest erupt like yelps from an injured animal. Though distraught, she carried on because she had to for her boys.

Faces of Grief

Death gave Aileen a respite after that, but when it raised its ugly head again, it was a wolf with fangs so large and sharp she cried out aloud in pain and abject misery.

Another magnificent April day dawned; it was the birthday of her eldest son, Floyd, in 1964, and she had planned a family dinner. Jimmy, her youngest—a paratrooper in the U. S. Air Force—couldn't be there, but Aileen knew he would call to wish Floyd "Happy Birthday." A call came, but it was not from Jimmy—it was from an eerily solemn voice, telling her Jimmy had landed in high voltage wires after a routine parachute jump. Electrocuted upon impact, his body was burned so badly his casket could not be opened.

"I was numb," Aileen recalls. "For days I had no feelings at all—I guess I protected myself by refusing to think, to feel, to even believe the awful news.

"It was different from Grover's death," Aileen explains. "Although a husband cannot be replaced, another husband can find a new place in your heart. A child, though, is part of your body and can never be replaced."

Johnny Phillips, Aileen's middle son, thought *he* was going to be the one to die from an airplane fall. At the age of 15, Johnny had dreamed of slamming into the ground after falling from a plane. In the terrifying nightmare, Johnny morphed from 15 to 21 years old as he watched his own funeral following his plummet to the earth. From the night of that awful dream, Johnny was convinced he would die at the age of 21. Not wanting to leave a wife and children behind, he refused to get married. And, when he decided to enter the military, he joined the Navy to avoid being in airplanes. As luck would have it, he ended up stationed in Newfoundland, where he flew on Early Warning Aircrafts patrolling between Iceland and Greenland or the United Kingdom, on the lookout for Russian aircraft. One night, as part of a 23-man crew, after having worked two four-hour shifts (separated by a four-hour stint in the kitchen), Johnny headed to his bunk to catch some sleep. His eyes bleary from staring at radar screens, he dropped into deep dreamland and almost immediately saw his brother Jimmy. Together, they were playing happily, as they had in their younger days; but just

176

before Johnny awoke, Jimmy grasped him in a bear hug and whispered, "Goodbye, Johnny." As if he sensed what was happening to his brother thousands of miles away, Johnny woke up crying. He hoped it wasn't true, but he knew his brother was gone.

A few hours later when Johnny's plane returned to base, landing on the sub-zero runway, a man in a suit stood at the end of the frigid steps. Johnny's heart turned as cold as the mountains of ice he had flown over that day.

"Are you John Phillips?"

"Yes."

"I'm from the Red Cross, and I have some bad news."

"I know," Johnny replied grimly. "My brother Jimmy is dead."

The Red Cross representative was stunned—he had only received the news a couple of hours earlier. When Johnny told him about his dream, the man shook his head in disbelief. But there was never any doubt in Johnny's mind. He had misinterpreted the dream he had had when he was 15-years-old. The dream had foretold his brother's death—not his own— in the parachute disaster. Johnny would be 21 when *Jimmy* died; Jimmy was 19.

Despite Johnny's deep grief, he felt freed from his six years of fear that he would die at 21. Within days, he asked the girl he loved to marry him, and the wedding was hurriedly scheduled while Johnny was home on leave for Jimmy's funeral.

In a fog, Aileen went to her middle son's wedding within days of burying Jimmy, sitting in the church pew as the soloist sang, "You'll Never Walk Alone." I was there that day, and my own heart ached for her as I heard the words, "When you walk through a storm, hold your head up high." Deadened, Aileen listened to the singer remind her that at the end of the storm a golden sky and the sweet silver sound of a lark awaited her. How Aileen sat there that day I will never know, with her dreams tossed and turned, but she did, trying once again to be strong for one of her boys.

Eventually Aileen's grief pushed its way to the surface. "You have to grieve," she says. "The tears have to come and different situations bring them on." For Aileen, walking into her friend Hazel Williams' house, seeing Hazel's son Terry walk through the door struck her like a steel hammer. Reality hit: Jimmy would never come home again like Terry would. "The dam burst," she remembers, "and I cried and cried for a very long time."

The time between Grover and Jimmy's deaths was 19 years, and another 19 years passed before Aileen felt death's fangs again. But this time, two wolves attacked her within 10 days.

In 1983, she made a daily trek to the hospital to see Floyd, watching him caught in the clutches of cancer. The tumor in his brain was relentless, and Aileen wanted to be with him as much as possible. One night while visiting him, a grandson went to her home and found Chester, her second husband, dead of a heart attack. Another storm to walk through.

When she left Floyd's bedside to go to the funeral home, even though Floyd had been unresponsive for days, he nodded his head three times when she told him she would be back later. "I think he already knew Chester was dead even though no one had told him." Floyd died ten days later.

Two husbands, two sons—and Aileen still has one of the sweetest spirits I have ever seen. Somehow she still holds her head high despite the storms she has weathered. When I told her how I had always admired her strength and been inspired by her faith, she replied, "I've never felt strong going through a death. Knowing my husbands and sons were Christians and that they were in heaven made it easier, but the losses were still powerful and heartbreaking."

Catching her breath, Aileen concedes, "Death never gets easier. You keep grieving each one, but you learn to accept that life doesn't always suit you." After Grover's death, she was never again as angry toward God. "I believe I don't deserve—no one does—a life with no sorrow. We don't even deserve God's goodness." Alan Paton, in *Cry the Beloved Country*, seemingly agreed: "I have never thought that a Christian would be free of suffering." Paton added, "For our Lord suffered. And I have come to believe that He suffered, not to save us from suffering, but to teach us how to bear suffering. For He knew that there is no life without suffering."

Aileen appends another perspective: "In spite of tragedy and other heartaches, I've never gone hungry and I've always had family and friends to support me." In the midst of great sorrow, she can still find reason to be thankful. She also found solace in humor. When a flower arrangement in a small piano arrived at the funeral home just before Floyd's service—a tribute from a fellow musician, Lewis Kell—someone picked it up and turned it on, expecting a hymn. When "Beer Barrel Polka" sounded merrily from the twinkling keys, laughter filled the hearts of the family. A moment of levity in the time of grief was good for their souls.

Having experienced both sudden and slow deaths, Aileen doesn't know which one is worse. "You grieve a lingering death before the death, but the shock of someone dying suddenly stuns you. When either happens, you feel lost until you work your way through the grief. Sometimes it helps if you have to work your way through for other people."

Aileen knows "some people nurse their grief too long. You never get over losing a son or husband, but you can't stay in the state you're in when it first happens. The pain and the reality are still there, but you have to grieve and then move on." Her advice: "Don't dwell on the loss. Get busy. The fastest way to get on with your life is to do something for someone else."

Aileen also has advice for helping others as they grieve: "When a person dies, often people don't want to let the loved ones talk. They try to change the subject, or make statements like 'It's God's will' or 'Everything will be okay.' That's not what a person in deep grief needs to hear. "Just listen to them and let them talk or cry or whatever they need to do. Every situation is different. Don't say, 'I've been there,' or 'I know what you're going through.' You may think you know, but you don't."

When we are in the midst of trees bending beneath the weight of the wind, we should not try to right them with words or even gentle force. We should wait silently just outside the storm until the winds die down, until the trees begin to unbend, unloading their burden. Only when they are ready to right themselves can we help.

Chapter 34 (Part 1)

CARLA

LOSS OF A SPOUSE

"Why would a good God do something so senseless and awful?"

After almost seven years of marriage, Kelly and Carla were living life to its fullest on their 15-acre farm. A log cabin, a pond, and a horse barn cradled the young couple like two birds in a nest. Secure with themselves and with each other, they had it all.

Although his fulltime job was as a fireman, Kelly's real love was flying. With his own plane and his own airstrip, he was as close to heaven on earth as anyone could be when he soared through the air, an eagle with powerful wings. In his spare time, he offered flying lessons to those just dreaming of the life he had. If Carla could only use one word to describe him, it would be "adventuresome."

Carla Stewart, not shy about her independence, never wanted to be married, but after she met Kelly Gibson, that changed. Though they initially dated and broke up, they got back together when Kelly invited Carla to go flying with him in spring 1993. A year later, they married — and it was a marriage made in heaven. Carla not only had a man who adored her, she also had a mate who supported her love of horses. Her "someday" goal was to quit her job and manage her horse farm.

July 12, 2001, dawned like most other sultry summer days — hot and humid. After a long, nearly perfect, Fourth of July weekend, Kelly and Carla had settled into their regular work week. On an off-shift (Kelly worked 24 hours on and 48 hours off), Kelly came by Carla's office several times, trying to extend the holiday weekend for a few more hours by being with her. She finally told him he needed to stop interrupting her work, but she felt guilty about sending him away so she took him a piece of cake when she went home.

Usually eager to take off in a plane, Kelly seemed reluctant to fly that night, telling Carla he didn't want to head to the airstrip

181

for his scheduled teaching duties. A new student and a new plane weren't as attractive as staying home with Carla. When Carla urged him not to go, he reluctantly responded, "There's no one else to do it if I don't" and headed for the door. After he walked out, Carla saw he had left his Coke on the table and ran to give it to him — providing a second opportunity to say goodbye and their usual "I love you" at parting. They laughingly argued about who had opened the Coke — he hadn't intended to pop the top until he was airborne.

Late in the evening, Carla reflected to herself, "He should be here by now," but she put the thought aside. A little later, one of Kelly's friends called to ask if Kelly were flying in Resaca that night. Still, Carla didn't grow concerned until another friend called and told her she might want to call the sheriff's department — that there had been a plane crash. Even then, Carla thought Kelly was alright — that she might have to go to the hospital if he had been hurt, but never did it occur to her that she would soon hear news that would forever transform her life.

When the phone rang an hour or so later, there was so much static on the line she couldn't hear. Hanging up, she redialed the number. When the man on the other end of the line identified himself as the county coroner, Carla's heart sank, grasping what was coming. Kelly was dead. He had died on impact. The student who had been flying the plane was in the hospital, but Kelly was gone. (The student died the next day.)

Although it has been nine years, Carla's voice trembles as she says, "Kelly was supposed to be my 'forever.'" But now, forever would be without him. "I was just so shocked," she remembers with tears welling up in her eyes. Even so, she recalls her first thought was, "He had told me once he didn't think he would live to be 40." And on the night he died, Kelly was 39.

Carla's auto-pilot kicked in. She submerged her own despair and worried about everyone else. In her mind, she started making a list of everyone who needed to be called — first Kelly's brother, who would have the difficult task of telling his mother. Staying busy, worrying about everyone else and planning the details for two services (one at the funeral home and a memorial service at Kelly's hangar where his own plane still sat) helped Carla get through the first few days.

Today Carla summons up memories she thought were long buried. In the round pen with her horses, she says, with a jerk in her voice, she had occasionally wondered what life would be like without Kelly if something happened to him. But it wasn't real. It was pretend—just a game of "what if," never expecting the "what if" to become a move on the checkerboard of her life. Now, he was gone, and all she had were memories and her horses.

Kelly loved flying and Carla loved horses. Without him, Carla turned her full focus to her animals—instinctively, she knew they would accept her sorrow unconditionally. The horses didn't argue with her, when for a while, shock produced denial—"It wasn't really him. Someone will call and tell me it was a mistake—that Kelly wasn't the person who died," she told herself, knowing it wasn't true but finding respite in temporarily believing Kelly was still alive.

When her grief threatened to engulf her, when she could no longer stand people telling her it was going to be okay, she would get up early and work her horses, clean their stalls, stand with her head against their warm bodies. Friends told her she needed tranquilizers to get through her shock and despondency, but Carla's mother understood—she needed to process what had happened. "Even then," Carla says as she evokes the most painful time in her life, "I realized, 'This is my life—this is how it's going to be.'" The finality of Kelly's death lodged in her conscious and subconscious mind, and she knew she had to deal with her loss.

Always a strong Christian, for the first time in her life, Carla felt let down by God. Betrayed, she cried out, "God, I have always tried to do what's right. People at work gripe and complain about their husbands, but not me. I loved my husband—every fiber of his body and spirit. Sure," she adds, "We had an occasional tiff, but they were never bad and we both knew our love was greater than any disagreement we might have."

Like others faced with platitudes from well-meaning friends and family, Carla rebelled when people tried to convince her, "This happened for a reason."

"I wanted to scream at them," Carla exclaims, the fervor in her voice strong and sure. She couldn't believe there could be any reason God would take Kelly. "Why would a good God do something so senseless and awful?"

Carla worried about herself when she couldn't pray. She was too hurt by God to talk to him — and she certainly didn't want to listen to anything He had to say about taking Kelly. It was okay, her mother reassured her, everyone else was praying for her. Even when she couldn't turn to God, though, Carla remembers thinking, "God gave me my horses — starting with the Nevada mustang a neighbor handed over to her after its owner abandoned it — because He knew I would need them to comfort me when Kelly was taken." But it was still hard to depend on God. Why would He help her if He wouldn't leave Kelly on earth to be her companion? One day, though, when she saw a squirrel playing in the field, she knew she wanted to pray. Carla's not sure why the squirrel triggered a transformation in her spirit, but the frisky little animal scampered across her hardened heart, making paw prints of love.

Finally able to pray, Carla began the long journey back to life. The hardest part, she says, is that she no longer knew who she was. "I loved being Kelly's wife. I was proud of who he was and who I was to him. And I loved being who I was when I was with him. But I was no longer that person. I had to decide who I was now. For 28 years I had been Carla Stewart. And then for almost eight years, I had been Carla Gibson. Now, I was the 'horse whisperer,' but I knew I couldn't be that forever — that I had to get back on track to who I was — who I was going to become without Kelly."

Laughingly, Kelly had once told Carla, "If something ever happens to me, you'll marry the first cowboy who shakes his spurs at you." Not quite, but after eight years of living alone, Carla married Richie White about a year ago. It's a struggle, though, to shape a new life with a new husband. When she and Richie went to get their marriage license, the clerk asked, "Your last name will now be White?" A shock wave washed over Carla. Carla Gibson was her "forever name." For a second, she toyed with being honest, telling Richie she didn't want to give up "Gibson." She wanted to be Carla Gibson White, but she knew that wouldn't be fair to Richie.

Today, Carla is getting more comfortable with her new life. She's like an effervescent bubble — illuminated from inside with subdued shades of glistening hues. Her carrot-colored hair falls gently around her slender face in soft waves as she clearly and candidly describes where she is with life. Adjusting hasn't been easy, but she's getting there. Her e-mail address illustrates her fun-loving spirit is returning: daisypickingirl.

Admittedly a bit stubborn, the spirited Carla advises other mourners not to let anyone tell them how they should feel or what they should do. "Feel what *you* need to feel," she counsels. When people told her after Kelly's death she should move off the farm, back closer to family, her independent streak took charge. No way, the tousled-haired pixie declared to herself. She had planted roots with Kelly on their horse farm, and she wasn't going anywhere. Later, a friend told her, "I'm proud of you for staying there." It was tough and challenging, but for Carla it was right.

The fairytale marriage ended too soon, Carla says with regret. But, even though she lost Kelly, "I wouldn't trade our lives for anything." She adds with poignancy, "If it weren't for Kelly, I wouldn't be who I am today. Even though I was independent, I didn't think I could do a lot of things. But Kelly believed in me, and I learned to drive a tractor and how to mend fences," adding with an impish grin that Kelly even trained her to fly a plane. "If he hadn't taught me those things, I couldn't have kept the farm."

Carla concludes, "We just lived life — and loved every minute of it. Some of our best moments were in the air together, soaring above the clouds. If Kelly had to die, I'm glad he died flying." Her face radiant with memories of the life they shared, Carla will always treasure the time she had with Kelly, but she's learning to move on, to find new meaning in her life. In time, maybe she will find she can have another fairytale marriage.

Chapter 34 (Part 2: Kelly's Mom)

HAZEL

LOSS OF A CHILD

"I grew up believing that heroes never die. On July 12, 2001, I was proven wrong."

Wade Gibson, Kelly's younger brother

If Kelly and Carla had a fairytale marriage, Kelly and Hazel had a storybook mother and son relationship. He called and popped in to see her frequently, often just sitting and talking to her. She loved going places with him, flying to Nashville, Atlanta, and other places for concerts and other fun activities. "We were so much alike," Hazel remembers, "that he could read what I was thinking, and I could read what he was thinking." They even liked the same things, including Carla.

Hazel loves Carla — the daughter she never had; three sons and two grandsons, not a girl in the brood. But the relationship between Kelly's mother and her daughter-in-law made up for it in spades. Today, Hazel still stays in regular contact with Carla, and she totally supports her remarriage, even encouraged it.

Like Carla, Hazel couldn't comprehend Kelly had been killed in a plane crash. In bed, sound asleep, Hazel had been jarred by the jangling of her telephone. Groping to pick up the receiver and get it to her ear, Hazel heard the voice of her youngest son, Wade, telling her to come to the door. It took her a moment to realize what she was hearing, but in the background an incessant pounding on her front door penetrated her consciousness.

"Why are you calling me on your cell from my front porch?" Hazel questioned, still groggy.

"Just open the door, Mom," Wade pleaded. Now fully awake, no longer staggering sleepily, Hazel rushed to the door and saw Wade's anxious face.

"Kelly has been in a plane crash," Wade whispered in disbelief. When Wade added that Carla had told him one person was alive and the other person dead, Hazel knew in her heart

186

Kelly was the one alive. If one person had survived the crash, it would be Kelly.

But her teeth chattered the entire drive from her home in Woodstock, Ga., to Kelly and Carla's home in Trion. When the death call came hours later, she heard the tragic news in disbelief. She doesn't remember much about the next few days, just what seemed like hundreds of fire trucks passing by in tribute. On the back of the last one an empty helmet and bunker suit formed a stark reminder that one of their brotherhood was gone. As the loud siren faded slowly into the still air, Hazel's heart grew fainter, too. And, then, the last tribute appeared in the sky, three planes in formation. When one peeled off, another part of Hazel was stripped away with it.

Kelly's father (Hazel's ex-husband) flew in from California for the visitation but mysteriously disappeared before the funeral. Looking back, Hazel wonders if he just couldn't stay, if his guilt for the kind of father he had been was just too much. When his youngest son had called him to share the news, he had said, "That's the worst news I've ever heard" and then abruptly hung up the phone.

Hazel understands, recalling, "I kept saying, 'I want Kelly here. I don't want him to be gone.'" She would go home, touch his picture, and feel his presence. But it wasn't like touching his skin, feeling the warmth of his body.

"I talked to God so much," Hazel recalls. "I wanted to understand *why*."

Pausing, uncomfortable, Hazel shared her innermost feelings: "Why would it be Kelly and not his dad?" As her friend Bonnie said, "I can't understand why it could not have been Vic...*everyone* loved Kelly. He was so good, so giving."

But soon, Hazel turned from questioning God to thanking Him for giving her Kelly. She knew she could either become bitter or turn it around and be thankful for the 39 years she had with Kelly. "Born on Easter morning in 1962, he blessed my life; he was a gift from the beginning." I told myself, "That's what I need to be thinking." But, still, it bothered her when friends tried to console her by saying, "He's in a better place." And when one man told her, "At least he died doing something he loved," she struck back at him in rage: "He might have been doing something he loved, but he didn't want to die doing it." Today, she feels badly she reacted that way, but at the time, she just couldn't stand to hear the words.

Her anger was never directed at God, Hazel says, but when her grandson, now 21, joined the Marines three years ago, it hit her hard: "If we have to go through this again, I don't know if I can take another loss." Looking back, Hazel says she should have been thinking more positively, thanking God for Doug, not thinking about his being taken away. Thankfully, Doug survived a tour of duty in Iraq and another one in Afghanistan. Hazel slept more peacefully when he finished his Marine service in May 2011.

At her worst times, Hazel says she cried out loud—not just silent tears but sobs that shouted against the night. She remembers sitting on the bathroom floor, weeping uncontrollably. When she managed to control her outbursts and even hold the silent tears inside, Hazel says she lived in a shell for a long time. Then the terrorist acts hit on September 11, 2001, and she totally fell apart. She grieved for the people who lost loved ones that day, taking their sorrow on herself, engulfed and crushed by the massive devastation. Acknowledging it did take her mind off Kelly, Hazel was so upset she retired at the end of the year. Numb, she started "knitting like crazy." She knitted afghans, stockings, caps, dish cloths, and anything else she could think of—she still has four afghans under her bed, she confesses with a smile.

Finally, Hazel realized she had to get out of the life she had lived with Kelly and get another life. It took her a long time, though, to use the word "dead." The day she first said, "Before Kelly died..." is emblazoned in her memory. She remembers feeling surprised, astonished even, as she said the words. For several years she didn't want to say anything about him, to hear her voice saying his name aloud; but now, she says with a mother's pride, she talks about him as much as she can.

Today, Hazel says keeping Kelly's memory alive is effortless—it's just there. "Every day, it just seems like something reminds me of him—a certain kind of car, a

Hazel

motorcycle, a plane flying overhead" — and when that happens, Hazel thinks to herself, "Kelly would know what kind of plane that is by listening to its engine."

But visiting Carla, looking out the window at the runway — at the hangar Kelly built — still brings tears to Hazel's eyes. And sometimes she cries all the way home after leaving Carla. Some of the tears, though, are for Carla, whom she so dearly loves. Strangely, another trigger that causes Hazel to weep is listening to church hymns. "I used to think the song service was one of the best parts of going to church," she says, regret shading her voice, "but now I can barely get through the beautiful music."

Hazel has nothing but good memories of Kelly — how when he smiled, he smiled all over, lighting up a room; how he never got mad when anything happened, always rolling with the punches; how he always took care of what needed to be done; how he walked with a lot of energy; how he went out of his way to help others; how witty he was; and most of all, how he loved her and spent time with her. She's still sad that he is gone, but she's sure he brightened God's kingdom when he landed his plane.

AUTHOR'S NOTE: The FAA report revealed that the student pilot at the controls of the plane had a 0.0012 level of marijuana metabolite in his blood and a 0.0529 level in his bile. The plane had made three full-stop landings and takeoffs before the fatal clipping of tree limbs on the fourth take-off.

Chapter 35

CONNIE

LOSS OF A SPOUSE

"I thought I could love him enough...I thought Robbie and I
could love him out of the dark cloud that hung over him."

The signs were there, subtle and steady, but Connie missed
their significance—a reality she will regret the rest of her life.
One day, in December 2003, her husband David told her, "To
make it, I'm going to really need you to support me." Without
questioning him, Connie told him she would always be there for
him 100 percent. Later, she says, those words came back to haunt
her. Even then, though, she thinks she almost knew what he was
saying. But she didn't want to accept it, so her reassurance was
brief though firm.

Four months later, on an unusually hot day during April
2004, David Kennedy came in from working outside and told
Connie he wasn't feeling well. Brushing him aside, Connie told
him it was just the heat spell. Later that week, after a verbal
altercation, she thought, "We need to have a long talk and sort
this out. Tomorrow night (Friday), we can do that."

She knew something was wrong, but she didn't know how
wrong.

The next morning, Connie went through her regular routine,
preparing coffee and breakfast for David, but he seemed out of
sorts. When he hugged her before leaving, it didn't feel right—
like a child who surrenders to a hug but stiffens his body,
holding back from the warmth that usually comes with an
embrace. And when he said, "I love you sweetie," Connie says it
sounded different than she had ever heard him say the words
before. Late leaving, Connie and David rushed out, but feeling
uneasy, she called him on the way to work.

"He was so disconnected...cutting me short, like he didn't
want to talk." They talked again at lunch, when Connie

reminded him it was their son's senior prom night and he needed to get home early to see him off. David didn't argue, but he was still distant, like he didn't have the energy to talk. Or, maybe he just seemed disinterested. Before the conversation ended, their cell phone reception cut them off. Looking back, Connie wishes she had insisted they meet for lunch. A thousand times she has said, "If only..."

Excited about her son's big night, Connie left work early, around 4 p.m., and headed home. On the way, she called her husband's cell repeatedly — 15 times. When he didn't answer, she says, "I knew instantly what had happened." The certainty she felt was unequivocal.

At home, she waited alone for the inevitable. David always called when he was going to be late, so she knew he wasn't going to walk through the door. And he had threatened suicide before. When her son came home just before midnight, she broke the news: "Your daddy didn't come home tonight. I fear the worse."

"He was dead," Connie whispers with firmness. "I knew it. I knew he had killed himself. I just didn't know how or where." She called the sheriff's office.

Three days later, David's body was found. He had gone to an isolated location and parked, running a pipe from his exhaust back through his window. He had also overdosed on amitriptyline, an anti-depressant drug. Later, Connie realized he had not been taking his medication, saving it up for an overdose. But she was confused when she found he had his passport and $1,000 in cash on him when he died. Had he considered running away and then decided just to end his life? "Now," she thinks, "I'll never know."

David didn't leave a note, but Connie knew. She had no doubt her husband died from mental anguish. For years, he had suffered severe bouts of depression, and recently he had been diagnosed as bipolar, possibly schizoid. During their marriage, David had been to seven counselors.

But none of that mattered to Connie. "I thought I could love him enough...I thought Robbie (their son) and I could love him out of the dark cloud that hung over him."

The strong love transmuted into anger that their husband and father had taken his own life, leaving them to deal with his loss. After hearing about the suicide, Robbie's first words were, "How selfish of him."

"We both felt like he did it to us," Connie recalls. People who take their own lives never realize how horrible it is for those who are left behind, she adds. She bemoans that David, like other victims of their own hands, couldn't see suicide was a permanent fix to a temporary problem. "Why," Connie asked her husband repeatedly, "why?"

After 24 years of marriage, Connie lost her identity. A successful manager, Connie's real image of herself was: "David's wife." A role she was proud to play — "We were best friends and confidants, sharing everything," she says fondly. But now, a part of her had been chopped off — an arm severed and the bleeding wouldn't stop. She was still a mother and a Christian, but she was no longer a wife. "My purpose in life had been to make him happy. I counted on him and relied on him. He was *my special man* and meant so much to me."

Like other couples, Connie and David could talk without words. A touch or a look conveyed thoughts that didn't have to be spoken. But it was the words Connie missed most after David's death. "I could tell him the good, the bad, and the ugly, and he never condemned me. He was always in my corner — whatever happened, he was there for me." Now, alone, Connie's life had an unbearable void. Her soul mate was gone.

She cried all the way to work each day, went into the restroom and bawled at lunch, and then sobbed all the way home. But she made herself keep going. She started writing in a journal, beginning with, "Why did God let this happen to me?" A steadfast Christian, her infuriation with God erupted like a spewing volcano. The emotional burden she carried had to have an outlet, and God became the simmering point. So filled with deep sadness she couldn't eat or sleep, Connie's lithe frame became even slimmer.

Friends who still had their husbands at their side tried to tell Connie David's death was God's will. Furious, it was not what

Connie wanted or needed to hear. She knew she had to allow her rage to run its course, that it would subside in time.

It distressed Connie she had not been able to "fix" David. Finally, she came to realize after you live with someone who is emotionally disturbed for more than 20 years, you think your life is normal. When that person is gone and you realize what a relief it is not to deal with the rollercoaster ride of up again, down again behavior, guilt seeps in. Another burden to add to a load already weighing her down.

Knowing that lying around feeling sorry for herself wasn't helping, Connie pushed herself to get up, first tackling her house that she had let go. Then, she forced herself to go to a bereavement group, and there she found not another soul mate, but "soul friends," people who understood her anguish, her anger, and her remorse.

It's now been six years since David took his own life, leaving his wife and son to deal with the aftermath. Connie's anger and deep sorrow didn't destroy her faith. Instead, it became stronger when she realized she couldn't depend on herself to get through her grief. Church members ministered to her; one man became a surrogate father for her son, while others went out of their way to befriend him. Turning to scriptures she had memorized in her youth, Connie found a different experience with God than those she had known when she was on the mountaintops of life. Knowing life doesn't end with death gives her faith she will see David again—and he will be well. Until they are reunited, Connie's prayer today is to be happy, healthy, and whole.

As she talks softly about her journey through grief, Connie exudes a quiet confidence. She's been tested with fire, and she survived the flames. She knows now that she couldn't "fix" her husband's life; and despite all of her plans for the future being cancelled, the life she has left is worth living. She still thinks about David every day, but the pain is softer now and the tears flow less often. She's even made it to the center of the bed, which she carefully avoided for several years after David died.

Recognizing each person must map out his or her own pathway through grief, Connie advises others not to isolate themselves too much—to seek out friends and family, to join a bereavement group, to find a singles group for sharing activities. Connie says to widows: "Work hard to establish a social life even if it's a lunch bunch with other women. That can be your new beginning. Getting connected with people will do wonders for a grieving soul." She acknowledges holidays are terrible, but she's mindful they are only 24 hours and you sleep part of that time. And, she says, misery is optional. Connie firmly believes, "Grief is also a gift—perhaps the most awful of all gifts; but it can open your heart to others who are grieving. You can minister to them in a way that no one else can. You become uniquely qualified to walk with others down the path of despair and to encourage them along the way."

As a Hospice volunteer, Connie speaks with grieving people on a regular basis. "I have been where they are. I can give them courage and hope. And I can listen. This is the most important single thing you can do for someone who is grieving...listen."

For those whose loved one was emotionally disturbed, Connie is resolute: The person you loved was ill—depression, bipolar disease, and other mental illnesses shouldn't have stigmas. They eat away at you, but, like cancer, they aren't diseases you contract by choice. And, treatment for emotional distress, like chemotherapy and radiation for malignancies, doesn't always cure the chemical imbalance that causes the disease in your loved one's head.

Neither should suicides be viewed as shameful. In David's situation, Connie believes God decided her husband could not make himself better, and he took him to a place where he would be healed. Suicide adds to the angst of mourners, but it should not be an embarrassment.

"It will get better," Connie says with the voice of experience, "even if you think it won't right now. It will. Grief does subside; your deep pain will lessen. But," she cautions, "you have to be intentional about working through grief. You have to take charge of your own life and your own future. You can have hope," Connie adds, "that you won't always feel this bad." Whether this year or next year or five years from now, a turning point will occur, and the pain will lessen. For Connie, being thankful God has answered her prayer to be "happy, healthy, and whole" is enough to be grateful to be alive.

Chapter 36

GORDON

LOSS OF A SPOUSE

"I believe a part of you goes with them – a part of you
disengages and departs never to return."

Gordon's face lights up when he talks about Anne, the first woman with whom he ever had a real relationship. Both were 30 years old when they were introduced by Gordon's mother, who worked with Anne for eight years before it occurred to her to try to hook up her tall, handsome son with the lovely brunette. Gordon and Anne dated for about a year and a half before marrying and settling into a quiet life together. Although they were active in church and had a number of friends, they enjoyed each other so much they spent most of their time together.

For twenty years, Gordon and Anne were best friends as well as husband and wife. Philosophically, they behaved like fraternal twins.

Anne had never been sick a day in her life, so when she started dragging her left leg, she didn't think much about it. Maybe just tired or perhaps she had turned it the wrong way and hadn't noticed. But a couple of months later, she was on the floor working on something, and when she tried to get up, she fell back. A trip to the doctor didn't find any problem, but Gordon insisted Anne go again. No answers. On a third trip, Gordon became more insistent – the doctor needed to do a scan. Neither he nor Anne was prepared for the results.

At age 50, Anne was diagnosed with lung cancer. Even worse, the cancer had metastasized to her brain. Stage 4 cancer with only a five to seven percent chance of survival. What others would have considered a death sentence, Anne considered a challenge. Why shouldn't she be one of the five to seven percent who survived? Gordon agreed. Anne had the will and determination to make that happen.

Gordon

Through surgery, chemotherapy, and radiation, Anne never complained. For her, not whining about how she felt was a badge of honor. She was stubborn, a fighter. She refused to consider the possibility she couldn't beat the odds. And, for one and one-half years, she did well. Even when she could barely get out of bed, she went on with life as if she would be around forever. Six weeks before she died, looking pale and wearing a wig, she went for a job interview. Some thought she was crazy, but Gordon supported her totally — if she wasn't ready to give up, he certainly wasn't going to tell her to stop looking toward the future.

Gordon and Anne didn't talk about death, even though Gordon says, "Part of me accepted she was going to die, but part of me put it in God's hands: If He decides she will live," he thought, "she will live." Gordon continues, "I fought with myself about it, but I never totally believed she was going to die until about two weeks before her death." During that time, he admits, Anne was obviously aware her death was imminent, but the only statement she made was, "I'm scared." Still, she never cried, never complained. Gordon says she was the most valiant person he has ever known. "Her dogged determination to live was nothing less than heroic."

Even at death's door, Anne and Gordon still didn't talk about the end. It was only in the last week, when Anne was comatose, that Gordon lovingly told her it was all right to go, that he would be okay.

He didn't just tell her once. He lay down beside her for hours, telling her over and over again how much he loved her and giving her what she needed most: his permission to let go of earthly life. Does he regret not telling her this when he could be sure she would hear him. "No," he says with a sense of peace on his face, "I was told it was not the right thing to do (to not talk about Anne's death), but I at no time wanted to concede something for her that she didn't want to concede."

Gordon was with his beloved Anne when she died at 1:30 p.m. on April 23, 2006. A couple of friends were present, along with his brother. Hospice and his minister arrived within 15 minutes. What Gordon remembers most that day cuts like a sword, and even after four years, the pain in his heart fills his eyes with tears. "What was most horrific for me was the body bag. It doesn't seem dignified; it doesn't seem right." Appalled, Gordon was adamant when they tried to put Anne in the body bag: "For God's sake," he whispered, "put something on her." And the Hospice representative, who had been with Gordon and Anne throughout her last days, tenderly dressed her.

Gordon's angst is seared in his soul. Watching his cherished wife, even beautifully clothed, be zipped up in a cold, dark body bag reinforced the finality of his loss. "It was like someone had hit me and then hit me even harder." She was dead and it was going to be forever — at least on this earth. Two blows that beat Gordon to the ground, leaving him aching.

When Gordon received Anne's ashes, he says with a poignant smile, "I put them on her chair in the living room and told her, 'We're going to watch our favorite television show.'" He says he did that for a couple of days before her ashes were entombed at the Forest Hill Cemetery. Crazy, he wonders? No, Gordon needed to talk to Anne. He knew she couldn't answer, but it made him feel better to commune with her. "I still talk to her," he says, "about little things and big things." He had talked with her for 22 years; he almost knew the words with which she would respond.

How did he get through the first few days? "I'm not sure I did," he says as he reluctantly steps back in time. "I immersed myself in activities, because I would have gone crazy sitting home alone. My closest friends almost kidnapped me, forcing me to get out of the house. I didn't want to go, but I did. I was so sad, so hurt, so devastated."

When he did go out with his friends, often something happened to trigger his fragile emotions. One night, he went to a play with friends Gene and Faye Wolfe. "And, the house was packed, but wouldn't you know it, the seat beside me was empty." And his loss struck him again. Anne should have been sitting there, but Anne was gone, and he was alone.

When he was tempted to stay home to avoid such triggers, Gordon forced himself to think what Anne would have wanted him to do. "Heavens, no," he says with conviction, "she would not want me to sit home and dwell on my misery. I was, of course, doing it for me, too, but mainly I was doing it for Anne. I'd talk to her before I left, kissing her picture and letting her know I would be back soon. Many times, I would think something like, 'My hair's a little long. Anne would want me to have my hair cut.'"

Those were moments of reverie, talking to Anne as if she were still beside him. "But most of the time, I felt as if I were in a vortex, a black hole that was so deep and so awful I couldn't bear it. Not only was I in the whirling hole, but I had a hole inside me." His soul was engulfed in agony. "I never in my life thought I would experience that kind of hurt. I had had disappointment and losses in my life, but this was different. It was as if I didn't know if I would make it."

Sitting outside on an unusually warm early fall day, Gordon's face reflects his ongoing grief. With sunlight illuminating his face, he looks back, his eyes still clouded by memories of how he felt, averring, "I believe a part of you goes with them—a part of you disengages and departs never to return." He describes the aftermath this way: "If a man loses his leg, he learns to live in another way. If you lose your spouse, how can you learn to live in a world where she no longer exists?" And yet, Gordon says softly in amazement, "How selfish it would be to want her back the way she was."

The days of grief wear on; the journey through loss is still tough, Gordon says. "You can't escape the connection—a piece of furniture, a car, a scene—all reminders of what was and what could have been." The emotional responses still come: the intensity doesn't change, but the frequency slows down.

Gordon cried a lot after Anne's death, and most of the time he cried alone. Anne's parents, from a different part of the country, were not emotional people. That made it more difficult for him. "I wanted more 'team crying,'" he recalls. People who grieved in the same way he did—even if not at the same deep level.

Missing Anne beyond measure, Gordon remarried after two and one half years but now admits it was probably a mistake. He met his second wife at a church committee meeting and now realizes neither of them was ready for another relationship. They parted ways after a short time, but they are still friends. They just were not matched philosophically the way he and Anne were; being friends works better than being married.

Gordon grasps now that Anne will always be a part of him. And that's perfectly okay with him. He talks to her, makes decisions after considering what she would advise, and honors her memory in myriad ways. His first real relationship — and although there may be another, Anne will everlastingly hold a unique place in Gordon's heart. As Rosemary Rogers noted, "First romance, first love, is something so special to all of us, both emotionally and physically, that it touches our lives and enriches them forever." The love Gordon and Anne shared, even though now washed in a river of grief, wove a scene in the tapestry of Gordon's life that will never fade.

.

Chapter 37

JOY

LOSS OF A SPOUSE

"For several weeks I felt like Paul was just gone to a meeting somewhere and would walk through the door at any time."

Joy — a fitting name for a perky lady whose smile radiates happiness and contentment with life. She was married 36 years to Paul, a highly intelligent, analytical person whose leadership skills were honed early. A planner, he typically had a plan mapped out, whether for vacations or work, but he was always willing to change that plan as needed.

That adaptability would have been helpful when his retirement plans were interrupted by brain cancer, but the kind of disease he had, glioblastoma multiforme IV, took that part of his brain first. Once it started, Joy says, "The analysis of what to do next was totally left up to me as the portion of the brain affected was the right frontal lobe that controls memory, thought process, and analytical thinking." In hindsight, Joy believes that might have been best. If Paul had questioned every decision the doctors made, as would have been in character for him, it would have made matters much more difficult. As it was, he just accepted whatever Joy and their daughter Leigh Anne thought best.

Still, Paul's planning mode had ensured he and Joy had thought through decisions like donating their bodies to science, and he had taken care of all the paperwork years before. As much as she didn't want to let him go, she knew from his living will she could not unfairly prolong his life. Toward the end, he couldn't speak due to the increased swelling of the brain in the affected area, and Joy knew he wouldn't want to continue in the physical shape he was in.

The last night of Paul's life, Joy and Leigh Anne made a final trip back to the nursing center about 10 p.m. He was sleeping peacefully, but his breathing was very shallow. Telling him she would be okay, Joy said goodbye. When the phone call came at 2:30 a.m., she was not surprised. She drove back to the nursing center with her daughter and Paul's mother to say final farewells. In an atmosphere filled with care and concern, "The center staff had done a beautiful job in preparing for our visit. There was a fresh pot of coffee, some cookies, low lights, clean linens and Paul," Joy recalls gratefully. She also remembers how hard saying goodbye was for Paul's mother. As with other parents who lose children, it just seemed out of the natural order. And age doesn't make any difference.

Although Joy felt somewhat prepared for Paul's death, she walked through the next few days in a daze. Since his body was transferred the next day to Memphis for total body donation, she didn't have the typical funeral home arrangements to make. Instead, she and her daughter worked on the obituary, answered e-mails, let people know about his death, and made plans for a celebration of his life.

Looking back, Joy thinks her shock came more from Paul's initial diagnosis than it did from his death. Yet, denial set in for several weeks as she felt like he was just gone to a meeting somewhere and would walk through the door at any time. And, she says, ""I don't really think that feeling is totally gone yet."

It's still hard to believe Paul, a healthy, vigorous man who kept himself in excellent shape, was attacked by cancer. After the diagnosis, Joy is glad they spent the last 11 months of his life touching base with friends and family. Many were able to attend the Celebration of Life to share their love for Paul. For Joy, the celebration was a signal that she could start to move on. She had planned something Paul would have approved of, and it was not only a tribute to him but also an assurance people would continue to support her.

Fortunately, Paul left financial matters in excellent shape, so Joy has not had to grapple with any of those problems. The biggest challenge she faces now is how to best help Paul's parents, emotionally, physically, and financially. "They counted on him so much," she says, "and after he retired, he would always stop in and visit each day, so they really felt a deep emptiness without him." Joy tries to fill this void, helping them with business affairs and visiting them daily, but Paul was their rock.

Always a practical person, Joy doesn't dwell on the "what if's" but instead looks to "what's next." She believes her final acceptance will be when she receives Paul's ashes and can take them to some of their favorite places to truly say goodbye. In some ways, though, she now understands why others choose burial so they have a physical place to visit.

Joy misses Paul in many ways, but most of all she misses talking to him about all facets of life. "He was my sounding board, which I miss greatly." But Joy is moving on, accepting that his death "put me in charge of my own life." Paul was always the decision-maker, which Joy attributed to his being an only child, and in adulthood his family always did what he planned. Now, Joy realizes that even though she always thought of herself as an independent person, she set herself up for a dependency-type relationship by letting someone else make the decisions for 36 years.

"I never truly lived on my own," she notes. "I went from living at home, to college dorm life with suitemates, to getting married. I always felt I missed out on 'something' by not living on my own. Now that I am by myself, I am learning all sorts of things about keeping the house, cars, finances, etc." But that doesn't change her desire to keep Paul's memory alive. She has established an endowed scholarship fund at the college where they both worked and is donating some of his possessions to various causes. She's serving out his term on a local United Way board of directors and has accepted a term on a leadership board he was responsible for founding.

Joy has made it through a difficult journey with strength and grace. To others facing terminal illnesses of family members, she advises doing research so you can talk intelligently with doctors. Understanding the process of the illness also helps prepare for what is to come. She emphasizes this doesn't mean you should lose hope—just that by thoroughly understanding, you subconsciously start coping. Joy also suggests that death and final wishes be discussed if possible, preferably long before needed. On the practical side, she recommends knowing where all financial documents are stored, making sure they are in both names, letting others help when they offer, and most of all, staying busy. Returning to work, having productive work to consume her time and thoughts was a huge benefit, Joy concludes.

Chapter 38

LINDA

LOSS OF A SPOUSE

"If this is God's will, why am I not at peace?"

Linda is soft-spoken, and despite her deep-rooted grief, her face glows when she talks about Mike. Linda and their son Dusty were the center of her husband's life; everything he did was for them. Although quiet, he was Linda's rock—the person she knew would always be there for her. After almost 33 years, she could set a clock by his comings and goings. He was that dependable. And, they did almost everything together. They had good friends, but they were comfortable just being by themselves, so that's how they could usually be found.

At 55, Mike had had a bout with congestive heart failure, and he was diabetic, but neither a doctor nor a sign in the sky signaled his life was to be cut short less than two years later. The hours ticked by like any other day, and in the evening after returning home from work, Linda and Mike shared their day's events, as they did every day. In bed, they said their prayers and cuddled as they drifted off to sleep.

At 3 a.m. Mike woke Linda, telling her he couldn't breathe. Linda immediately called 911 and then helped Mike down the stairs to wait on an ambulance. As they sat in the living room, Linda reached out to Mike, wanting to hug away his pain. But Mike put up his hands, warding her off, and she realized his struggle for air was so severe he feared any pressure from her arms might stop his breathing altogether. Seconds later, as Linda told Mike she loved him, he looked at her with love that didn't want to let go. His life gurgling up in his throat, he whispered, "I love you, too," and fell onto the floor. Linda sat beside him, holding his head up to make his breathing easier. And, with his last gasps, Mike weakly murmured, "I'm going to die and I don't want to die." Although Linda tried to reassure him, it was too late. He couldn't hear her; he was gone.

Seven months later, Linda still hears those words in her head, "I'm going to die and I don't want to die," like a recording stuck on one line. She sits in the living room in the chair where he sat and relives the scene of his death. Sometimes she moves to a chair across the room where she can look at his chair, but the horror of the scene and the terror in Mike's words don't change. Though Mike was a devout Christian and Linda is sure he didn't fear death, the words haunt her. She knows his concern was for her and Dusty, that he didn't want to leave them, but the dread in Mike's voice, the alarm he sounded, rattles relentlessly in her head.

Today, Linda talks about the stages of her grief. Shortly after Mike's death she dreamed of being with him again. In the dreams, she knows he is dead, but he is doing things with Dusty and her. Her subconscious mind couldn't mesh the denial of his death with a life without him. Her conscious mind knew Mike was dead, but her subconscious allowed her to deny his death for brief respites when life seemed normal again.

Linda also went through anger, and she cites one incident at visitation as the second night following Mike's death came to an end. Friends and family insisted she take home the food that had been brought to the funeral home, and even though inside Linda rebelled, she dutifully followed the path others felt she should trod. As she loaded her car, she angrily spoke to Mike, "*You're* supposed to be here to pack up this food." In life, Mike was always there, the perfect gentlemen who helped her with everything. As illogical as it sounded, with his body lying in the funeral home, Linda lashed out, her subconscious again throwing her into a partial state of denial.

And, the denials didn't stop. They just took other forms. Linda remembers thinking, while working in her yard one day, "If Mike comes back, how can we repay the insurance money? Maybe we could sell our house..." Illogical denial, mixed with bargaining. "If God will just give Mike back to me, I'll figure out a way to make this work."

In the days after the funeral, friends and family tried to be helpful, asking about wills, insurance policies, and other necessary business affairs that needed tending. "I wanted to scream," she says. "I don't even know my name. I don't want to get out of bed. How can I make decisions?" And yet, she suddenly wanted all of her financial matters in order. "I wouldn't have cared if I died," she candidly confesses, "but I wanted everything set up so business affairs would be easy for Dusty." She wasn't contemplating suicide, but she had just as soon be dead as alive. Knowing death was not a likely option at the moment, Linda began wishing six months would pass quickly, assuming she would be better then. But she wasn't.

As with other widows, the reality of life alone set in after family and friends returned to their own lives. Suddenly, she was worried about whether the heat would go out when snow and ice started to accumulate on a frigid, January night just days after Mike's death. She knew a kerosene heater sat in the garage, but she didn't know how to light it. Another one of those innumerable things Mike always handled. The list is interminable—putting the garbage out, taking her car for repairs, opening up the swimming pool in the summer... little things and big things; things she knew he did, and things she didn't know he did. All on her shoulders now. So much to learn; so much to cope with. Left to deal with doorbells that ring in the middle of the night with no one there; security alarms that go off at 3 a.m.; the rip-off man taking her money and not cutting her trees; getting stuck in a body suit and no one to help (that's funny now, but it wasn't when she thought she was going to have to call 911 to get her out.) Where was Mike when she needed him?

Depression hit Linda like a huge boulder, knocking her into a place she had never been. When she first went back to work, she says she didn't want to go home at night. "If they hadn't locked the doors," she admits, "I would probably have spent the night there."

Unwilling to be a victim of misery forever, Linda tried to pull herself out of her gloom. She prayed a lot, exercised, and went on a diet. But she couldn't make herself happy. Depression held her captive, and her tears flowed as steadily and as often as rain in the jungles of the Amazon. Even when she could stop the torrent streaming from her eyes, a trigger would unleash a new surge. She had subscribed to *Sporting News* magazine for her husband for his birthday, and now, every month when she opens the mailbox to find a copy there, grief grabs her again.

But Linda has made progress. She knows now she can survive the unthinkable — because she has. And, it helps her deal with the small problems in life as she compares the worst possible thing that could happen, losing Mike.

Linda's faith remains strong, although she has had lots of questions for God. And for herself: "If this is God's will, why am I not at peace?" For the first time, after Mike's death, she realized that talking about the comfort God brings is much easier than having to live it. "A whole different story," she adds.

The hardest part of adjusting to Mike's absence is loneliness. "I just feel so alone," she says with heartrending sadness. Driving by neighbors' homes on Labor Day, watching families gathered around barbeque grills to celebrate the holiday, Linda felt so alone she went home and sobbed. Alone. No one to share her day with. No one to cuddle with in bed.

Despite her sense of seclusion from the world, despite feeling empty and forlorn, Linda has made it to the point she knows it is possible to survive. That's what she tells others who lose their spouses. "There were times I didn't want to face the day, but I did, mainly for my son." Putting one foot in front of the other, forcing herself to go to work, kept Linda moving through grief. She will always miss Mike, and the life ahead of her isn't the one she had anticipated, but she's working on finding a way to carve a new path. She's not there yet, but she's headed in the right direction.

Recently, Linda found a song that touched her heart so deeply she wanted to share it with others. Heart trembling, she stood before her church's congregation and sang, "You're Still God," written by Margaret Becker (published by C. J. Shetley Music). The words tell the story of her grief: She thought this would happen to anyone but her. She never dreamed she would carry this heavy burden on her knees, never thought she would be standing where she stands today. She freely admits, as the writer of the lyrics does, that she has never known this kind of heartbreak, has never felt this kind of pain.

Linda

But the chorus of the song echoes her trust. Though shaken and torn, she knows God is still God when her eyes have cried a million tears, when her last hope has disappeared. She knows, as the song proclaims, God will make a way somehow. Linda adds, as the song does, "You're still God, and You're holding me right now."

It's not just the words of trust that spoke to Linda; it was also its acknowledgment that even when hearts cannot find reasons for trials, God's watching his children. He's proven faithful over and over, and she can trust Him even when she doesn't understand.

Chapter 39

SHELBY

LOSS OF A SPOUSE

"For the whole first year, I kept thinking, 'If I could just die, I could be with Garland.'"

The hot June sun seared the parched hay as Garland made his first round of the day, cutting the tall stems, readying them for the bailer that would pick them up the next day. A retired chemical engineer, at 67 he loved his days on his farm in Cedar Grove, about 30 minutes from the Chattanooga home he shared with his beloved wife Shelby.

Shelby worried about Garland as she saw him off that morning. Concerned the medication he was taking for early stages of dementia would make it dangerous for him to drive the tractor; she had lain awake the entire night before. At one point, she even thought about taking the keys to his truck and throwing them into the woods so he couldn't go. But she knew that would cause problems. And, at least, she thought, once he got to the farm, his neighbor Billy would be there to help him in the hayfield.

As she kissed Garland goodbye, reminding him of the roads he needed to take, Shelby promised to join him at noon the next day, bringing lunch. She needed to do some work on the little house on the 300-acre farm — once that was done, she could stay with him when he needed to do several days of work. Then she wouldn't have to fret so much.

When she arrived at the farm the next day, Garland was still in the fields, so Shelby busied herself in the little house. A half hour later, Billy showed up without Garland, saying he hadn't been able to help the day before and was just now getting to the farm. Even then, Shelby assumed Garland was trying to finish a section of pasture before coming in for lunch. When Garland did not show up in the next hour, though, she sent Billy to look for him in the remote part of the farm where she knew Garland was working. Billy was to tell Garland he needed to stop and come to lunch.

Standing on the porch watching for Garland and Billy to return a little later, she saw Billy sprinting back over the hill, shock suppressing the smile he always wore. Alarmed, Shelby asked, panic coloring her voice, "Where's Garland?" When Billy told her there had been an accident, she frantically started running toward the hill, but Billy's burly arms pulled her back. Gently he told her Garland was dead — his body lying beside the tractor, blood covering his face, lungs punctured in three places. Stunned, Shelby managed to call one of her sons, Blake. And then...

"I just walked through that little house over and over for hours. Blake says I kept saying repeatedly, 'Oh, my sweetheart...oh, my darling. What am I going to do without you?'

"Somehow I made it through the next few days, but like the hours immediately after Garland's death, I can't remember much. Friends told me I kept whispering in agony, 'I loved Garland so much. I loved every inch of his body. I loved every breath he took.'"

Shelby does remember cutting blue hydrangeas from the garden — flowers Garland and she had lovingly grown together — for his casket. Seeing them there, a blanket over his broken body, was like an ice pick in Shelby's heart.

"In the days after the funeral, I was a walking zombie. I refused to answer the phone. I didn't want to talk to friends or family. Some avoided talking about Garland, apologizing when they inadvertently mentioned his name — they didn't understand I wanted to hear them reminisce, to recall their memories of Garland. But everyone feared upsetting me even more. And their calls were filled with strained silence and stilted words. So I begin to let the jarring ringing of the phone fill the air, unanswered."

Cut off from the world, Shelby staggered around the house in her gown, looking out the window toward a nearby mountain range, seeing but not seeing. Finally, she found a big decorative box and began putting in Garland's things—little notes he had sent her, birthday and anniversary cards, ·awards he had won. With every scrap of paper, Shelby remembered the life they had shared, tears sometimes coming in torrents and sometimes more softly, like gentle rain. "I didn't know if I could face life without Garland. We had always thought we would grow old together, and now I was left alone."

At night, Shelby couldn't sleep except for short spells, but one night about two weeks after Garland died, she dreamed about him. *I could feel someone kissing me tenderly on my neck and face, as delicately as butterfly wings brushing a flower. Joyously, I whispered, "Honey, honey, it's you." And then he picked me up and I could feel him carrying me toward the ceiling, saying "It's all right, Shelby. It's all right." I kept thinking we were going to hit the ceiling, but before we did, I woke up.* Shelby doesn't know if this dream was her husband's way of letting her know he was in heaven or if it came from the sleep medication she was taking, but she likes to think it was a sign from Garland.

Shelby had one other possible sign when she went back to church just five days after Garland died. Her son Eric was with her, and as they sat down (avoiding the pew where Garland and Shelby always sat—something she still does), Eric nudged her, pointing to a verse on an overhead screen displaying announcements at the front of the church. It was Garland's favorite verse, Isaiah 26:3-4: "Thou wilt keep him in perfect peace whose mind is stayed on thee because he trusteth in thee. Trust ye in the Lord forever for in the Lord Jehovah is everlasting strength" (KJV). Today Shelby ponders if the selection were a coincidence, or had God dictated the verse to be displayed that day? She will never know for sure, but it comforted her as she sat there, her whole world caved in.

As she talked about her husband in 2010, Shelby recalled thinking during that church service, "If God would just let Garland be here for 24 hours so I could tell him how much he meant to me, how good he was to me...." Like most people, Shelby has regrets, wishing she had told Garland she loved him more often, had been kinder, less stern, not as snappy, more like her tenderhearted husband. "I was just too independent," she bewails.

Today, she misses all the little things — like talking by phone at the end of the day when Garland was traveling on business, sharing what had happened. She misses her best friend and companion who always had her back. She misses talking to him about their children. After six years, Shelby admits that's probably never going to change.

In bereavement groups Shelby attended, grievers discussed how they thought they would feel better after a year — after they had been through all of the birthdays, anniversaries, holidays, and other special days. When that didn't happen, they said it would be better in two years. But, it's been six years and Shelby still grieves. She made it past the worst of her depression after her doctor suggested she take an antidepressant, but even now her heart hangs heavy in her chest any time she thinks of Garland and the life they could be living. The grief is a little softer, its edges less sharp, but it still hurts.

Through attending bereavement groups where she listened as young wives told about raising children alone after losing their husbands and where she heard older ones talk about the horrors of watching their husbands suffer, Shelby realized she had much to be thankful for — 44 years with a loving husband, two grown sons and grandchildren, no financial worries. It helps, she says, but it still doesn't take away the longing or the loneliness. Even though she dates other men, she hasn't found anyone who could replace Garland and doubts she ever will. Laughingly, she admits for the first couple of years she took pictures of Garland to show her dates, talking about him incessantly. "I just didn't realize how crazy that was — I was so consumed with my grief I thought my dates would want to hear about my love for Garland.

"For the whole first year, I kept thinking, 'If I could just die, I could be with Garland.' A big red rubber hose caught my eye every time I went into the garage, and it was only the thought of my sons that kept me from hooking it to the exhaust pipe of my car and simply going to sleep. I just couldn't let them think I was that weak." Like Friedrich Nietzsche, Shelby found the thought of suicide consoling: "In that way one gets through many a bad night."

"Unable to kill myself, I began writing a series of letters in my journal to Garland, telling him how I felt about his death and how I was trying to cope with it. I still write to Garland sometimes, and I talk to him regularly. Just last week, as I walked in my yard, I told Garland, 'Just look, Garland. Those trees we planted have grown so much since you died.' It's a one-sided conversation, but I believe Garland hears me and smiles."

Shelby's advice to those who lose spouses: "Join a support group. My family and friends all wanted to help, but they didn't know what to say or do. In a bereavement group, where everyone has lost a loved one, your grief is understood. These people have been where you are or are where you are now. They listen with their hearts; they identify with what you are saying. When you cry, express regret, talk about your depression, they comprehend the essence of your grief. When they offer comfort and support, they are empathizing, not just sympathizing."

Chapter 40

JERRY AND JUDY

JERRY: LOSS OF A SPOUSE AND A SIBLING

JUDY: LOSS OF A SIBLING

"I will never, ever, ever not miss her. I don't know that I will ever stop grieving."

Jerry

"Losing a sibling is like losing a chunk of your childhood."

Judy

Jerry Ransom's eyes glow when he talks about Debby, the petite brunette who was the love of his life for more than three decades. An identical twin, Debby Levan was born in Michigan but grew up in a bedroom community of Chattanooga and married Jerry, who also had ties to the area. Together they had two children, Jeremy, now 29, and Melissa, who just turned 33. Like all couples, Jerry and Debby had their ups and downs, but their marriage was rock solid. Two years after her death, Jerry says, that he will never, ever, ever not miss his wife. He's not sure he will ever stop grieving.

But Jerry's sorrow started four years before Debbie slipped away on a cold December day as Saturday night faded into Sunday morning. Jerry never believed Debby was going to die — even up until the last few days, even after Hospice came to help care for her, he kept telling her she would outlive him.

Perhaps it was denial, or just wishful thinking, but Jerry always thought Debby would win her cruel battle against cancer. After all, she had fought the ambush of tigers on her heels more than once and sent them scurrying.

The odyssey through cancer started innocuously with a small hip problem after Debby stepped off a curb the wrong way in November 2004. A scan showed nothing, so Debby and Jerry weren't worried. But the nagging hip pain continued to grow worse, and the following May she was diagnosed with breast cancer—even worse, it had metastasized to her hip. The war was on, and Debby set her jaw, determined to beat the animal craving her life. She had a mastectomy and hip replacement with pelvic reconstruction, as well as radiation and chemotherapy. And, for a while, she felt better.

But the tenacious tigers kept scratching at her door, time and time again. She had surgery for brain tumors and again got better. Then, the unrelenting cancer invaded her pelvis again. Still, Jerry says, "No matter how bad it got, I always thought she would get better." And she did, time and time again.

When Debby's doctor suggested calling Hospice, Jerry still didn't realize the end was near. And Debby refused to give up: "I'm fighting this." Jerry says the entire time she was sick—through multiple surgeries and rounds of radiation and chemo—the only day she didn't get out of bed was the day she died. Weak, sick, fragile—it didn't matter. She forced herself to get up every day. In her last days, she still refused to give up. When someone tried to talk to her about plans for her funeral, she responded, "There's not going to be any funeral home stuff!" That day she was in and out of consciousness, but when Jerry asked if she could squeeze his hand if she knew he loved her, her grip was strong, the message clear. She died early the next morning.

Jerry says his faith helped him cope, but he concedes it is difficult to believe God allowed Debby's suffering. He doesn't think God chose Debby, singling her out for horrendous pain. Deep down, he knew it was all right. At the funeral home, he told friends, "Today is a good day and tomorrow (the day of Debby's funeral) will be an even better day." People who haven't walked the path Jerry trod, taking care of his wife's every intimate need and more, may not understand, but he knew what Debby had been through. He recognizes, too, that though he never admitted it even to himself, he had subconsciously resolved himself to Debby's death somewhere along the road of her illness.

With a deep sigh, Jerry says he would have gladly traded places with Debby. Not that he wanted to die, but he would have willingly taken on the burden of her pain if she could have been set free. It was the desire for her suffering to be relieved that carried Jerry through the first few days after Debby's death. Christmas was just days away (Debby's funeral was on December 17), and Jerry's face takes on a look of pain as he recalls how tough it was to get through the holidays without her. A high school principal, he recalls that for the first time in his days as an administrator he couldn't wait for school to start again.

Jerry still lives in the house where Debby died, but he knows he needs to move. He says they bought the house after she became ill because their previous home had two levels and Debby couldn't negotiate the stairs, so all of his memories in the new house are stained with Debbie's pain. After a poignant pause, Jerry adds, "Man, I miss her. I don't miss her the way she was at the end, but I miss her." And all this house has are memories of her the way she was at the end. Memories like open sores that are still tender. Memories he would like to fade into the past.

Today, two years after Debby's death, Jerry says he's moving on with his life, despite his continuing grief. Still, he says, almost reluctantly, "There is one thing I cannot do. I cannot be alone in my house. I have to be doing something with someone all of the time." A strong person, a "fixer" who has spent his life making everything right for others, his inability to save Debby sinks him into depression when he is alone. As long as he keeps moving with people around him, he makes it all right. But home alone, he misses Debby unbearably. It hurts — he freely admits.

꿈

Just over a year after Debby's death, Jerry found himself about to lose another beloved member of his family — his younger brother. Johnny had a close brush with death 25 years previously when he dived into the shallow end of a swimming pool. Unbelievably, his broken neck did not leave him a paraplegic. His luck ran out, though, when a pain in his neck sent him to the doctor. No one knows if it was related to the long-ago accident, but when the doctor couldn't get his blood pressure to register, he was hurriedly admitted to the hospital.

He never walked out again. Four months later, he died of pulmonary fibrosis and internal bleeding.

Easter, the day that promises resurrection, dawned bright and clear that April morning. At the hospital, Johnny kept pointing up. Understanding what he was trying to communicate, the nurse gently told his parents, "I think he's ready to go." Johnny's mom, her heart breaking, held Johnny's hands, and, in Judy's words, "with the sweetest, most reassuring smile, looked into his eyes and told him she loved him and said simply, 'It will all be okay.' So simple and so true," Judy adds. Then, Johnny's dad took his son's hands, and with tears blurring his eyes, told him he loved him. He then reassured Johnny he would be going to a place where he would have no more pain or suffering — that he would be able to breathe freely once again. The picture of his resurrection undoubtedly beneath his clouded eyes, Johnny squeezed his parents' hands.

Johnny's oldest son, Wesley, watched helplessly, said his own sad goodbye, and then made the final, inescapable decision. The next morning the respirator would be slowly cut back, then turned off. No one in the family wanted to let Johnny go, but they all knew nothing else medically could be done for him. No one could bear to watch him suffer with no good end possible. And, after all, as Judy had lovingly told her brother when the end was near, "You are going on the biggest adventure of all." Torn between letting go and sending Johnny on to reunite with his dear grandparents and others, the family was ready to put aside their desire to hold on and set Johnny free from suffering.

When the sun begin to climb across the spring sky the next day, the family — parents, siblings, son Wesley and stepson Daniel, Johnny's fiancée Donna, and his beloved Aunt Madge — gathered for one last time with Johnny. Johnny's younger son Jason, who had visited his dad regularly and had already said his farewell, wasn't present, but he was in constant contact by phone.

After their parents had left, late that night Jerry and Judy stood beside Johnny's bed, knowing he could never recover. Spirits sinking with love and concern, they asked if he was ready to go and if he wanted the respirator removed. Johnny squeezed their hands, and, complying with his wish, they asked the nurse to begin slowing down the rate of oxygen. As the evening turned into another new day, just after midnight, Jerry asked his brother to do something for him: "Tell Debby I love her." Then, the machine gave Johnny his final fragment of pure air. With two short breaths, Jerry knew Johnny was gone. Judy remembers looking at Johnny and thinking, "'This is Johnny, and he is dead. The person in this bed is *dead*, and it is *Johnny*.' It was so hard to believe." Time stood still as Judy tried to force herself to face the unbelievable, for as Shakespeare said, "Grief makes one hour ten."

Unable to escape the reality that Johnny was gone, Judy's tears surged like breakers, blinding her until she had to pull her car to the side of the road while she was driving. Even though she managed to return to work within days, coming home each evening opened the floodgates on her grief. "I would lie on the bed, watching a DVD of Johnny's life from the time he was a baby...I listened to a CD of his funeral over and over...I looked through boxes of pictures, trying to find one I hadn't seen before, trying to hold on to a piece of him...I listened to a CD his son had made of his favorite music." All efforts to hold tight to the life that had been entwined with hers and Jerry's since her little brother arrived as a bundle of joy in their family.

When her tears subsided, Judy says she felt as though she had the flu: "exhausted, sick with grief." Sleep scurried away from her each night, and when she finally trapped it in the wee hours of the morning, she would awake with a start at 3 a.m., thinking, "Who died? Somebody died, who was it?" Then, like an icy splash of water striking her face, her startled, sad mind would respond, "It was *Johnny*."

Nine months after Johnny's death, Judy's belief is secure that Johnny has been transformed in his new life, resurrected to health and happiness. But the tears of grief sometimes strike when she least expects them. As Sylvia Plath said in *The Bell Jar*, Judy just knows, "...if anybody speaks to me or looks at me or looks at me too closely, the tears will fly out of my eyes and the sobs will fly out of my throat...I can feel the tears brimming and sloshing in me like water in a glass that is unsteady and too full." The tears may last a long time. After all, Judy laments, "Losing a sibling is like losing a chunk of your childhood."

Today, Judy finds herself chased by feelings about Johnny — "They are all over the place." She's learning to capture them, trying to bring them to a place where they can be more easily managed. "A few weeks ago while waiting for my turn at the Geek Squad at Best Buy, I was antsy and pulled out a little notebook and started writing about the last moments before he died. Then another time I wrote a little more, then while waiting in my car for a store to open, I wrote more. It did feel like I was grabbing all those random thoughts and putting them into one place."

Looking back, Jerry says he may have been more emotional about Johnny's death than Debby's. Still suffering from his wife's death, Jerry had entered into a relationship that ended just before Johnny died. The combined losses put Jerry down for a while, he recalls. He couldn't sleep, and at work he was a walking zombie.

Part of his grief was watching his mother and father. His 83-year-old mother Jean had never been one to show her emotions, but when Judy went home to tell her parents Johnny was gone, Jean broke down. As bad as their grief was, Judy and Jerry know their parents' grief was on a different tier. Their mother "finally let it go," Jerry says, unable to hold back the wellspring of tears. Her husband John tried to tell her Johnny was all right, that he wasn't suffering any more, but that didn't help Jean. "I know that, but I'm supposed to have three children, not two. He can't be gone; he can't," she uttered in abject misery.

Johnny was 57 years old, but he was Jean's youngest child. He was still her baby. And he was gone. Jean's grief sounded from deep inside her — unfathomable sorrow and yearning. Judy says it reminded her of something she once heard about a mother who cried the "'cry of the ages,' the cry that mothers make when they have lost their child." Primeval — from the darkest caverns of the soul.

Children are supposed to bury their parents — burying your son is against the natural order of life and death. A flower should live in full bloom before fading. Trees should grow old before falling and turning to dust. Nature's cycle should not be interrupted.

Chapter 41

MUFFIN

LOSS OF A SIBLING

*"I was not prepared. You would have thought I would have
been, given his many close encounters with death."*

Muffin Liskovec never met "can't do" even once in her six
decades of life. A trim and slim dynamo with long, brunette hair
framing her face in soft swirls, she never met a challenge she
couldn't handle, a mountain she couldn't climb, or an enemy she
couldn't conquer. Perhaps that explains why, given the many
health issues her brother Charlie endured, she never allowed the
thought of his dying to penetrate and grab hold until just a few
days before his death.

Charlie had been sick for 16 years, beginning with prostate
cancer in 1993, and in recent years he had suffered from kidney
failure. Muffin had hoped to indirectly donate a kidney to him in
a paired kidney donation exchange, but by the time a potential
matching pair was identified, Charlie was too ill with other
problems to risk the trauma of a kidney transplant.

Charlie had endured numerous physical problems over many
years, and the family had gotten into a rhythm with intermittent
hospital stays. So after Memorial Day, when Muffin and her
husband Eddie visited Charlie in Georgia just before heading to
Michigan for a surprise 80th birthday party for Eddie, they were
shocked to learn nothing else could be done medically. Even
then, Muffin says, "I heard the words, but really could not
comprehend what was being said...or I would not *allow* myself
to truly believe what was being said. God had brought Charlie
out of so many 'near death' situations during the past 16 years,
most of them within the previous three years, I was sure He
would provide a miraculous healing this time, as well."

Torn between staying with her brother and going to the
gathering 14 hours away where Eddie's children, grandchildren,

and great-grandchildren had already gathered, Muffin agonized, knowing if she left she might never see her brother again. Charlie made the decision for her, urging her to go, adding, "Promise me you'll come back to rub my feet some more," bringing a smile to Muffin's face. Saying a prayer to God, asking that Charlie's valiant fight not end while she was away, Muffin left with fear in her heart.

Just hours after the celebration in Michigan ended, the dreaded call came: Charlie had made a turn for the worse—he might not live much longer.

"I was devastated," Muffin recalls. "It was my worst nightmare come true. I was a 14-hour drive from him, and I wanted to see him and speak to him before he died." Shaken, Muffin kept thinking, "We are losing him and there is *nothing* I can do.

"*I was not prepared.* You would have thought I would have been, given his many close encounters with death. Knowing my brother was a Christian, assured he would immediately be with Jesus upon taking his last breath, provided a tremendous amount of comfort. But it did not relieve the sorrow and grief of feeling him slipping away from us."

Immediately after receiving the call, 80-year-old Eddie and his 62-year-old wife Muffin determined to drive non-stop to try to make it to Columbus, Ga. before Charlie died. It was an excruciating trip, which they made in less than 10 hours, stopping only for restroom breaks. When they walked into Charlie's room, Muffin's heart cried out, "We made it!" As she had promised a few days before, she immediately began massaging Charlie's feet. Although he was semi-conscious, Muffin was able to tell him she loved him and was extremely proud of him.

Looking back, Muffin wonders how she could have survived if she hadn't made it back to Georgia before Charlie died. She acknowledges it was more for her than Charlie: "I feel at that point, he was probably somewhere between still being in the earthly realm and the heavenly realm. He did react to some of what family and friends would say or ask him...a slight movement of the closed eyes or a faint nod of the head. A large single tear ran down his cheek as we prayed with him and his much beloved granddaughter Izzy led us in singing "Jesus Loves Me." Muffin says she has often wondered why Charlie shed the tear. She knew he was not afraid to die because he trusted God, so she believes he was overcome with sadness at leaving his family.

Getting through the first few days was rough. Despite being forewarned, losing Charlie was still a shock. "It was the *finality* of it that took my breath away," Muffin recalls, the horror of the realization still echoing in her words. She remembers being in a daze, "intellectually knowing he had died but emotionally not coming to terms with it."

Surrounded by family and friends kept her moving and doing, speaking and responding, but Muffin says she didn't really comprehend and assimilate the loss in those early days after Charlie's death. She thinks that's a good thing. "It would be too overwhelming to feel the brunt of the loss full force from the minute it happened."

Going back into Charlie's home, seeing his shoes and socks, his electric wheel chair, his lift chair, and his hospital bed — all just as they had left them when he had to be rushed to the hospital, hit Muffin like a boxer's punch to her gut. "If I had only known it would be the last time he would ever be home," she laments, "if I had only known he was dying, there are so many things I would have said to him.

"I wanted more time. That was, and still remains, the regret that gnaws away at me ...that I did not verbalize how much I loved him and how proud I was of him. I should have said, 'Too bad if this makes you a little uncomfortable, you need to know how I feel!'"

Muffin and Eddie stayed with her brother's wife Shirley for about eight days after Charlie died. Since they had already been with the family for the two and one-half weeks prior to that, they needed to return home. And, Muffin realized, it was time for Shirley to have her alone time to begin dealing with all that had happened. But leaving was hard. "Of any time after Charlie's death, leaving their house was the most difficult. I hated it. I felt that I was losing my connection with him — it felt like he was dying all over again. I knew it was time for us to leave and that staying would not accomplish anything, but it was extremely painful and sorrowful. I think it was only then that I felt the full brunt of my loss and the finality of it."

Muffin still goes to Charlie's grave each time she and Eddie visit his wife, Shirley. "It hurts to go, but it helps, too. It's a time during which I can express how I am feeling, how I loved him, and how much I wish I could have been able to donate a kidney for him. I don't feel I can say these things any longer to anyone else...they have heard it from me before. I feel safe verbalizing my thoughts at Charlie's burial place. I know he cannot hear me. I know only his body is there, but it helps. For me, it is what I need to do. I can release those emotions that have built up over time."

Today, Muffin enjoys speaking naturally of Charlie. And, her heart is warmed when she hears from others who loved and admired the 6'3" man who worshipped God through his singing, who had a grin that could illuminate a room, and who loved — and in Muffin's words, "I do mean LOVED" — chocolate chip cookies so much he always refused to share the big tin Muffin brought him every Christmas. "It was bittersweet," Muffin says, knowing how many other lives he made better and realizing his own grandchildren would miss his touch in their lives.

Still, Muffin says, "I am thrilled and comforted now, one year and four months after his death, to hear his name spoken, to hear someone tell a story about Charlie, or to state he is missed. It does not make me sad. It comforts me to know he has not been forgotten. He fought such a valiant fight to live through all of his physical difficulties, and he did it with such grace and trust in God, that he was a mighty witness to many, not only among the members of the church, but also among the doctors and nurses, who sensed his peace despite the sickness, uncertainty, pain, and weakness he was bearing."

Today, Muffin says softly she misses Charlie as much now as she did the first week of his death. She also still has some bouts of depression related to her frustration at not being able to help him receive a kidney transplant and for her failure to speak up and tell him how she felt about him.

"It amazes me that the grief, tears, and feeling of loss can be as profound now as they were when he died," Muffin admits. "The spells of sadness come and go," she says, noting she is dealing with them in her own way. She doesn't talk about it with anyone. It is too private. She feels it is something she has to journey through on her own.

"It helps," she says, "for me to try to visualize Charlie in Heaven, fully understanding all things, with all of his questions answered and having a whole body with which he sings for the glory of God."

In an effort to make something positive out of a negative, Muffin is seriously considering following through with donating a kidney, becoming an altruistic kidney donor in memory and in honor of Charlie. "We, as a family, know the emotional roller coaster that is the life of the person (and his family) who is in need of a transplant to sustain life," she avows, "so it has been forming in my mind that giving someone a healthy kidney for a second chance at a healthy life would be a fitting tribute to Charlie and would soothe the wound of not being able to help him. I feel the need to make this decision soon since I am not getting any younger [Muffin is 63]. I am praying about it and trust God will give me a sense of peace in whatever decision I make."

As for now, Muffin knows Charlie fought the good fight, was faithful and trusting to the end, and he is now safe with Jesus. She will never forget how special he was to her and other family members on earth, and with a determination that once propelled her career, she has thrown her time and energy into keeping his memory alive. She purposely mentions "Pop" when she visits his wife, children, and grandchildren. Currently, she is creating a "Pop Memory Book" for Izzy, the oldest of Charlie's three grandchildren and the one who will most likely have a vivid memory of him since she was five years old when he died. The book will contain photos of Izzy and Pop, stories of special times they spent together, little things Pop did for her that she may have forgotten, and a re-creation of the many times he demonstrated his love for her.

As she works on the book, Muffin sometimes still pauses, wondering why Charlie had to suffer. Sustained by knowing God loves Charlie more than anyone, she takes comfort that it was time for him to be released from his pain and suffering. "It was not the healing on earth for which we had prayed, but he *is* healed and no longer has a body that is failing him." That, and the belief Charlie lives eternally and that someday, his family, having the same faith he held so dear, *will* be with him again, lifts Muffin when grief pulls her down momentarily.

"Sounds like 'pie in the sky' to those who have never experienced a personal relationship with Jesus," Muffin concedes, "but I know that it is true." She adds she doesn't know how anyone deals with the eternal loss of a loved one without that promise from God. "Why would you want to risk loving another, only to lose them, at any time, with no hope to see them again, ever? Life after death is what sustains each of us who has lost a loved one." Muffin resurrects memories long dimmed by time, remembering how she felt when her mother died. "She had accepted Christ only a few years before her death. She did not want to die, but like Charlie, she did not fear death — she was peaceful and not afraid. What a gift that is for those who are left behind."

Chapter 42

ALISA, DARLENE, AND KAY

LOSS OF A SIBLING AND PARENTS

"Kids," their dad said, emotion filling his voice, "We've always preached His grace is sufficient and now we have to show it."

On a blustery fall day, with leaves rustling their message that autumn was approaching, I pulled into Darlene's driveway. Located in the historic Shepherd Hills area of Chattanooga, Darlene's stately Georgian home provided a lovely backdrop for the trip back in time the sisters were about to take.

The three sisters bear no resemblance — Kay, the oldest, is tall with soft ringlets of hair framing her face, her animated appearance concealing an inner strength; Alisa, the middle of the three, is the shortest but clearly the strongest willed; Darlene, the youngest, of medium height with long, casually styled brunette hair and probably the most laid back. Two siblings are missing today: Brenda, the eldest Durrance sister, who lives too far away to be here, and Dennis, who was the "light of our lives," Kay says with a smile as wide as the Brooklyn bridge. Darlene and Alisa jump in, agreeing Dennis' fun-loving ways, his genuine love for people, and his unequivocal love for each of his sisters, made the family whole.

Darlene quickly adds, with a deep-throated chuckle, that Dennis was not perfect. With laughter lighting her eyes, she recalls how he once put her on the floor with a fork because she had eaten his French fries. "His beautiful red hair came with a quick temper," she admits, but all three of the girls, now grown into womanhood, stress Dennis' temper wasn't "that bad." His brotherly love always won, and while he might be momentarily mad, he quickly forgave his errant sisters their willful ways.

The most mischievous of the five children, Dennis often tried his pastor father's patience. One night after church, he and "Dar" decided to see how many of their friends they could crowd into a telephone booth with them. Packed like sardines, barely able to move, they panicked when the man who owned the restaurant where the phone booth was located came to the door with a shotgun. Somehow they managed to unfold their tangled legs and arms and jump out of the booth. Their dad had let them drive the new car his church had just purchased for him, and they all jumped in and tore out of the parking lot. Sandwiched into the back seat, Darlene suddenly looked shocked as she spied Dennis at the other end of the seat. "Who's driving Dad's car?" she gulped. With a scared smile, Dennis responded, "I thought *you* were driving it."

It's not the only time "Brother Durrance" had to deal with his impish son. One night Dennis and a friend drove through a drive-in liquor store and when the clerk opened the window to take their order, they egged him. It was hilarious—until they pulled in Dennis' driveway and his dad was standing there in his boxer shorts (something he apparently did frequently as his son arrived home after a prank). "Tiny" Durrance, who was a solidly built six foot tall mass of anger, pointed his finger in the window at his son and grunted in a tone that harbored no resistance, "They want you at the police station, and I'll be right behind you." Dennis' friend later said he was more scared of Bro. Durrance than he was of the police.

Dennis always had funny stories—and he was usually at the cusp of them. One day while crossing a waterfall, he fell over the side, disappearing. His friend just knew he was gone forever when he couldn't see him. Dennis, way down below, was so terrified he couldn't yell for what seemed like an eternity, but he finally croaked out, "Keith, I'm down here…"

Despite Dennis' antics, being the only boy in the family had its advantages. Everyone doted on him, and he could get away with a lot his older sisters couldn't. Kay, who taught Dennis when he was in high school, bemoans the way he was, although a dimple threatens to reveal she treasures the memory of having him in her classroom, even if he did play a lot. At night, she would complain: "Mom, why don't you and Dad make Dennis make A's—you made *us* do it." Her mom, Vivian, would just shake her head, responding, "We're happy with "C's" — he's a boy, Kay."

Kay couldn't stay upset with Dennis long; he was just too loveable. One day she jumped on one of his classmates for writing on his desk. He hastily informed her Dennis had written on *his* desk. And, sure enough, he had. When Kay challenged him, asking him how he could put her in that position, he just put his arm around her, and sweetly said, "Oh, Kay..."

Sometimes the girls managed to turn the table on Dennis, making him the brunt of a joke instead of the other way around. When Dennis turned 16, even though his sisters had never been given a new car, he thought his dad would buy him one. After all, he was the only boy in the family. Among the gifts he opened, one box had a key with a key chain. "Dennis' eyes got big — real big," Dar recalls with a twinkle in her eyes, "and he sprinted to the street. Sitting there was a toy car. He just about killed us," she chuckles.

In the end, the love the kids felt for each other is undeniable — even after 30 years, they can't talk about the night Dennis died without tears welling up in their eyes.

The February night had turned chilly in Florida, where Alisa, Darlene, and Dennis lived. Darlene and Dennis had graduated from Truett McConnell College the year before, and their dad had rented them a house to share with Alisa. Because the house had only two bedrooms and because Dennis was planning to leave to continue his education at Sanford within a few months, he offered to sleep in an unheated room in the garage. In Ocala, Florida, the temperature rarely dipped below 40 degrees, so he wasn't concerned. Besides, he had to get up at 3 a.m. each morning to go to his temporary job stocking shelves at Publix.

But this particular night, it was unusually cold. Dennis wanted Alisa to prepare one of his favorite dishes, but she told him it took too long and was just too much trouble. Instead, she convinced him they should grill hamburgers — it was easier and the clean-up would be faster. It was a trade-off that would come back to haunt her.

About the time they finished eating, Dar got a call from somebody at Truett McConnell College and went inside. After talking a while, the person asked to speak to Dennis, but Dar told him Dennis had probably already hit the sack since he had to get up at 3 a.m.

Outside, Dennis kissed Alisa on the top of her head, telling her he was sorry he got upset because she wouldn't cook what he wanted. Alisa was left alone to do the clean-up, and as she stood at the kitchen window, she saw Dennis walk by carrying the hibachi. "Where's he going?" she thought. And then she realized he was probably going to empty the ashes.

When Alisa got up the next morning to go to work, she saw Dennis' car still sat in the driveway. She walked to his door and when she heard his alarm clock still going off, "I knew something was wrong," she utters with difficulty, the memory still tender. Panicked, she ran to get Dar. Together, they opened his door and saw Dennis face down on the floor. "I went hysterical," Alisa remembers with pain penetrating her soft voice. "I tripped over the hibachi trying to get to the alarm."

"I knew he was dead," Dar recalls tearfully, "but I called 911 anyway. We lived in a fairly remote area, so I told the dispatcher I would drive to the end of the road and leave my headlights on so they could find us. It took forever for the ambulance to get there." Sitting alone in her car, her heart beating wildly, Dar prayed, "God, don't take him yet. He's the only boy," hoping and praying that she was wrong, that Dennis wasn't gone.

Picking up the story as Dar's emotions begin to build, Alisa remembers that, although Dennis' back was cold, when she tried to turn him over, she thought his chest was warm. "Maybe he's still alive," she hoped, her emotions overruling her head.

When the EMTs arrived, they kept asking Dar and Alisa, "Where is the note?" They didn't have a clue the medics thought Dennis had committed suicide. When a detective arrived, he explained that people often committed suicide the way Dennis had died.

Astounded, Alisa told the detective: "Dennis had gotten in bed and had set his alarm to get up the next morning. He was looking forward to finishing his bachelor's degree at Sanford. There is no way he committed suicide."

Dar says neither she nor Alisa even thought about the hibachi being the cause of death, even after Alisa tripped over it. Dennis had cut his eye at work a couple of weeks previously and was still wearing a patch, so they first thought a hemorrhage had erupted in his eye.

In retrospect, Alisa, Dar, and Kay know that having the suspicion of suicide hanging over Dennis' death made their grief worse. Not that they ever believed it was even a remote possibility — they just knew others were thinking that and it hurt to have Dennis' memory marred with such thoughts.

When they finally realized the smoldering hibachi Dennis had obviously carried to his room for warmth had been the cause of his death, Alisa says she assumed Dennis realized what was happening and tried to get out. But the coroner said he was probably gone within 30 minutes after lying down — that involuntary muscle movement probably caused him to roll out of the bed. The sisters were relieved the coroner believed Dennis just thought he was going to sleep.

Dar had the terrible task of calling her Dad. When she told him Dennis was dead, all he could say was, "What? What?" Later, they learned their mother had awakened about 3 a.m., thinking something was wrong. And, strangely, sometime during the night Alisa had sat straight up in bed, thinking, "What is going on?" She wondered, "Did I just have a bad dream?"

One by one, the family got the bad news. Kay was teaching at Keystone Heights when Brenda's husband came to tell her. She stood perfectly still for a moment, but when her brother-in-law told her to stay there until he could tell her principal, she took off down the hall. "I just had to get away from there," she recalls. "I remember thinking, 'If I can just get away from Robert, it won't be true.'"

In shock, the four girls awaited their parent's arrival from Georgia. Kay remembers, "I was concerned about both of my parents, but more about Dad. This was his son; his only son."

When Vivian and Bro. Durrance arrived, the Florida house was packed, but they went straight to their girls, hugged, and took them into a bedroom.

"Kids," their dad said, emotion filling his voice, "We've always preached His grace is sufficient and now we have to show it." Then, Dar says, "We all knelt and prayed. The horrible loss was still there, but we felt better."

`"Dad wanted us to exhibit strong faith," Kay recalls. Later, back in church, Bro. Durrance said he had always believed Romans 8:28, but he questioned how Dennis' death could possibly work for good. After all, God had been tugging on Dennis' heart to pull him into the ministry; and although Dennis had not made a commitment, he had told his dad, "If the Lord wants me, I'll do it." But he wasn't quite ready, Kay says, because he told his dad, "The Lord better be loud about it."

Bro. Durrance told his flock, "I've dealt with people in grief all my life, but I have never been tested the way I have now been tested." But in the end, despite his enormous grief, his timeworn beliefs sustained him.

As strong as their faith was, it didn't prevent the sisters' anger. Alisa says she was first angry with herself for not cooking Dennis' favorite dish (perplexingly, she can't remember what that dish was) inside instead of pushing to grill hamburgers on the hibachi. Then, her anger turned to Dennis: "How could he have done something so stupid?" she bewailed. Then, she raged against God. "I don't know how long it lasted, but I was furious God let this happen to us. Our dad was a minister, and we were all good people. For a long time, it just seemed so senseless, so stupid." Over and over again I berated myself, "Why didn't I cook that stupid dish that night? All of this could have been avoided." Tearfully she says, "Some of it came back to me."

Dar responded differently. "I remember being afraid to be angry with God—afraid something else would happen. But deep inside, I was angry God didn't step in to prevent Dennis' death." It helped her that Dennis had such strong faith. "But I did feel we got cut short."

Kay, the teacher, felt bad that she wasn't there to save Dennis. "My faith was so strong I thought, 'If I had been there, if I had only been there—just like Paul lay down on that child—I could have saved him.'" She knew she could not have revived

Dennis, but in her distress the thought became almost real. But she wasn't there, and she couldn't have saved him.

"I had a hole in my heart for months—it felt like an actual hole," Alisa remembers. "We'd been a family, a close family, so long, we had a huge void. I knew it would never be right again." Kay agrees, recalling thinking, "We'll never be happy again. We all entertained each other, but it was Dennis who could make us roll on the floor giggling."

Looking back, Dar says, God gave Dennis' parents and sisters special time with him. Because of his eye injury, he had taken time off from work and driven to Georgia to spend two weeks with his parents just prior to his death. And she treasures the time she and Alisa lived with him. "God had a hand in Dennis' death," she believes. "Mom and Dad had just moved in January before Dennis died in February. It was good they could return to their new church, where they were enveloped by a loving church family."

Today, the girls remember how life changed for the family, in ways big and small. Alisa still can't set an alarm clock—hearing it go off would be more than she could bear, resurrecting memories of the morning she heard Dennis' alarm clock ringing incessantly, knowing something was terribly wrong even before she entered his room. And, "It was a long time before Dad grilled anything," Dar recollects.

Still, Alisa remembers, "Mom and Dad were so much more mature in their faith than we were. Mom stayed with us for a week or so after Dennis' death, and I was just amazed at her strength."

But the girls have no doubt their parents had their moments, too. They were just in private.

Among other regrets—Dar thinking if she had only taken the telephone to Dennis; Lisa thinking if she had only cooked inside—the girls all bemoan they did not have a chance to say goodbye. And it was the same with their parents, when they died. "Now," Kay says, "if I had known, there are so many things I would have said."

They had the opportunity with their dad—he told Kay, "I think this is it"—but Kay insisted to him he would be better the next day after the doctor drained fluid off his lungs. And Alisa says, "I thought we would all sit down on his bed and he — our father, the strong minister — would walk us through his death." When cardiac arrest took his life, Kay felt bad she hadn't said what she should have said instead of placating him. "I still have nightmares about that."

As bad as it was losing their parents, it paled by comparison to their loss after Dennis' death. You expect parents to die, but never your younger brother. Alisa remembers going back to work, not sure whether she could do it or not. And she certainly didn't want people who hadn't known Dennis to offer condolences. It was more than she could bear. "I felt I was in a place I didn't need to be, like I was a stranger going in each day. People meant well, but inside I raged, 'You didn't know Dennis — you don't know our loss.'"

When people tried to tell her they understood, Kay says she thought: "No, you don't. You can't understand. He was our only brother. He was the light of our lives." Dar remembers sitting in the den where she and Alisa had sat with Dennis, sometimes silently and sometimes sobbing. She couldn't stand it and moved down the road within a short period of time. It was still hard, though, driving by the old road where they had lived.

The girls concede that even though they didn't want anyone asking how they were doing immediately after they returned to work, when people stopped asking, they wanted to scream, "Don't you know I am still dealing with this?" Emotions torn and raw, rationality eluded them.

When Kay married four or five months after Dennis' death, the girls' sadness is reflected in the wedding pictures. They put a lighted candle on the altar in Dennis' memory, and the sight of it inside the sanctuary threw them into a crying spell as they stood in the vestibule. When a family member admonished them, "Shape up. This is Kay's day," they still couldn't stop crying. "Dennis should be here," they mourned. Then they remembered — as they did many times when they were filling buckets with tears — Dennis couldn't stand to see them cry. When one of them said, "Dennis would hate this!" smiles spread across their faces, lifting their spirits.

They put on the best faces they could and the wedding went forward. It helped, Kay says, that she had a new life to look forward to. She still struggled with Dennis' death, but Dar and Alisa, without anything to help fill the void, took longer to be able to go on with their lives. "I just wasn't whole," Alisa says with sorrow still bubbling to the surface. And Dar says, "Even when I met Tom (now her husband), and began a wonderful relationship, it still didn't fill the hole left by Dennis' death."

Christmas was especially bad, even though it was 10 months after Dennis died. When the Christmas cantata began, Kay says she burst out crying. "I had to get up and leave."

Looking back, Dar, Alisa, and Kay saw several indicators Dennis must have subconsciously realized he would not live a long life. A few days before his death, he told someone he loved his girlfriend Kelly but would never marry her. "I don't know why," he said, "but I just don't think I will."

And, earlier he had told Kelly as he put her on the bus to go back to college a few weeks before he died that she should marry Kevin, the boy she dated before Dennis. Kelly recalls she was boo-hooing when she got on the bus. "I didn't feel like I would ever see him again."

And, in a strange twist, he had told his grandmother, "As long as I live you'll never go into a nursing home." With a hint of a somber smile, the grandmother later told Bro. Durrance, "I guess he was right."

Today, 30 years later, Alisa, Dar, and Kay say they thought it wouldn't be tough to talk about Dennis' death. After all, they said, they talk *about* him all the time. They tell their children about what a crazy guy he was. They tell stories on him and on themselves. That's how they keep him alive. But going back to that night, reliving the shock and horror, awakened memories best forgotten. Better to remember Dennis in happy times. And, they say, to them he will always be 20—a prankster, a fun-loving, people-loving young man who made their lives special.

The roots of the Durrance sisters' faith didn't grow on top of the ground; they were imbedded deep in the earth and in their souls. Sorrow burned fiercely when Dennis died, and it still smolders, but they have found the truth of Peter's words: "And the God of all grace, who called you to his eternal glory in Christ, after you have suffered a little while, will himself restore you and make you strong, firm and steadfast." (I Peter 5:10 NIV)

Chapter 43

PAM

LOSS OF SIBLINGS AND PARENT

"I felt God had deserted me. Why should I worship him?"

When I reconnected with Pam Stone at a high school reunion, her first words stunned me: "Oh, how Anna would have loved being here with all of you." Her remark hit me hard, because I had lived out-of-town for the past 20 years and only recently had learned of Anna's death in 2004. Anna, a schoolmate and friend during our 12 years in school together, had disappeared from my life, and it was as if her spirit appeared in her place when Pam spoke her name. I felt uncomfortable, even a little embarrassed that I had not kept in touch with Anna over the years. But truth be known, I hadn't stayed in touch with anyone from my high school days.

Later, as I talked with Pam, I learned she had dealt with not one, but multiple deaths over a short period of time. When I asked her to tell me about those deaths, she began this way:

"To tell about the loss of my family, I have to start at the beginning." She notes the Stone family was not anything special — pretty much like every other family. A loving mother and father and three children: Anna, the oldest; E.J. III, affectionately called "Butch," the only boy; and Pam, the youngest and a tomboy.

Like most families, the Stones lived a routine life: school, pets, vacations, and an adequate amount of fun. Anna was an indoors person, enjoying reading and making sure everything was neat and clean. Butch occupied himself with scouting, racing at the local drag strip, and learning to fly. Pam loved the outdoors and adored her pony, Dewdrop, and later her horse, named Red.

Mr. Stone, E. J. Jr., adored his children and made sure they had opportunities to see lots of North America — from Canada to the Great Lakes to the Ozark River. He and Mrs. Stone, Martha, taught the value of family, and the whole crew always gathered for holidays and special occasions, even after the kids married and grandchildren entered the picture.

The Stone family faced death many times over the years as grandparents, aunts, uncles, and friends died. But Pam says, "None of that prepared us for what would happen during a short four-year period from 2001 to 2005."

The sad saga started when Butch was diagnosed with cirrhosis of the liver. With family love and support, he dealt with the ongoing illness and hospital stays, but finally a transplant appeared to be his only hope for a normal life. In 2001, he checked into the hospital to remove a buildup of fluid, not an unusual occurrence. An unfortunate fall brought serious complications, and the family received a report he was not expected to make it through the night. Pam recalls, "Well, they forgot to tell Butch that, and he pulled through." A few days later, the family thought he was gone, but he rallied again, eventually getting well enough to be scheduled for the transfer to Emory for the long-awaited liver transplant.

Twice the doctors predicted Butch wouldn't make it and he did; this time they predicted he would and he didn't. Before he could be moved to Emory, Pam somberly remembers, "The phone call you don't want to receive came. His heart had just given out and they could not revive him. My big brother was gone. He was the rock I had turned to when I was growing up; he taught me how to drive; he told me everything would be okay when I was a senior in high school and still had not found that someone special. He was there to support me when my marriage ended and then to help me through a bout of depression. He encouraged my attending college late in my life and getting a career and standing on my own two feet."

Pam's bulwark, big and strong and supportive. "How was I going to go forward without a big brother?" And, Pam worried about how she would help her parents deal with the loss of their son. "I had always heard the saying, 'Parents should never outlive their children,'" she recalls, "and never would that saying mean more."

Everything was tough without Butch—Thanksgiving, Christmas, even church services. "It was very hard to try to understand why my brother had to die. God was not being fair." And it was only to get worse.

E.J. Jr. moved like a downhill snowball after his son's death. Within three months, he went from a fully functioning adult to stage four Alzheimer's, compounded by Parkinson's disease. The physically powerful, vital man who had been the glue that kept the family together, changed and aged as his wife and children watched helplessly. "He died but just didn't leave."

In 2004, routine surgery for an Achilles heel injury sidelined Anna for three weeks, leaving Pam to shoulder the burden of caring for their father and mother alone. But Anna loved her job—and the children she taught—too much to stay away long, so as soon as the doctor released her, Anna returned to school. Riding the halls in a wheelchair was exhausting, but it was worth it to Anna. Pam talked with her by phone the night after she returned to school. Although Anna was fatigued, her day had been good. The kids in her classroom worshiped Anna and lined up to help her.

Anna's second day back at school started normally. Pam had a doctor's appointment that afternoon and thought about calling to check on Anna on her way home, but she decided to wait until after choir practice that night so they would have more time to talk. At church, she left her cell phone in the car and was surprised a few hours later that she had 10 missed calls and messages. When James, Anna's husband, answered the phone in the Erlanger Hospital waiting room, Pam was a little unnerved. And when he told her, "Anna is dead," all she could think was, "I'm dreaming; none of this can be true." But it was. Anna had slid out of her wheelchair to the floor of her classroom, dead from a blood clot that had gone to her heart or lungs. From the recesses of her mind, words Anna had said just days before echoed in Pam's mind: "I am here to help and I am not going anywhere," committing to help Pam care for their parents.

Now Pam had to repeat what she had thought was the worst message she would ever have to deliver to her parents: "Anna is dead," just as she had told them their only son had died.

Pam

Her parents were already in bed, so she had to get them up to tell them once again they had lost a child — this time their eldest. "I watched them age before my very eyes."

The loss of her second sibling hit Pam hard, too. "The emptiness I felt when I lost Butch was now twofold. I was the lone child left." And anger appeared in battalions — rage at the doctors, resentment at the world, fury at God. But deep within Pam, she knew she could be angry at God, and he could not only take it but would respond with compassion.

Numb inside and out, she barely made it through the funeral service. Feeling totally alone, she cried night and day. "Why would God do this to my family?" she cried out in frustration. She had always been active in church and now, "I felt God had deserted me. Why should I worship him?"

Pam says in her desolation she visited the cemetery and argued with both Butch and Anna, whose bodies now lay side by side. "Why did you leave me alone?" she remonstrated. And didn't they care their deaths were a catalyst for their father's ALZ? "How dare they?"

Daily, Pam watched her daddy disintegrate. He wandered outside at night, re-fought battles from his days in World War II, grabbed his wife's hand and twisted it, oblivious to her pain. That last incident broke Pam's will to keep her dad at home. "It was almost like I was giving up," she says remorsefully. In three short years, "I had said goodbye to Butch and then to Anna, and although Daddy was alive, I had to say goodbye to him as well. A part of me was dead and happiness was not something I felt."

Blinded by grief, Pam made the difficult decision to place her Dad in a nursing facility in December 2004. He would last four months. By the beginning of March 2005, he stopped taking nourishment, and the family knew E.J. Jr.'s shadow was shortening as the sun began to set on his life. Watching her dad slip away was more than Pam could bear, and she could no longer force herself to visit him, an admission she makes with regret sifting through her voice like sand in an hourglass.

Two weeks later, the phone call came announcing E.J. Jr.'s passing, and another funeral was on the horizon. Pam recalls she and her mother "went through the motions of greeting people at the funeral home with smiles on our faces, but," Pam adds forlornly, "for me there was not one in my heart."

Losing three dearly loved family members in a short four-year period has taken its toll on Pam. Even now, though she knows fancying her dad back as he was may be selfish, Pam says, "I want them all back with me." She goes to the cemetery often to talk with Butch, Anna, and her father. With her mother now in the early stages of ALZ, she still gets mad at Butch and Anna for leaving her to handle family issues. But knowing her brother, sister, and father are together helps. A friend dreamed she saw them together and happy. They told her not to worry that everything was okay with them now. "Is it okay? I don't know. All I really do know is that the sadness that started in my life in 2001 is still here today in 2010. Sometimes I think I can't go on without them, but I get up, say a prayer to God, and ask Him to watch over me and mother and for just a minute I am not sad."

Chapter 44

SUZANNE, MELISSA, DEBBIE, AND BO

LOSS OF A SIBLING AND A PARENT

"With a parent, you know they won't always be there, but I never thought I would lose a sibling. I never thought about one of us dying."

A vase of sunflowers, Anna's favorite, sat on the dining room table, and a green stuffed frog—a remnant of Anna's life—rested on an end table, watching silently as Anna Watson's siblings chatted easily about their sister. The warm banter back and forth signaled a closely knit group, love and candor casting a glow over their words as they painted the story of Anna's life, illness, and death. They won't forget Anna. Just as they all wore purple, Anna's favorite color, at her funeral, Suzanne has donned purple today as a reminder.

The oldest of Foy and Doris Watson's clan, Anna married, but it didn't last, reinforcing her sense that love shared was love lost. She had learned early on the love and attention showered on the first born had to be spread around as the family welcomed each new child. The arrival of Suzanne four years after Anna's birth was a pivotal point in Anna's life. It didn't help any that the second-born was an extrovert, popular at school, and a strong student. Looking back, Suzanne realizes she took a lot of attention away from Anna and that probably created some resentment. As child after child made entrance into the family, Anna moved farther and farther to the rear. The one area in which she excelled was dance—"It was a part of who she was," Suzanne shares, "even as an adult."

A teenager in the 60s, Anna fell in love with the Rolling Stones and the Beatles, and George Harrison's death hit her hard because, he, like she, was searching for meaning. Typical of the age, Anna had a rebellious streak, even burning her Bible to flaunt her unorthodoxy. For a time, she escaped home and lived with her grandmother, a wise woman who treated Anna like an equal, who saw Anna's potential and wanted her to be the best she could be. From her grandmother, Anna heard family stories and family facts, and she became the keeper of family history. Within that history, Anna's resentment toward her parents burned deep in her heart, and even as an adult, Debbie remembers Anna telling her, "Dad doesn't like me."

Suzanne says, with poignancy, "Anna's personality and experiences made her vulnerable to dependency, including her long-term addiction to smoking." But it was more than that that shaped Anna. When Doris and Foy began their downward descent toward divorce, Anna was old enough to recognize what was happening. The rest of the kids didn't understand what was going on, so Anna carried the burden alone as everyone else went merrily about their lives outside the home. Neither Doris nor Foy saw how miserable Anna was, that she didn't fit in at school, and that her early onset of pubescent acne was a source of deep embarrassment. Foy worked long hours away from home, and Doris was too busy shuttling the other kids from one place to another to notice Anna's struggle with life. Anna was different, and she knew it. She was often the scapegoat of the other children's pranks, the brunt of their jokes.

Even as an adult, Suzanne says, "There was Anna, and then you had the rest of us." Yet, the love and closeness they all felt embraced Anna as an integral part of the family. That started with weekly dinners around the family's kitchen table, when everyone shared what had happened that week. This was one time pecking order mattered — the oldest always went first. But the dinners also served, Bo remarks, as a time to calibrate where you were on the "ladder." How well you were doing in comparison with your siblings. Sometimes Anna didn't think she measured up to everyone else.

As siblings, Anna, Suzanne, Melissa, Debbie and Bo played off one another. Bo describes it like shooting fish in a barrel. "We all knew what everyone's pressure points were." And the greatest fun, he says with a cragged grin, was getting Anna fired up about something. Looking back, Bo remarks Anna could be demanding, spiteful, and cantankerous — but with a laugh, he says, "We spiced that up and made it fun." Clearly, the give and take, even though sometimes tinged with tension, had love as its undergirding. Losing Anna was unexpected and hard.

Although the family knew Anna suffered chronic obstructive pulmonary disease (COPD) for more than 10 years, Anna was very private about her health, and it wasn't until seven or eight months before her death that her strenuous struggle with breathing became apparent. Sitting in church one day, Debbie noticed Anna had to use her muscles to lift her chest to breathe. Even then, although the siblings talked about it (mostly in terms of "If only Anna would quit smoking"), they didn't realize how sick she was. Anna once told Debbie that smoking was her only friend, adding, "If I didn't have that, I wouldn't have anything."

When Anna sat on the sofa at family gatherings and asked someone to bring her coffee or something else, they just thought she was being Anna — lethargic and demanding. When she remarked, "I'm not going to live a long life," no one really paid much attention. But Anna was serious, and it didn't really matter to her if she lived or died, sometimes asking, Debbie recalls, "Why would God put me here for this?" A deeply spiritual person, Anna often didn't express herself as a traditional Christian, one more piece of evidence she saw herself as different.

The week she died, Anna left a voice mail for Suzanne, saying she wasn't feeling well. She sounded desperate, telling Suzanne she couldn't get up, so Suzanne went by to check on her that afternoon. Shocked by what she saw, Suzanne struggled with what to do with her obstinate sister. Much sicker than Suzanne expected, Anna managed to rouse herself and refused to go to the hospital. The next day, Anna's employer called Bo to say Anna hadn't shown up for work. Bo assumed she had gone to the doctor, but he dropped by after work to see how she was feeling. Walking in, he spotted Anna with her head down, sitting at the kitchen table, unresponsive. After calling for an ambulance, Bo phoned his other sisters. Over the next few days, Anna had only one period of wakefulness, a brief time of coherent thinking, but it was enough to fool her siblings that she was going to be all right. Except for Bo, a physical therapist whose medical background kicked in, the siblings thought she would come off the ventilator.

When the end of Anna's life could no longer be denied, the family gathered around her bed, and in her last lucid moments, Anna gave her final orders—what was to be done with her beloved dog Lucy, her remains, her memorial service, a celebratory party, and other details to be handled after her death. Then, after they had made the joint and undisputed decision to take her off the respirator, each of Anna's siblings had private time with her in the ICU, telling her how much they loved her, bidding her farewell.

The dynamics between siblings in large families take interesting turns, and the grieving process was no different. At Anna's funeral, Bo avowed, "It's all right." He had said what he needed to say to Anna. He had no regrets and no unresolved issues. Even though he was 12 years younger, Bo had spent a lot of time with Anna both when he was young and after they were adults. He treasures his memories, but he doesn't look back except with fondness, laughing about Anna—how she always feared losing her job (at her funeral, he said with a crooked grin, she finally did, fulfilling the truth of her words), how she never missed an opportunity for a "pit" stop when they traveled together. Sometimes it appeared Anna didn't take teasing well, but no doubt she knew it came from love and probably relished it more than she let anyone know—it put her at the center of attention—a spot she had been forced to give up early in life.

Debbie's relationship with Anna had been different. "Anna drove me nuts," she says with a shy smile. Still, she has no regrets. Anna was who she was and Debbie is who she is. Honest to the core, Debbie says, "I felt it was okay because I couldn't have done anything different in our relationship."

Melissa had some anger after Anna's death; upset she never quit smoking even when she knew what it was doing to her. Debbie shares some of that anger, grieved that Anna put her family in a position where they had to deal with her life choices. Debbie, a social worker, says she tried to "fix" Anna, but it didn't work. So, she's had to work through guilt she didn't do more or that what she did wasn't right.

Suzanne, her eyes filling with tears, murmurs, "I'm just glad we had a chance to say goodbye." After she left Anna's room for their "one-on-one," Suzanne told her husband, holding back tears, "I don't have anything to ask forgiveness for; I have no regrets. I'm just glad I could spend this time with her — it was a blessing." And, she's thankful there was no dissension among her siblings when they decided not to use heroic means to save Anna — to pull the plug on the respirator instead of letting her suffering continue.

After Anna's death, Melissa sorrowfully fulfilled Anna's last order: Don't let my dog Lucy live in pain. Going home to Lucy after the funeral, Melissa's heart broke as she saw the grieving dog. Already ill herself, Lucy had given up when Melissa took her from Anna's house only days earlier. Within days, Melissa, Debbie, and Suzanne had the heartbreaking responsibility of having Lucy put to sleep. Together, they said a prayer over Lucy and then sent her to be with Anna.

Later, as Anna requested, all of the siblings took Lucy's ashes, mixed them with Anna's and the ashes of Anna's other dog and a cat that had died earlier, and scattered most of them at Anna's gravesite, each taking a handful and saying something to or about Anna as they let the ashes tenderly sift through their fingers. Anna's best friend took a small bag of ashes and fondly flung them into the ocean, and Melissa and Bo will soon take the remaining bag of ashes, hike up Sunset Hill, and let the dust that remains of the Anna they loved take flight.

Today, 11 months after Anna's death, all that Anna asked, except that last scattering of ashes, has been done. The series of remembrances and tasks to be completed helped the siblings grieve. As Suzanne says, "We were still doing things for her." But now, "all of a sudden, we don't have anything else on our list for her."

Suzanne continues, "I never thought I would lose a sibling. I never thought about one of us dying. With a parent, you know they won't always be there, but Anna was still young at 61, and I wasn't expecting her death. With five kids, the relationships are intricate. Still, we were closely knit — always there for each other. It doesn't seem normal and right for Anna not to be here with us." Sitting still, Suzanne lets the love and the loss wash over her. "The memories and the missing will always be right below the surface," she concedes, "emerging at times unexpected and also at times I feel the need to feel the loss again."

Bo credits his parents with preparing his sisters and him for their mother's death and for Anna's. "No topic was off limits in our house," he recalls. "As a family, we had talked about death and dying. We were taught to be realistic about death; we know death is an inevitability we all face. For me, there was no tension between letting Anna go and leaving her here. I knew she couldn't recover, and I knew she would want us to let her go."

Bo, Debbie, Melissa, and Suzanne are glad their father reconciled his differences with Anna ten years before her death. Even though losing Anna was hard, Foy Watson didn't have to regret the early strain in their relationship; "the come to Jesus" meeting they had years earlier settled all that. The kids are thankful their dad had those years of good times with Anna before she died. Debbie says with a sigh that Anna's death changed *all* of the siblings' relationship with their father. He's more sensitive and open to them, and their relationships are even stronger and deeper than previously.

Together, Foy and his kids closed one more door on Anna's life. As she wished, her remaining funds went to Pet's Placement in Red Bank. The donation they made in her memory created a wonderful "meet and greet" room for potential pet adopters and their hopeful adoptees. A plaque in Anna's memory was hung in November to serve as a reminder of Anna's love for her animals.

With that done, the siblings continue to keep Anna alive by telling tales whenever they gather. They're a fun group; they know how to laugh at themselves and at each other. With easy banter, talking about Anna, it's almost as if she is in the room, waiting for her chance for a rejoinder. And, when they're out shopping, one will remark, "I would never buy that," adding with a wicked grin, "but Anna would." They mimic each other's mannerisms and joke about their fallacies, but the love they share is undeniable.

"People live on in us," Bo says gently, his voice filled with affection. Compassion and care coloring their voices, his siblings agree.

~

Her voice still reflecting incredulity, Debbie says, "Facing mother's death was almost surreal. So many signs we didn't recognize. When the doctor said the word, 'Hospice' to us, we looked at each and said in amazement, 'Hospice?'" In denial, the siblings hadn't faced the inevitability of their mother's death, even though her lungs had surrendered to the cancer that had infiltrated them.

Doris was independent, strong, and private. Although she was in the final stages of cancer, she lived alone until two weeks before her death. When she finally moved in with Melissa, Suzanne says she knew in her heart her mother would never leave. Even so, when her mother said, "I hope you haven't brought me over here to die," her conscious mind still denied the end was near. But Doris knew, and soon after her children got her settled in at Melissa's, she just gave up.

Debbie refused to let Hospice workers wear their Hospice tags, not wanting her mother to know and not wanting to admit to herself that Hospice meant the end was near. But when Doris asked to see her ex-husband, reality began to set in. Foy came and spent time alone with Doris, and the children think both their mother and father found peace that day after an acrimonious divorce and its awful aftermath that had clouded the past four decades.

When the calls went out that Doris' breathing was getting shallower and shallower, her death imminent, all five children quickly assembled at her bedside. Bo read the 121st Psalm, their mother's favorite, then each took a turn saying goodbye. Debbie says she told her mother it was okay, that her children would be all right. After her death, the adult children sang two songs, "Michael, row the boat ashore," and "If I had a hammer." They sent their mother off on a journey across the river in song, and they comforted themselves with the words, "If I had a bell, I'd ring it in the morning; I'd ring it in the evening; I'd ring out the love between my brothers and sisters...."

As they would later with their sister Anna, the siblings had a chance to say goodbye. A gift they will treasure forever. And, in Ann Radcliffe's words spoken in 1764, their mother Doris undoubtedly found, "There is some comfort in dying surrounded by one's children."

As the siblings walked outside into an unusually bright day of November sunshine, Debbie recalls Bo remarked, "What a beautiful day." They all knew it didn't compare to the splendor their mother was experiencing as she entered heaven.

Chapter 45

SHERRY

LOSS OF PARENTS

"Two years have passed, and it is still hard for me to believe I wanted him to die, that I even prayed for it."

Almost 40 years ago I penned these words and the ones that follow. While writing this book, I discovered the tear-stained paper, faded with time, and I was struck once again with disbelief that I could have wished for the death of a father I held so dear.

As far back as my junior high days, I had feared his dying. As he grew older, as I too matured and faced the fact he had to die someday, I began to have an uncontrollable feeling that I couldn't stand to give him up. If he was late coming home from the hayfield, I insisted on getting in the car and driving the 25 miles to our farm to make sure he was all right. And all the time I was speeding along, I would be filled with terrible dread that I wouldn't be able to exist without him.

And yet, a few short years later I stood in the hall outside his hospital room and prayed for him to die. Even before that — perhaps a year before — I had wanted him to die. But not then. I couldn't stand the thought of his dying after endless days of agonized staring into space. I had prayed then, in the early spring, that he be given one good summer before the end came and he was taken away forever. And, he had had that summer. He hadn't been well, but he had been able to go for short rides in the car and for an occasional visit to the farm. And sometimes, rarely, he came out of his self-imposed sanctuary long enough to take a brief interest in a cow or a garden. It was hard, even then, to watch him — to see a spark of interest in life for a brief flash — and then see him retreat behind the blank stare once again.

Faces of Grief

Now, finally, two years later, I am beginning to have memories less drenched with the despair of his last years. When my younger sister Sylvia, now 20, remarked recently our mother didn't want her six-month-old grandson wearing overalls, I responded that our dad would have gotten a kick out of seeing him decked out in overalls. And then suddenly, I could hear him saying to Bart when he came in dressed in something else: "Where's them overalls, boy?" When I repeated the words aloud, Sylvia and I laughed spontaneously, for we could both see and hear the warmth and merriment with which our father would have spoken. Now, recalling our words, I am once again overwhelmed with sadness our father never got to see Bart. A man with three daughters, a mischievous little boy would have been the apple of his eye.

It's hard to go back far enough in my memory to find the man who would have cherished seeing his grandson in overalls. The years of gloom seem to have blotted the good times away.

For four years, my father bravely fought the cancer cells that had invaded his lymphatic system. In the fifth year, the hospital stays became more frequent and longer in duration. More than 100 miles away, the Veterans' hospital became our home-away-from-home. Leaving at the end of each day, I walked down the bright flower-bordered sidewalk with tears trickling from my eyes and a choking feeling clutching my throat. I felt so helpless. What could I do? Nothing except be by his side as much as I could. I tried taking his favorite foods — homemade yeast rolls and fried apple pies — but even the small pleasure of enjoying my goodies was denied him, as the tumor expanded to fill his stomach capacity. It was ironic — what he needed most, food and medicine, only caused him more agony.

And so the days wore on — pain and more pain — with no hope of relief. His eyes clouded by inner torture, my dad lost all interest in the world about him. How heartrending it was to see my father — once a joking, loving man who knew no selfishness — turn into a shell of a person who wanted to

*withdraw from life. A man who resented happiness and
laughter.*

*It was the sense of helplessness that overwhelmed me in
the end. I can still hear the words he uttered in a tortured
whisper when I tried one day, with enormous difficulty, to
lift him up in bed: "I'm still human, you know. I'm not a
creature." The words cut like a razor-sharp sword. My
attempt to carefully and tenderly move him had felt brutal to
his fragile, pain-ridden body. Skin stretched loosely over his
skeleton like a man long-imprisoned in a concentration
camp, the slightest touch or movement was insufferable.
Inside, I cringed that he thought I had been unfeeling and
cruel. Was I being selfish to want my father to live when the
quality of his life was wretched, perpetual pain and abject
anguish?*

*My family and I struggled as long as there was
meaningful life to struggle for, but in the end, I prayed for
my father's release from his tormented existence. Even if it
meant losing him. His doctor told us, in the wee hours of the
morning just after he died, that my dad had been ready to let
go. He wanted, as I wanted for him, to die.*

*Time heals some scars, but I never remember my father's
unyielding suffering without a sorrowful sting in my soul.
Were it not for the assurance he is in a new body now, my
misery would be unbearable.*

*Yes, I prayed for the death of my dearly beloved father. I
owed him that. He loved me — and my mother and two
sisters — in Browning's words, "to the heights and depths his
soul could reach, while passing from death to eternity." We
loved him no less. We loved him so much we preferred to lose
him to life on this earth than to have him suffer
unmercifully.*

~

I learned, many years later, that Saint Teresa of Avila was
right, "Pain is never permanent." At the time of my father's
ordeal, time moved as slowly as a redwood tree stretching its
arms toward the sky. Its roots deep into my soul, I wondered for

years if my father's hellish hurting would forever discolor my memories of the fun-loving, hard-working, caring man who shaped so much of the person I was to become. Thankfully, even though at the time I couldn't envision it possible, time softened the suffering and re-colored the fabric of his life with the joy and happiness he brought into mine.

Before that happened, though, my sisters and I had to face another brush with death. Within months of our father's passing, our mother was struck with cancer. It was almost too much for us to bear. Flavia, my older sister, remembers wanting to hurl her fist toward the heavens, crying out, "This isn't fair, God! How dare you make us go through this again?" But our mother's faith was strong. She never questioned God then or years later when Parkinson's disease robbed her of her ability to speak or move. Always believing God would heal her, she waited patiently for renewed health. It wasn't to come on this earth, and when my sisters and I had to make the heart wrenching decision not to allow heroic measures to keep her alive, we were comforted in believing she was dancing in heaven, finally able to have power over her limbs again. We even joked that she was talking the ears off God and everyone in His kingdom—all that she not been able to say during the time her voice had been silenced by Parkinson's was rolling helter-skelter from her tongue.

Still, as with my father, it is difficult to remember Mother without the thought being tinged with sadness at the disability she suffered. Having lost both parents through slow, torturous illnesses, I once thought that those who lost loved ones quickly were blessed. I've since discovered there is no good way to give up anyone you hold dear. The heart aches both with watching someone suffer and with their death. While different, the pain that comes on the heels of sudden death also stings sharply.

As Rabbi Harold Kushner said, "Pain is part of being alive, and we need to learn that. Pain does not last forever, nor is it necessarily unbearable, and we need to be taught that." In the awful angst over suffering—or in the clutches of grief—perhaps we can find hope in those words. Or, in knowing, as Shakespeare affirmed, "This, too, shall pass."

Chapter 46

WANDA

LOSS OF A PARENT

"I will always be thankful and believe God's last great gift to her was the swiftness of her going."

Cleo Dalrymple, not blessed with worldly wealth, had an abundance of all that money could never buy — three healthy children who loved each other and loved her, three wonderful grandchildren, many faithful friends, a loving church family. She never focused on the financial security she did not have, instead cherishing the many blessings God bestowed on her. Her outlook on life reigned positive, even when she went through her first bout with cancer in 2003.

Two years later, she was diagnosed with bladder cancer, but she never faltered in her faith or in her optimism. Still, she may have begun to feel like Job when she broke her hip in March 2007. A nurse, who was a friend of the family, said Cleo had enough strength to heal the broken hip or fight the cancer, but not both. Yet, Cleo did not accuse God of deserting her, and until about a month before her death, she kept pushing herself — driving her car, going to church, doing pretty much what she wanted to do. But when the cancer metastasized to her bones, the pain she had tolerated so well became almost unbearable. Finally, she conceded to her daughter Wanda she did not want to live with that kind of hurt.

Wanda says her mother had a strong pain threshold, "and the pain must have been awful for her to say that." Cleo wasn't a complainer — about anything.

Looking back to answer an unanticipated question, Wanda is sure her mother felt some depression, but she never expressed it. "She accepted this challenge in her life the way she did all of her challenges," Wanda says. "She knew God was not going to put more on her than she could bear, and that whatever happened,

He would not leave her to bear it alone." With conviction Wanda adds, "I know she believed that with all her heart."

The last day of her mother's life, Wanda was still in denial. Called to the hospital, she was met by a family member, who hugged her and told her how sorry he was. Wanda's response: "Don't worry. She'll be fine. I'm sure she'll be going home tomorrow." She had no idea how bad her mother was.

In the hospital room, the siblings watched their mother's agony as she thrashed on the bed in pain. Even seeing Cleo suffer, Wanda and her siblings stayed securely in denial; they didn't perceive their mother's death was imminent. They were convinced, as the doctor was, a blood transfusion would "perk her right up." But everyone was wrong. Cleo slipped into a coma, never to awake on earth again.

Forcing herself to turn her thoughts backward, Wanda realizes she hadn't prepared herself for her mother's death. Even though she was 84, and "common sense told me she wasn't going to live forever," Wanda admits, "it's one of those head/heart situations. I was just not expecting it when it happened."

Straightforward and unequivocal, Wanda admits her grieving was different from her brother and sister. Cleo had lived with her son Richard for many years, and he had given her the three greatest gifts of her life, her only grandchildren, so a special bond existed. His mother was an integral part of Richard's everyday life, a face seen daily. Her absence created a void felt intensely and continuously.

Wanda's sister Gloria is single, and Wanda is sure her mother worried about Gloria not having anyone to support her. On the other hand, Wanda had a good marriage—a husband who was there for her emotionally and financially—and she knew her mother was not concerned she would make it. Gloria's sense of loss after the death of her second parent was one of emptiness and abandonment.

But Cleo would be proud; her three children have been strong for each other since her death. Whenever one of them is in need, the other two are there.

Wanda

Having taken off the week before her mother's death, Wanda had no bereavement days left and had no choice but to return to work the day after her mother's funeral. Today, she realizes it was probably for the best. "It's hard to sit at your desk and scream," she says with soft laughter. Then, her natural humor taking a firmer hold, she adds, "Well, I have done that, but people look at you sort of strangely."

Despite the levity, it's easy to discern Wanda misses her mother. "I certainly feel I have lost my best friend, someone who would support me no matter how bad my mess was," she says. She adds a friend once told her that when she had lost both of her parents, she felt like the last person who would ever love her unconditionally was gone. Wanda understands that feeling.

Calling herself the "sometimes unlovable child," Wanda has tried to take her mother's place as much as she can. She reminds her brother and sister of birthdays and family get-togethers. On holidays, she fixes the favorite dishes for the family that her mother prepared. And, she talks to Gloria more than she ever did before.

She talks to her mother too, usually in the context of joking. When she goes to the grocery store and forgets to use her coupons, she laughingly tells her mother, "Calm down; I can use them later." Or, when she is cooking and doesn't understand the directions in the recipe, Wanda tells Cleo, "You need to come back for about two minutes."

Conceding many people won't understand, Wanda frankly admits she is thankful God took her mother the way he did. "I'm sure she was in pain at the end, but it could have been so much worse for a much longer period of time. I will always be thankful and believe God's last great gift to her was the swiftness of her going."

Wanda ends her thoughts on grieving the loss of her mother by stating bluntly she doesn't know how people get through the loss of a loved one without God in their lives. "I believe with all my heart and soul I will be with Mother and Daddy again one day. I believe they are together in Heaven and waiting on us. They raised us to believe this, and it's holding."

Chapter 47

FINAL THOUGHTS

The universe is change; our life is what our thoughts make it.
Marcus Aurelius Antonius, Roman Emperor, 121-180

Someone once described two kinds of birds that are said to fly over the California desert — hummingbirds and vultures. The vulture sees only rotting carcasses on the surface of the stones, but the hummingbird looks for tiny cactus flowers, hidden among the rocks. It buzzes back and forth until it spots the hidden blooms, almost lost in the crevices, and then flies low to scoop them up. Each bird finds what it is looking for. We may not have had any say in the death of our loved one, but it is up to us what we look for — and what we find — in the aftermath of grief.

On the other side of our journey through grief, we will either find ourselves forever fractured, or we will become stronger in the broken places. We can let our regrets haunt us, or we can forgive ourselves. We can be filled with self-pity, or we can find new purpose for our life. We can be resentful our loved one is gone, or we can be thankful for the years we had together.

An unknown author once noted that when the sun sends its rays from afar, they melt icicles in one part of the world and harden clay in another. In the same way, death can harden our heart's faith or melt the shards of ice imprisoning our hope. While the creator of the universe is tough enough to bear the brunt of our questions and not be wounded by our anger, we, on the other hand, need someone stronger than we are to lift us up when our burden is too heavy to carry alone. We need God much more than He needs us.

Yancey reminds us God is not deaf. While we may not hear a response to our cries for relief from suffering, "He has promised to set things right... Let history finish. Let the symphony scratch out its last mournful note of discord before it bursts into song."

Final Thoughts

We have only to believe Romans 8:18: What we see is less than nothing compared to the glorious eternity planned for us. "For in this hope we were saved. But hope that is seen is no hope at all. Who hopes for what he already has? But if we hope for what we do not yet have, we wait for it patiently." (Romans 8:24-25, NIV)

The hope of a reunion in a different realm makes it possible to survive our great loss—and to say with Paul: "Oh death, where is thy sting? Oh, grave, where is thy victory?" (1st Corinthians 15:55, KJV)

Francois de La Rochefoucauld reminds us, "One can no more look steadily at the death than at the sun." Finding a lifeline to grasp when the stark sunlight of sorrow threatens to blind us is our only hope. Yes, we are transformed by our loss, but what we become in the aftermath can be shaped and formed by belief that a higher power has an unseen plan for our lives and for those whose earthly bodies have turned to dust.

SOURCES

Chapter 1

Crane, Stephen. "The Open Boat." *Major Writers of America Vol. II*. New York: Harcourt, Brace & World, Inc., 1962.

Crass, Robert. *La Requiem*. New York: Ballentine Books, 2000.

DuMaurier, Daphne. http://www.dumaurier.org. Accessed 9/21/2010.

Humphreys, Josephine. Quoted in Hickman, Martha Whitmore. *Healing After Loss: Daily Meditations for Working Through Grief*. New York: Avon Books, 1994.

O'Sullivan, Sonja. Quoted in Hickman, Martha Whitmore. *Healing After Loss: Daily Meditations for Working Through Grief*. New York: Avon Books, 1994.

Chapter 2

Hoppe, Sherry L. *SIPS OF SUSTENANCE: Grieving the Loss of Your Spouse*. Nashville, TN: Wakestone Press, 2011.

Chapter 3

Palmer, Parker. *The Hidden Wholeness*. San Francisco: John Wiley and Sons, 2004.

Manning, Brennan. *The Ragamuffin Gospel*. Sisters, Oregon: Multnomah Publishers, Inc., 1990.

Merton, Thomas. "The Road Ahead." *Thoughts in Solitude*. New York: Farrar, Straus, & Giroux, 1956.

Tillich, Paul. *The Shaking of the Foundations*. New York: Charles Scribner's Sons, 1940.

Chapter 4

Kübler-Ross, Elisabeth. *On Death and Dying*. New York: McMillan and Co., 1969.

Chapter 5

Goodall, Jane. *Reason for Hope: A Spiritual Journey*. New York: Warner Books, 2000.

Kübler-Ross, Elisabeth and Kessler, David. *On Grief and Grieving*. New York: Scribner, 2005.

Chapter 6

Caldwell, Taylor. *Prologue to Love*. Garden City, New York: Doubleday & Company, Inc., 1961.

Fitzgerald, F. Scott. "The Crack-Up." In *Major Writers of America, Vol II*. New York: Harcourt, Brace & World, Inc., 1962.

Chapter 7

Sources

Bayly, Joseph. *The Last Thing We Talk About*. Elgin, Illinois: David C. Cook
Publishing Co., 1981.

Caldwell, Taylor. *A Prologue to Love*. Garden City, New York: Doubleday &
Company, Inc., 1961.

LaHaye, Tim. *How To Win Over Depression*. Grand Rapids, Michigan:
Zondervan Publishing House, 1977.

Merton, Thomas. "The Road Ahead." *Thoughts in Solitude*. New York:
Farrar, Straus, & Giroux, 1956.

Whitman, Ardis. "Resources to Last a Lifetime." *Woman's Day*. New York:
CBS Publications. 1963.

Unruh, Allen. "The Power of One."
http://voteyesforlife.wordpress.com/2008/05/12/the-power-of-one-
by-dr-allen-unruh/ Accessed 9/15/2010.

Chapter 8

Bayly, Joseph. *The Last Thing We Talk About*. Elgin, Illinois: David C. Cook
Publishing Co., 1981.

Caldwell, Taylor. *Prologue to Love*. Garden City, New York: Doubleday &
Company, Inc., 1961.

Kübler-Ross, Elisabeth and Kessler, David. *On Grief and Grieving*. New
York: Scribner, 2005.

Kushner, Harold. *When Bad Things Happen to Good People*. New York:
Schocken Books, 1981.

Moss, Aron. Quoted in Yancey, Phillip: *Where is God When It Hurts*. Grand
Rapids, Michigan: Zondervan Publishing House, 1997.

Chapter 9

Lewis, C. S. "Petitionary Prayer: A Problem Without an Answer," in
Christian Reflections, edited by Walter Hooper. London: Geoffrey Bles,
1967.

Yancey, Phillip. *Where Is God When It Hurts?* Grand Rapids: Zondervan
Publishing House, 1977.

Chapter 10

Bayly, Joseph. *The Last Thing We Talk About*. Elgin, Illinois: David C. Cook
Publishing Co., 1981.

Fitzgerald, F. Scott. "The Crack-Up." In *Major Writers of America, Vol II*.
New York: Harcourt, Brace & World, Inc., 1962.

Chapter 11

Alborn, Mitch. *Tuesdays with Morrie*. New York: Bantam, Doubleday, Dell
Publishing Group, 1997.

Chapter 12

Bayly, Joseph. *The Last Thing We Talk About*. Elgin, Illinois: David C. Cook
Publishing Co., 1981.

Finkbeiner, Ann K. Baltimore. *After the Death of a Child: Living with the Loss Through the Years.* Maryland: John Hopkins University Press, 1996.

Kübler-Ross, Elisabeth and Kessler, David. *On Grief and Grieving.* New York: Scribner, 2005.

Mitchell, Ellen and Rita Volpe. *Beyond Tears: Living after Losing a Child.* New York: St. Martin's Press, 2004.

Redfern, Suzanne and Gilbert, Susan K. *The Grieving Garden: Living with the Death of A Child.* Charlottesville, Va.: Hampton Roads Publishing Co., 2008.

Chapter 13

Bayly, Joseph. *The Last Thing We Talk About.* Elgin, Illinois: David C. Cook Publishing, 1973.

Collins, Judy. *Singing Lessons.* New York: Simon and Schuster, 1998.

Fine, Carla. *No Time to Say Goodbye: Surviving the Suicide of a Loved One.* New York: Broadway Books, 1999.

Kübler-Ross, Elisabeth and Kessler, David. *On Grief and Grieving.* New York: Scribner, 2005.

Menninger, Karl. *Man Against Himself.* New York: Mariner Books, 1956.

Noel, Brook and Blair, Pamela. *I Wasn't Ready to Say Goodbye.* Naperville, Illinois: Sourcebooks, Inc., 2008.

Chapter 14

Bayly, Joseph. *The Last Thing We Talk About.* Elgin, Illinois: David C. Cook Publishing Co., 1981.

Worden, J. William. *Children and Grief: When A Parent Dies.* New York: Guilford Press, 1966.

Yancey, Philip. *Where is God When It Hurts.* Grand Rapids: Zondervan Publishing House, 1977.

Chapter 15

Lutzer, Edwin W. *How To Say No To A Stubborn Habit.* Wheaton, Illinois: Victor Books, 1984.

MacDonald, Gordon. *Rebuilding Your Broken World.* Nashville: Thomas Nelson Publishers, 1990.

Chapter 16

Cool, Lisa Collier. "Forgiving the Unforgivable." *Reader's Digest.* 2004.

Manning, Brennan. *The Ragamuffin Gospel.* Sisters, Oregon: Multinomah Publishers, 1990.

Marrow, Lance. "Pope John Paul II Forgives His Would-Be Assassin." *Time Magazine,* January 19, 1984.

Smedes, Lewis. *The Art of Forgiving.* New York: Ballentine Books, 1996.

Chapter 17

Bayly, Joseph. *The Last Thing We Talk About.* Elgin, Illinois: David C. Cook Publishing Co., 1981.

Sources

Cornwell, Patricia. *Black Notice*. New York: Berkley Publishing Group, 1999.

Kübler-Ross , Elisabeth and Kessler, David. *On Grief and Grieving*. New York: Scribner, 2005.

Lutzer, Edwin W. *How to Say No to a Stubborn Habit*. Wheaton, Illinois: Victor Books, 1984.

Shakespeare, William. *The Winter's Tale*. In Arden Edition. Pafford, John Henry Pyle, ed. London: A & C Black Publishers, LTD., 1966.

Chapter 18

Bayly, Joseph. *The Last Thing We Talk About*. Elgin, Illinois: David C. Cook Publishing, 1981.

Waitley, Denis. *Seeds of Greatness*. Old Tappan, New Jersey: Fleming H. Revell Company, 1983.

Chapter 19

Kübler-Ross, Elisabeth and Kessler, David. *On Grief and Grieving*. New York: Scribner, 2005.

Chapter 20
Chapter 21

Caldwell, Taylor. *Prologue to Love*. Garden City, New York: Doubleday & Company, Inc., 1961.

Schuller, Robert H. *The Inspirational Writings of Robert H. Schuller*. NY: Inspirational Press, 1986.

Seligman, Martin E. P. *Learned Optimism*. NY: Simon and Schuster, 1990.

Chapter 22

Manning, Brennan. *The Ragamuffin Gospel*. Sisters, Oregon: Multnomah Publishers, 1990.

Chapter 23

Holzer, Hans. *Ghosts: True Encounters with the World Beyond*. New York: Black Dog and Leventhal Publishers, 1997.

Goodall, Jane. *Reason for Hope: A Spiritual Journey*. New York: Warner Books, 2000.

Guggenheim, Bill and Guggenheim, Judy. *Hello from Heaven!* New York: Bantam Books, 1995.

Hoppe, Sherry L. *SIPS OF SUSTENANCE: Grieving the Loss of Your Spouse*. Nashville, TN: Wakestone Press, 2011.

http://www.members.core.com/~ascensus/docs/jung1.html Accessed 10/12/2010

http://oaks.nvg.org/jungdreams.html Accessed 10/12/2010

Kübler-Ross, Elisabeth and Kessler, David. *On Grief and Grieving*. New York: Scribner, 2005.

Jung, Carl Gustaz. *Dreams*. Translated by R. F. C. Hall. Princeton, New Jersey: Bollingen/Princeton University Press, 1974.

Puopola, Sonja Tita. *Sonja's Ring: 11 Ways to Heal Your Heart*. Minneapolis, Minnesota: Publish Green, 2010.

Chapter 24

Frankl, Viktor E. *Man's Search for Meaning*. Boston: Beacon Press, 1959.

Hoppe, Sherry Lee with Dennie B. Burke. *A MATTER OF CONSCIENCE: Redemption of a hometown hero, Bobby Hoppe*. Nashville, Tennessee: Wakestone Press, 2010.

Merton, Thomas. "The Road Ahead." *Thoughts in Solitude*. New York: Farrar, Straus, & Giroux, 1956.

Waitley, Denis. *Seeds of Greatness*. Old Tappan, New Jersey: Fleming H. Revell Company, 1983.

Chapter 25

Hoppe, Sherry L. *SIPS OF SUSTENANCE: Grieving the Loss of Your Spouse*. Nashville, TN: Wakestone Press, 2011.

Merton, Thomas. "The Road Ahead." *Thoughts in Solitude*. New York: Farrar, Straus, & Giroux, 1956.

Chapter 26

Hickman, Martha Whitmore. *Healing After Loss: Daily Meditations for Working Through Grief*. New York: Avon Books, 1994.

Merton, Thomas. "The Road Ahead." *Thoughts in Solitude*. New York: Farrar, Straus, & Giroux, 1956.

Chapter 27

Cary, Phoebe. "Nearer Home." In Stedmen, Edward Clarence. *An American Anthology 1787-1900*. Boston: Houghton Mifflin, 1900.

Kübler-Ross, Elisabeth and Kessler, David. *On Grief and Grieving*. New York: Scribner and Sons, 2005.

Manning, Brennan. *The Ragamuffin Gospel*. Sisters, Oregon: Multinomah Publishers, Inc. 1990.

Final Thoughts

Yancey, Philip. *Where is God When It Hurts*. Grand Rapids: Zondervan Publishing House, 1977.

Permissions

Sherry L. Hoppe, Ed.D.

Sherry Hoppe is the primary author of *A Matter of Conscience, Redemption of a hometown hero, Bobby Hoppe; Sips of Sustenance: Grieving the Loss of Your Spouse;* as well as authoring self-help books on grief and addiction, a devotion book, and several books on higher education issues.

Dr. Hoppe's first career was as a counselor before getting her Ed.D in higher education and entering the academic world. She is the retired president of Austin Peay State University and served as president at Roane State College and Nashville State College.

Made in the USA
Columbia, SC
31 October 2017